HYMNS TO THE DANCING ŚIVA

HYMNS TO THE DANCING SIVA

A Study of Maṇikkavācakar's *Tiruvācakam*

GLENN E. YOCUM

South Asia Books
1982

Published in United States of America by:
South Asia Books
Box 502,
Columbia,
Missouri 65205

In arrangement with
Heritage Publishers
4-C, Ansari Road, Daryaganj,
New Delhi-110002, India

Printed by
Printox, H-30, Sector IX, NOIDA,
Ghaziabad (U.P.)

To

Stuart and Shanta

Acknowledgements

It is impossible to mention all the people who contributed to the development of the ideas presented in this book. Many will have to go unnamed. Before recognizing thos whose assistance has been most immediate, a note of gratitude is due the University of Pennsylvania without whose financial support in the form of a four-year University Pre-Doctoral Fellowship and a Penfield Scholarship, it would not have been written.

My first acquiantance with Tamil came during a year I spent at Jaffna College, Sri Lanka, in 1967-68. Among the many colleagues and friends there, who answered my numerous questions with unfailing patience and kindness, special thank belong to W.L. Jeyasingham, Sabapathy Kulendran, and Sebaratnam Tambiah, who in their various ways guided my early interest in Tamil religious texts. At a later stage of my study I was indebted to several scholars in India and Sri Lanka for their generous advice and hospitaliiy—V.A. Devasenapathy, K. Kailasapathy, the late V. Varadarajan, Ratna Navaratnam, and G. Vanmikanathan.

I am especially grateful to my former teachers at the University of Pennsylvania; to my Tamil teachers over a four-year period—M. Shanmaugam Pillai, N. Kumaraswami Raja, and S. Vaidyanathan; to Charles S.J. White, Donald Swearer, and the late Dorothy Spencer; and to my dissertation committee—Ludo Rocher, David McAlpin, and Guy Richard Welbon. In particular, Professor Welbon, who served as my supervisor, was of great help with his generously detailed comments on my work and his sure-handed guidance during the final stages of writing.

To DeAnn Yocum belonged the burdern of typing the manuscript, a task she performed with accuracy, efficiency, and good cheer.

March 20, 1982 **GLENN E. YOCUM**

Contents

Much Madness is divinest Sense...
To a discerning Eye...
Much Sense...the starkest Madness...

Emily Dickinson

At the still point of the turning world. Neither flesh
nor fleshless;
Neither from nor towards; at the still point, there the
dance is,
But neither arrest nor movement. And do not call it
fixity,
Where past and future are gathered. Neither movement
from nor towards,
Neither ascent nor decline. Except for the point,
the still point,
There would be no dance, and there is only the dance.

T.S. Eliot, *Four Quartets*

Oh! blow my Coale with thy blesst Bellows till
It Glow, and send Loves hottest Steams on thee.
I shall be warm; and thou mine arms shalt fill
And mine Embraces shall thy Worship bee.
I'll sacrifice to thee my Heart in praise,
When thy Rich Grace shall be my hearty Phrase.

Edward Taylor,
Preparatory Meditations

1

Introduction

T.S. Eliot wrote that "to apprehend/ The point of intersection of the timeless/With time, is an occupation for the saint —/ No occupation either, but something given/ And taken, in a lifetime's death in love,/Ardour and selflessness and self-surrender."[1] Tamil Śaivas commonly refer to Māṇikkavācakar as a saint, and there is good reason to believe that the apprehension Eliot speaks of, was given to this devotee of the Hindu deity, Śiva. The expression, in time, of Māṇikkavācakar's apprehension of the eternal is a collection of Tamil poetry which bears the title *Tiruvācakam* ('Sacred Utterances'). It is the temporal dimensions of Māṇikkavācakar's vision which will set the major themes of this essay. To be sure, Māṇikkavācakar was a mystic whose thought and expression point to a quality of experience attested in mystical literature the world over.[2] But, here the principal intention is not so much to argue *sub specie aeternitatis* for the congruence of Māṇikkavācakar's experience with that of other mystics or, à la Eliot, 'saints' (although, on occasion, parallels will be alluded to), as it will be to arrive at an understanding of the particularity, the uniqueness, of Māṇikkavācakar's world-view and style of life.

Māṇikkavācakar is a figure of major importance in the history of Indian religion. The Tamil tradition of devotion to Śiva reaches its apex in his *Tiruvācakam*. This is so not simply because of the intrinsic merit of his poetry and thought, nor is it solely due to the continued popularity of his hymns among Tamil-speaking devotees of Śiva down to the present day. Māṇikkavācakar is of added interest to the historian because, in him, the Tamil Śaiva tradition builds a bridge to new emphases. Although Māṇikkavācakar certainly was not a systematic philosopher, his poems reflect a more coherent philosophical perspective than those of most of his Nāyaṉmār predecessors.[3] He represents the culmination of the Nāyaṉmār tradition of devotional poetry and, as such, his thought is the basis for the later philosophical elaboration and systematization of Tamil Śaivism in the Śaiva Siddhānta philosophy. While it is sometimes claimed that a significant stimulus for Rāmānuja's *visiṣṭādvaita* philosophy came from the devotional lyrics of the Tamil Vaiṣṇava Āḻvārs,[4] there is an even closer connection between Śaiva Siddhānta and Māṇikkavācakar. As Kamil Zvelebil has said, the "*Tiruvācakam* is the culmination of Śaiva *bhakti* hymnic literature, and, at the same time, the beginning of the specific system of Śaiva Siddhānta philosophy. It has always played an enormously influential role in the entire spiritual culture of Tamilnad."[5]

Māṇikkavācakar's claim to prominence in the Tamil Śaiva devotional tradition rests, however, not so much on his philosophical acumen—at least not for the common man who sings his hymns—as it does on the intensity of the experience. He is not primarily a philosopher but a devotee — indeed, for Tamil Śaivas, the bhakta (devotee) par excellence. The reason for this can be found not merely in the fervor of his expression but in the fact that the hymns of the *Tiruvācakam* communicate a sense of personality. Here we have hymns which are not chiefly occasion pieces composed to praise the manifestation of a god's presence at a particular temple. Rather, the *Tiruvācakam*, more so than the songs of the Nāyaṉmārs, presents a coherent and consistent picture of the struggles and triumphs, the tribulations and ecstacies, of one devotee. One comes away from the *Tiruvācakam* with the distinct sense of having engaged the vital thoughts and feelings of another person.

This does not mean we know everything about Māṇikkavācakar which we should like to know. There are questions, indeed many of them, which do not find answers in the *Tiruvācakam*. These are, for the most part, related to uncertainties about historical details of birth, status, and chronology of events — issues which, at best, are only implicitly resolved through a study of the *Tiruvācakam*. The dearth of such information notwithstanding an identity emerges. One knows who

Māṇikkavācakar is, although he may not know exactly where and when Māṇikkavācakar was born and where he died.

For the historian of religions, to encounter another human being at the level of his deepest experience is far more helpful in understanding him and his religion than a precise chronology of his life. For the modern-day pious Tamil Śaiva, such a life provides a paradigm, a model, for his own self-understanding and way of relating himself to ultimate reality. Indeed, in another sense, 'saints' are those uncommon figures who have mediated such understanding to their contemporaries and subsequent generations.

This study of the *Tiruvācakam* will be an essay in the history of religions. The goal will be to understand a religious tradition as it is reflected in the life of one man. In a very real sense, all history is based upon individual lives. It is in them that the interconnections between historical periods and the influence of various traditions can best be glimpsed. It is only there that the 'structures', 'forms', and 'patterns', which frequently are the concern of *Religionswissenchaft*, are lived.

This historical study of Māṇikkavācakar, then, will not be a chronicle but an essay in understanding (*Verständnis* in Dilthey's sense). Attention will often be focussed on the various influences at work in Māṇikkavācakar's thought. Indeed, he is historically interesting because of the complexity of the influences which he creatively weaves together. The attempt here will be to 'place' him in the religious history of India. But all this will have failed, if it does not contribute to our broader aim of coming to know the man himself. Consequently, the heart of the essay will be a detailed examination of the *Tiruvācakam* itself in an endeavor to present Māṇikkavācakar's thought-world systematically, to order life into manageable, comprehensible forms — all the while seeking to avoid any distortion or reduction of his experience into something which it is not.

In a sense, one could say this is an exercise in translation, in rendering the expression and experience of a Hindu poet a millennium removed from us in time and a world removed from us in cultural orientation into our present-day style and language. Assuredly this is no easy task. Yet, our age, perhaps of all ages, is in a relatively advantageous position to succeed in such an effort—because of its vastly enhanced opportunities for first-hand experience of cultural and religious differences, and because of its sophisticated conceptual tools, many of which were unavailable to previous interpreters of 'strange' places, customs, and ideas.

The discussion will, as already indicated, keep close to the text of the *Tiruvācakam*. There will be frequent citations of passages and numerous translated selections. No exposition, however, claims—or at least should claim—to be purely expository. As noted, that in which we are engaged is translation in the broadest sense. And no translation is literal. It is always interpretive as well.[6] The interpretation presented will be aided by perspectives gained from a variety of disciplines—principally from the history of religions, philology, and anthropology. I make no claim to possess a single hermeneutical key which will produce the desired goal of understanding. The methods which I make use of are varied but, I believe, coherent. They reflect to a large extent my own particular intellectual journey. The only overriding criterion for such methods is that they do not foster reductionist assumptions about the nature of religion. If, in fact, what one does is to reduce religious experience and expression to epiphenomena of social reality, economic patterns, or the dynamics of the psyche, he vitiates the already cited intention of understanding, of translating the past into present possibility.

With regard to achieving understanding, a few methodological remarks/assumptions are in order. There must be a fundamental willingness to enter into, to empathize with, to attempt to experience vicariously, a form of religiosity which may, at first blush, appear to be quite alien to our usual perceptions of reality. This is akin to what the British historian Hugh Trevor-Roper has called "historical imagination", "the capacity to migrate into distant foreign minds."[7] What is necessary is a readiness to think, feel, and will in Māṇikkavācakar's terms—a kind of total sympathy, which is anything but an easily won, nebulous 'intuition'. In this regard, the advice of a respected Islamicist is well taken: "Encyclopaedias, it is true, all too readily turn the mystery and livingness of things into terms and technicalities, and this destroys them. Truly to know the Muslim in his faith we must somehow linger in the precincts of his prayer, kindle to the accents of the Qur'ān reciter, and feel the pulse of the fast of Ramaḍān. But, outsiders as we are, we need for these interior ventures the discipline of academic statement. Sympathy and scholarship must excite and complete each other. Only by their partnership are religions understood."[8]

Beneath the acquisition of scholarly, linguistic and historical tools which are of great importance for persons of our time and place in coming to understand Māṇikkavācakar, there must be a response to the basic humanity he shares with us. It is this response, even more than the knowledge of languages and historical study, which makes understanding fully possible. Our common humanity is what allows us to think that we can live our way into (*erleben*, *einfühlen*) the world of a Māṇikkavācakar. If we can open our humanity to the humanity which meets us there, we shall have made a significant first step toward our goal of understanding. As Dilthey so perceptively remarked, understanding depends on "the rediscovery of the I in the Thou."[9]

If understanding of 'alien' religious phenomena is to occur, two closely related methodological maxims need to be followed. Both are associated with the general perspective of the phenomenology/history of religions. First, a crystallization of what has already been stated and a basic premise of phenomenological study is that one must bracket out, hold in abeyance, his own values when attempting to understand the religion of another person. One does not judge but rather seeks to empathize with, to put himself in the other's position. Consequently, normative questions about the ultimate truth or falsity of the belief or practice under study are suspended. Scrupulously fair *description* is what is aimed at. Secondly, a point repeatedly stressed by Mircea Eliade and his followers deserves reiteration, namely, "that a religious datum reveals its deeper meaning when it is considered on its plane of reference not when it is reduced to one of its secondary aspects or contexts."[10] While religious phenomena have social, political, economic, and psychological dimensions, one misses their intent, their essential meaning, if he tries to explain them as nothing more than the effect of one or a combination of these secondary aspects; for religion basically has to do with the sacred, with an 'other' dimension transcending ordinary, social, political, economic, and psychological levels of existence. Religious phenomena present themselves as ways of connecting man with the transforming power of reality itself. They are concerned with 'salvation'.

One of our leading questions then must be: What does it mean to be a devotee of Śiva? Here Eliade's wisdom is again welcome, because answering that question well will not leave its questioner unchanged.

> Obviously the historian of religions himself will feel the consequences of his own hermeneutical work. If these consequences are not always evident, it is because the majority of historians of religions defend themselves against the messages with which their documents are filled. This caution is understandable. One does not live with impunity in intimacy with 'foreign' religious forms, which are sometimes extravagant and often terrible. But many historians of religions end by no longer taking seriously the spiritual worlds they study; they fall back on their personal religious faith, or they take refuge in a materialism or behaviorism impervious to every spiritual shock. Besides, excessive specialization allows a great number of historians of religions to station themselves for the rest of their days in the sectors they have learned to frequent since their youth. And every 'specialization' ends by making the religious forms banal; in the last instance it effaces their meanings.[11]

The goal is to vivify foreign religious meanings, and when such forms do come alive they cannot be kept at arm's length. A similar point about the study of other religions is made by Wilfred Cantwell Smith from his distinctively personalist methodological perspective:

> . . . to study man is to study oneself, even when one person studies another (or one society another) separated by much space, or time, or both. What great men and women have produced makes available to us lesser men and women a vision by which we overcome, in part our lessness. There are facets of our common humanity that lie

> dormant in most of us until awakened by our coming into touch with others' attainments.[12]

This study, though certainly specialized, in Eliade's sense, has no intention of rendering religious forms banal. A genuine 'rediscovery of the I in the thou'' reconstitutes the 'I', making discovery a self-discovery. Lest the reader be misled, I am not laying claim to having had any 'mystical' experiences myself on the basis of my encounter with the *Tiruvācakam*, although I shall speak of Māṇikkavāckar as a mystic. Neither am I at all sure that I have been the subject of a 'religious' experience, unless the term be so broadly defined (as, in fact, I personally should like to define it) as to include modes of awareness which in our secularized culture usually have no connection with traditional religious institutions. Yet, despite doubts about my own mystical or religious experience, there is something in Māṇikkavācakar which strikes a responsive chord in me, a resonance which is, in large measure, the result of long and occasionally arduous study of Tamil texts and of the cultural milieu in which Māṇikkavācakar flourished. It also reflects a deep sense of affection for the people of the Jaffna peninsula in Sri Lanka, where I had the good fortune to live for a year and where my interest in Tamil Śaivism and the *Tiruvācakam* was first kindled. Certainly this undertaking has enlarged my self, and thanks to an involvement with Māṇikkavācakar's 'thou' I believe my 'lessness' has been somewhat lessened. A modest but unanticipated result of this process is indicated at the end of this chapter. But before concluding the introduction, some comments about available resources and more specific delimitation of the study are in order.

The *Tiruvācakam* has been translated into both English and German. I have had access to three translations but have not felt bound to their renderings and, in numerous instances, have departed from these translations. The oldest translation of the *Tiruvācakam* into a European language is G.U. Pope's.[13] Although Pope used a style of late Victorian rhyming poetry which rings stilted and uncongenial to modern ears, one cannot gainsay the considerable knowledge of Tamil and literary facility, although in a style now outdated, commanded by this great nineteenth-century student of Tamil language and literature.[14] The introductory sections and especially the lexicon-concordance accompanying Pope's translation are quite useful, although the introduction is hardly systematic but rather a hodgepodge collection of more or less valuable 'notes', the whole oddly designated an 'Appendix'. Pope was a child of his times, and his comments and translation do not transcend his Victorian and missionary biases, particularly on erotic motifs in the text.

Similar criticisms can be brought against the German translation by another missionary, H.W. Schomerus.[15] In this case, prudery about sexual matters is not so pronounced as with Pope, although the need to assert the superiority of Christianity, sometimes in a rather dogmatic, abrasive fashion, is an unfortunate characteristic of much of Schomerus' work on Tamil religion.[16] For Schomerus, the task of comparative religion is to make judgments about relative value, about inferiority and superiority. Needless to say such agendas do little to foster understanding. Schomerus also sometimes takes rather large liberties with the text and in these instances his translation can only be called 'interpretive' in a negative sense.

To date, the best translation of the *Tiruvācakam* is the recent one by G. Vanmikanathan, a native Tamil-speaker and a practising devotee of Śiva.[17] Again, the literary style is sometimes wanting, although it accords more with modern poetic tastes than those of Pope and Schomerus. For the most part, Vanmikanathan's renderings seem accurate, though he occasionally imposes an unnecessarily and anachronistically orthodox Siddhāntin view on the text, a tendency shared at some places by Pope and the philosophically-inclined Schomerus.

While one offers new translations of material already available in European languages because he senses the inadequacies of existing translations and feels that his own efforts are an improvement on prior deficiencies, my debt to Pope, Schomerus, and Vanmikanathan is a considerable one. Especially, during the last few years, when I have not enjoyed the advice of a Tamil teacher close by, the above translations have helped me over some particularly knotty problems, although I repeat that I often, perhaps sometimes stubbornly, did not follow their lead. All this is to say that I am indebted to these translations but am fully responsible for any inaccuracies and infelicities which blemish my own.

A work which does not appear in the footnotes of my essay but nevertheless has been consulted throughout this study is *Tiruvācaka Oḷineṟi* by Va. Cu. Ceṅkalvarāya Piḷḷai.[18] Basically, this is a concordance of the text. Although the selection of headings and entries sometimes leaves one rather bemused, and although experience has taught that this work must be used cautiously since the textual citations are sometimes inaccurate and often not comprehensive, *Tiruvācaka Oḷineṟi* has nonetheless been of most welcome assistance in ascertaining examples of certain usages and concepts. This work is a good example of traditional scholarship coming to the aid of 'modern' scholarship.

The Tamil commentaries on the text have been of limited value for reasons explained in chapter 3. Two works on Māṇikkavācakar, in European languages, to which I have had access, have proved of little help for rather different reasons. H.W. Schomerus' *Meister Eckehart und Māṇikka-Vāśagar: Mystik auf deutschem und indischem Boden* is somewhat less marred by the invidious comparisons which characterize his other work, although in the final chapter, Schomerus cannot resist the temptation of scoring points against both Māṇikkavācakar and Eckhart from his Protestant neo-orthodox theological perspective.[19] More bothersome is Schomerus' tendency to interpret Māṇikkavācakar as if he represented the fully evolved Śaiva Siddhānta position, which historically would be justifiable only if the poet lived three centuries later than he did. Many of the categories which Schomerus uses in his discussion of Māṇikkavācakar's thought are quite simply not to be found, even *in nuce*, in the *Tiruvācakam*. Also I find the comparison of Māṇikkavācakar with Eckhart, whose style is far more prosaic and philosophical and less 'mythical' than Māṇikkavācakar's, rather unilluminating. As a response to Rudolf Otto's *West-östliche Mystik*[20](which Schomerus criticizes for the choice of Śaṃkara as a point of comparison rather than "an Indian thinker who in the first place is a man of religious praxis", "a man of the heart" rather than "a man of the head"[24]), 'Schomerus' book is a failure. To my mind, Eckhart and Śaṃkara are more aptly compared than Eckhart and Māṇikkavācakar, not to mention the intrinsic superiority of Otto's study to that of Schomerus. Ratna Navaratnam's *A New Approach to Tiruvasagam* attempts to understand the text as 'great poetry'.[22] Her study is almost devotional in tone, and is concerned with establishing parallels with Western literature, some of which do not seem persuasive. For the purposes of this essay her work is not very helpful.

There are several aspects of the tradition about Māṇikkavācakar which it has not been possible to examine here. Besides the *Tiruvācakam*, another work is attributed to our poet. The *Tirukkovaiyār* is ostensibly an erotic poem, although it has traditionally been interpreted as an allegory of god's love for the soul. The poem is not an easy one and, as can be imagined, is a far less accessible form of religious literature than the clearly devotional hymns of the *Tiruvācakam*. In order to discuss the *Tirukkovaiyār* in the context of a wider study on Māṇikkavācakar, I would first want to read the work carefully with a pandit, an opportunity I have not had. More thorough examination of the hagiographical literature about Māṇikkavācakar is also a desideratum. As outlined in chapter 3, there are several texts of comparatively late origin which relate stories of Māṇikkavācakar's life. Meriting systematic study as well is the contemporary expression of his status within Tamil Śaivism. One frequently sees his image, enshrined in South Indian Śaiva temples and hears his hymns sung by common people. The Piṭṭuttiruviḻā is a festival held in Madurai to celebrate an event recorded in the poet's hagiographies. Also, the veneration of Māṇikkavācakar is reportedly still strong at Āvuṭaiyārkōyil in Tanjore District, this being the site which is today identified with ancient Peruntuṟai where Māṇikkavācakar first encountered his guru.[23]

The interpretation of the *Tirukkovaiyār* as a religious poem, the poet's hagiographies, and his modern-day cult and high esteem among many Tamils are all aspects of the effect of his thought on later generations, undoubtedly a very important factor for assessing the significance of any religious genius and his written legacy[24]; for we would probably not deem the *Tiruvācakam* so worthy of study were it not for the powerful influence it has exercised and continues to exercise on the religious imagination of generations of Tamilians. Be that as it may, the inability to incorporate consideration of these aspects into this study does not detract from the arguments presented below; for it is the intent of this essay to understand Māṇikkavācakar in so far as possible, on his own terms, tracing probable historical influences, rather than in the terms of a tradition of faith which stems from the poet.

Finally, a word should be said about the quotations on the page preceding this chapter.[25] Although all three passages derive from times and places far removed from ninth-century Tamilnad, they were chosen for their resonance with themes which are central to the *Tiruvācakam*. In this, they witness a certain unity of the human spirit, revealing parallels which give encouragement to our attempts at understanding other men across time and culture. On a personal level, they indicate a happy and unexpected result of my study of Tamil poetry; for the *Tiruvācakam* succeeded where several English teachers failed, bringing me an appreciation of and a sense of excitement about poetry in my native language.

NOTES

1. From "The Dry Salvages", in *Four Quartets* in T.S. Eliot, *The Complete Poems and Plays: 1909–1950* (New York: Harcourt, Brace & World, 1971), p. 136.

2. For example, see the definition of mysticism ("the apprehension of *an ultimate nonsensuous unity in all things*, a oneness or a One which neither the senses nor the reason can penetrate"—p. 14-15) and the anthology of mystical literature in Walter T. Stace, ed. and commentator, *The Teachings of the Mystics* (New York: New American Library, 1960).

3. The principal exception among the Nāyaṉmārs is Tirumūlar, whose highly philosophical and enigmatic *Tirumantiram* often displays a markedly different outlook from that of the other Nāyaṉmār hymns. This anomalous figure of the Tamil devotional tradition is also considered to be one of the Tamil Siddhas, whose general religious orientation is uncongenial to bhakti. For a summary of the major themes in the *Tirumantiram*, see Kamil V. Zvelebil, *The Poets of the Powers* (London: Rider and Company, 1973), p. 72–80.

4. See, for example, references to the Āḻvārs and the *Divya Prabandham*, and the argument on p. 230–237 for the authenticity of the Gadyas and the *Nityagrantha* in John Braisted Carman, *The Theology of Rāmānuja: An Essay in Interreligious Understanding* (New Haven:

Yale University Press, 1974).

5. Kamil Zvelebil, *The Smile of Murugan: On Tamil Literature of South India* (Leiden: E.J. Brill, 1973), p. 206.

6. Cf. G. van der Leeuw's statement: "every exegesis, every translation, indeed every reading, is already hermeneutics", *Religion in Essence and Manifestation*, 2 vols., trans. J.E. Turner (New York: Harper & Row, 1963), 2 : 667.

7. Quoted in H.P. Rickman's Introduction to Wilhelm Dilthey, *Pattern and Meaning in History: Thoughts on History and Society*, ed. H.P. Rickman (New York: Harper & Row, 1962), p. 43.

8. Kenneth Cragg, *The House of Islam*, 2nd ed. (Encino, Calif. : Dickenson Publishing Company, 1975), p. 5.

9. Dilthey, *Pattern and Meaning in History*, p. 39.

10. Mircea Eliade, *The Quest: History and Meaning in Religion* (Chicago: University of Chicago Press, 1969), p. 6.

11. Ibid., p. 62.

12. Wilfred Cantwell Smith, "Methodology and the Study of Religion: Some Misgivings", *Methodological Issues in Religious Studies*, ed. Robert D. Baird (Chico, Calif: New Horizons Press, 1975), p. 23.

13. G.U. Pope, trans. and commentator, *The Tiruvāçagam or 'Sacred Utterances' of the Tamil Poet, Saint, and Sage Māṇikkā-vā çagar* (Oxford: Clarendon Press, 1900).

14. In his erudite and, for the moment, definitive *Handbuch* of Tamil literature, Kamil Zvelebil somewhat over enthusiastically states that "the best translation [of the *Tiravācakam*] into English remains that by G.U. Pope"; K.V. Zvelebil, *Tamil Literature* (Leiden: E.J. Brill, 1975), p. 145, n. 98.

15. H.W. Schomerus, trans. and commentator, *Die Hymnen des Māṇikkā-vāśaga (Tiruvāśaga)* (Jena: Eugen Diederichs, 1925).

16. In addition to the introduction to his translation of the *Tiruvāçakam*, the same tendency flaws his book on Śaiva Siddhānta: H.W. Schomerus, *Der Śaiva-Siddhānta: Eine Mystik Indiens* (Leipzig: J.C. Hinrichs, 1912). See also by the same author, *Indien und das Christentum, I. Teil: Indische Frömmigkeit* (Halle–Saale: Buchhandlung des Waisenhauses, 1931).

17. G. Vanmikanathan, trans. and commentator, *Pathway to God through Tamil Literature: I—Through the Thiruvaachakam* (New Delhi: Delhi Tamil Sangam, 1971).

18. Va. Cu. Ceṅkalvarāya Piḷḷai, *Tiruvācaka Oḷineṟi* (Madras: South India Saiva Siddhanta Works Publishing Society, 1967).

19. Hilko Wiardo Schomerus, *Meister Eckehart und Māṇikka-Vāśagar: Mystik auf deutschem und indischem Boden* (Gütersloh: Verlag C. Bertelsmann, 1936), p. 169–189.

20. There is an English translation: Rudolf Otto, *Mysticism East and West: A Comparative Analysis of the Nature of Mysticism*, trans. Bertha L. Bracey and Richenda C. Payne (New York: Meridian Books, 1957).

21. Schomerus, op. cit., p. vi.

22. Ratna Navaratnam, *A New Approach to Tiruvacagam*, 2nd ed. (Annamalainagar: Annamalai University, 1971).

23. See R.K. Das, who says of Āvuṭaiyārkōyil: "Inside the temple there is an idol of Manickavachakar, which is worshipped with all ceremonial rites and rituals"; *Temples of Tamilnad* (Bombay: Bharatiya Vidya Bhavan, 1964), p. 84. Mrs. Ratna Navaratnam also informed me in conversation (June 4, 1973) that Māṇikkavācakar's "conversion" is still celebrated at Āvuṭaiyārkōyil.

24. Wilfred Cantwell Smith has argued that the "career" of certain religious texts (particularly texts such as the Qur'ān and the Bible which have the status of scripture) is sometimes more important and worthy of historical study than the conditions surrounding their origins ("The Study of Religion and the Study of the Bible", *Journal of the American Academy of Religion* 39, no. 2 [June 1971]: 131–140). Smith's point could, in some respects, be applied to study of the *Tiruvācakām*, which does have canonical status in Tamil Śaivism as part of the *Tirumuṟai*. However, in view of the limiting factors discussed in the paragraphs above, the focus here will be on the *Tiruvācakam's* 'origin'. Studies such as the one undertaken here are necessary prolegomena (in this case lacking, unlike for the Qur'ān and Bible) to consideration of the *Tiruvācakam's* effects over time. At a rather more sophisticated level of analysis, Gerald James Larson makes similar suggestions with regard to the study of the *Bhagavad Gīta* ("The *Bhagavad Gīta* as Cross-Cultural Process: Toward an Analysis of the Social Locations of a Religious Text", *Journal of the American Academy of Religion* 43, no. 4 [December 1975], p. 651–669).

25. The full references to the three passages quoted are as follows: Emily Dickinson, from poem 435 in Thomas H. Johnson, ed. *The Poems of Emily Dickinson*, 3 vols. (Cambridge, Mass.: Harvard University Press, Belknap Press, 1958), 1: 337; T.S. Eliot, from "Burnt Norton" in *Four Quartets* in T.S. Eliot, *The Complete Poems and Plays: 1909–1950*, p. 119; and Edward Taylor, from Meditation 6, *Preparatory Meditations, Second Series* in Donald E. Stanford, ed. *The Poems of Edward Taylor* (New Haven: Yale University Press, 1960), p. 91.

2

Historical Background

When asked who Māṇikkavācakar was, my usual response is to say he was a Tamil Śaiva bhakti poet who probably lived during the ninth century of the Christian era. Tamil, Śaiva, bhakti—these are the factors which are formative for his and our historical interest in this chapter will focus on each in turn. Māṇikkavācakar was not unique or even original in being a Tamil Śaiva bhakta. Indeed, the sixty-three Nāyaṉmārs, who preceded him, are very properly described by the same terms.[1] In any case, to understand him is in no small measure to understand him as a worshipper of Śiva, as a bhakta for whom the appropriate attitude towards his god is that of total devotional love, and as a Tamilian deeply rooted in the cultural and literary forms conveyed in the Tamil language.

This chapter, though not concerned with Māṇikkavācakar himself, will introduce some of the themes and dynamics of his own thought and style. For example, the Vedic god Rudra may at first sight, appear to have little in common with the diety worshipped by Māṇikkavācakar. But the pattern, the underlaying structure, which Rudra manifests is, in important respects, similar to that of Māṇikkavācakar's god, external characteristics notwithstanding. That is, the immediately conspicuous features may be different, but the basic character is much the same. Likewise, with certain peculiarly Tamil forms of religious and literary expressions—surface dynamics, harmonics, and tempi may be transformed, although what one hears are really variations on a theme.

First, the Vedic background of the diety Śiva will be the focus of attention, followed by brief remarks on bhakti in the early

Sanskrit literary tradition. Finally, the Tamil background of Māṇikkavācakar's thought will be reviewed.

Rudra-Śiva in the Vedas

The development of the cult of Rudra-Śiva strongly demonstrates the tendency of Indian culture to assimilate various strands of thought and practice. While the purpose of this section is not to sort out the genealogy of Rudra-Śiva's individual features, there is little doubt that Rudra-Śiva became a convenient receptacle for diverse characteristics of widely varying origin. This process of assimilation is far from clear and, in the absence of exact documentation, there has been a good deal of speculation and conjecture about 'non-Āryan' and 'pre-Āryan' sources for Rudra-Śiva's character. Although our concern here is principally with the Vedic Rudra-Śiva, mention should be made of the well-known hypothesis adduced from the archeological evidence that a pre-Vedic 'Proto-Śiva' was known to the inhabitants of the Indus Valley Harappa Culture prior to the Āryan migration into the Indian subcontinent.[2] While this hypothesis does not command universal assent among historians of ancient India[3], it is referred to here as an indicator of at least the possibility that, from the very begining of Indian religious history, this god was both venerated and was a figure around whom religio-cultural assimilation occurred, processes still quite evident more than a millennium and a half later in Tamil Śaivism.

Entering the Vedic period of Indian civilization, while the *Ṛgveda* contains no direct mention of Śiva, it does speak of the god Rudra, who is the early Vedic predecessor of the later great Hindu deity, Śiva. In the early Veda, Rudra seems essentially to be a storm god and many of his features mentioned in the *Ṛgveda* reveal his destructive and wrathful tendencies.[4] The name itself probably means "the howler", derived from the root *rud* ('to cry' or 'howl'). This etymology, which is the one favored by the traditional Vedic commentators, would be consistent with Rudra's association with the storm and its elements of wind and thunder. Other meanings for the name, however, have been suggested, among them a derivation from the root 'to shine' (Grassmann); a suggestion connecting *rudra* with the Pali *ludda*—'fierce, savage' or 'hunter' (Gonda); and the argument that *rudra* means the 'red' or 'ruddy one'. All of these alternative etymologies can also be harmonized with various aspects of the storm. Since the principal concern here is not with Vedic etymologies but rather with the streams of influence flowing together in Māṇikkavāckar's thought, this issue need not be belabored further.

As to the character of the Vedic Rudra, the poets who composed the *Ṛgveda* present us the picture of an often unsavory figure in the three hymns dedicated exclusively to him and in the other sundry instances (about 75) where he is mentioned. Briefly stated, Rudra appears primarily as a fear-inspiring deity whose shafts of lightning slay men and cattle (*Ṛgveda* 1: 114: 10). Thus, in the *Yajurveda* he comes to be known as Śarva, the 'archer' (*Vājasaneyi-saṃhitā* 16: 18: 28), whose malevolent arrows (*śaru*) not only bring destruction to men and cattle, but in the *Atharvaveda* are said to be the cause of fever, cough, and poison (*Atharvaveda* 11: 2: 22, 26).[5] He is called 'the red boar of the sky' (*Ṛgveda* 1: 114: 5)[6] and "the Asura of the high Heaven" (*Ṛgveda* 2: 1: 6),[7] who commands legions of "clamouring, molesting, hissing, flesh-eating attendants."[8]

This dark side of Rudra's character, however, has its obverse. For Rudra can be propitiated, and, indeed, the absence of his wrath comes to be viewed as a positive phenomenon. Thus, in addition to the deprecations in the *Ṛgveda* asking that Rudra not afflict children and villages with disease (*Ṛgveda* 1: 114: 1; 7: 46: 2), he is also addressed as the one who not merely withholds injury but who, as the great physician possessing healing medicines (*Ṛgveda* 1: 43: 4; 1: 114: 5; 2: 33; 2, 4; 7: 46: 3), is capable of bestowing health and welfare:

> For, being the lord, he looks after what is born on earth; being the universal ruler, he looks after what is born in heaven. Protecting us, come to our protecting doors, be without illness among our people, O Rudra!
>
> May that thunderbolt of thine, which, sent from heaven, traverses the earth, pass us by! A thousand medicines are thine, O thou who art freely accessible: do not hurt us in

our kith and kin! (*Ṛgveda* 7: 47: 2–3)[9].

In the Rudra of the *Ṛgveda* we can see the fundamental ambiguity of the storm itself. Anyone personally familiar with the Indian subcontinent knows well the rather ambivalent hope with which the monsoon storms are awaited. The storm manifests both creative and destructive aspects. Its fructifying rain is, of course, a positive force which probably countributes to Rudra's assimilation of elements associated with fertility. Certainly the post *Ṛgvedic* development of this god is marked by his increasing identification with the earth and its aspects of creativity. Perhaps this connection with fertility accounts for Rudra's special, albeit ambivalent, relationship with cattle, prime symbols of fertility and wealth among the Āryan tribes—a relationship already evident in the *Ṛgveda*. Despite, or perhaps because of, his much feared power to slay cattle, Rudra is invoked as *paśupa*, the protector or guardian of cattle or animals (*Ṛgveda* 1:114:9). And in the *Atharvaveda*, we find applied to Rudra the more familiar form *paśupati*, which later assumes such central significance in Śaiva philosophical terminology (*Atharvaveda* 2: 34: 1; 11:2:1; 11:2:28; 11.6:9; 15: 5: 3).

Whether Rudra's association with medicine can be read into the 'healing' powers of the storm is open to question. It could be that the absence of the storm's destructive features was given a positive interpretation. Thus, when Rudra does not strike with thunderbolts and does not cause the outbreak of disease often attendant upon the monsoon rains, he is said to be protecting men and cattle, and to be making available his healing powers. Be that as it may, what is significant is that Rudra represents the unpredictable, rather capricious, and ambivalent power of the storm, in which inhere both good and evil possibilities. Thus, he can be both benign and malevolent. At this stage in the god's history, such uncanniness evokes more fear than it does love. There could be little better example of Otto's *mysterium tremendum et fascinosum* than the Vedic Rudra; he is the numinous par excellence.[10]

The passage quoted above is interesting for reasons in addition to the fundamental ambivalence of Rudra's character which it highlights. In it we note that already, at this early stage of the god's history, universal sovereignity is ascribed to him, a fact which adumbrates Rudra's attainment in the *Mahābhārta* of the status of **the great lord** (*maheśvara, mahādeva*). Were this an isolated instance in the *Ṛgveda*, it would not be so worthy of a comment. But in other passages, similar terms are used to describe Rudra, e.g., "ruler of this world" (*īśāna asya bhuvanasya—Ṛgveda* 2: 33: 9) and "father of the world" (*bhuvanasya pitaraṃ—Ṛgveda* 6: 49: 10).

Again, it is not difficult to relate the features of absolute sovereignity accompanied by basic ambiguity to the storm. The utter dependence of human welfare and indeed life on the monsoon rains in India is an observation that has frequently been made. In fact, there are some who have been tempted to see this dependence on the monsoon as the reason for the 'passivity' and 'pessimism' of Indian religions. That is certainly arguable. both regarding the accuracy of this description of the character of Indian religion and with regard to the analysis of its purported nature. In any case, our point here is that the fundamental ambiguity coupled with awesomeness of Rudra-Śiva's character is something shared by the nature of the storm itself. This does not mean Rudra is nothing more than the storm personified or that the later Śiva has direct connections with the storm. Rather, the claim here is simply that Rudra, Śiva, and the storm share a common structure of power, unpredictability, ambivalence, and a general tendency to subsume contrary elements in a single nature. Certainly, the argument that such a structural link exists makes one uncongenial to theories such as Arbman's, that Rudra-Śiva is really a primitive pre-Āryan death demon.[11]

The development of the post-Vedic Rudra-Śiva is clarified if we keep in mind this keynote of his nature. The accretion of sharply conflicting traits on him is not arbitrary, random syncretism, although it is true that elements of widely varying meaning stemming from disparate cultural backgrounds are included in his make-up. For, Rudra-Śiva is precisely that diety who absorbs all contrarieties into his own nature. The principal subject of this deity's theme, which underlies all the variations in his mythological development, is Rudra-Śiva's ability to symbolize simultaneously opposite aspects of human experience. Philosophically, it becomes tempting to relate this *coincidentia oppositorum*[12] in the figure of Rudra-Śiva to an essential unity underlying the alternating opposites of life. It is not surprising that many orthodox Śaivas have felt comfortable with an *advaita* philosophical position, although Māṇikkavācakar and his philosophical successors in the Tamil Śaiva tradition deviate in certain significant ways from such a monistic point of view.

A further listing of passages from the later strata of the Saṃhitā and Brāhmaṇa literature could be drawn up in order to elaborate the basic structure of this god. Rather than piling up references, however, a few passages of special note will be mentioned. In the *Yajurveda*, there appears a litany addressed to the hundred forms of Rudra. This passage, the Śatarudrīya (*Vājasaneyi-saṃhitā* 16: 1-66; *Taittirīya-saṃhitā* 4 : 5 : 1-11), depicts a rather fearful figure "incorporating a startling collection of paradoxical and incongruous, grotesque and terrifying attributes."[13] If this litany dwells primarily on Rudra's baleful, awe-inspiring (*ghora*) side, the *Vājasaneyi-saṃhita* also contains the first instance of the word *Śiva* used as a proper name for Rudra: "Śiva is your name. You are a medicine, a cure, for cattle, horses and men; good fortune for rams and sheep" (*Vājasaneyi-saṃhita* 3: 59, 63; cf. *Ṛgveda* 1: 43: 6).[14] *Śiva* means the auspicious or kind one. It has often been suggested that originally this term was applied to Rudra euphemistically as a means of propitiating his wrath. While there is some merit in this argument, I am more inclined to agree with Gonda that the names Śiva, Śambhu ("the helpful, benevolent"), and Śaṃkara ("the beneficent"), of which Śiva "in post Vedic times becomes the principal designation of this divine form, are more than euphemisms; for it is a part or side of his essential nature so to be."[15] Indeed, it is this very double-sidedness, this ambiguity, which best defines this deity — a constant from the *Ṛgveda* down to the Śiva of later Hinduism.

If Rudra is the god of the ambiguous and uncontrollable aspects of existence, he is also the god of the outsider. The association of that which is unpredictable and ambivalent in the natural order with those who are in some manner ritually and socially deviant is quite comprehensible, if not almost foreseeable. Again, this important trait of Rudra-Śiva's multifaceted personality is already in evidence in the *Ṛgveda*—at least in germ.

Ṛgveda 10:136 is an unusual and interesting hymn, for it introduces us to a form of religiosity quite different from that centered on the sacrificial fire. Here appear the longhaired ones (*keśin*), the 'wind-girt', silent ascetics (*muni*), who possess miraculous powers, the apparent precursors of *yogins* such as the later Siddhas. Certainly, at this stage, these *munis* could hardly be considered orthodox practitioners of the Vedic religion. Apart from the Soma hymns of the *Ṛgveda*, there is little suggestion that the attainment of individual ecstatic experience was a desideratum of the early Vedic poets and their followers. In this hymn, however, the *keśin-munis* are defined by their almost shamanistic kind of ecstasy. Penetrated by the gods (*devāso avikṣata* — v. 2), they glide along the wind's course and, in verse 5, are called god-animated or perhaps "god-intoxicated" (*deveṣito muniḥ*).[16] The seventh and the last verse of *Ṛgveda* 10:136 establishes the link between the *munis* and Rudra.[17]

The Śatarudrīya litany mentioned above affiliates Rudra with a host of offensive types. Here (*Vājasaneyi-saṃhitā* 16:21; *Taittirīya-samhita* 4:5:3) he is designated the lord of thieves, robbers, burglars, pilferers, pillagers, cut-throats, and other similar types — hardly the Vedic nobility or their priestly practitioners! He is, furthermore, associated with dogs and with the Puñjiṣṭas (fishermen) and the Niṣādas, "a wild non-Āryan tribe"[18] (*Taittirīya-saṃhitā* 4:5:4). Sometimes he is portrayed as roving the forests accompanied by wild animals, garbed in the skins of the beasts he has killed. Here, his *Ṛgvedic* cohorts of Maruts and Rudras are replaced by equally 'uncivilized' attendants, prefiguring the later myths which see him surrounded by various ghoulish and malicious beings (*bhūtas, pretas, rākṣasas*, and *piśācas*). The figures of Rudra-Śiva's retinue may change but the same meaning is restated each time: this deity does not reflect social or ritual property; he is the archetypal outsider.

Especially intriguing is Rudra's relationship with the Vrātyas. This rather puzzling group is mentioned in *Atharvaveda* 15:5:1-7, where Rudra, appearing in seven different forms (Bhava, Śarva, Paśupati, Ugra, Rudra, Mahādeva, and Īśāna), is mentioned as the protector of the Vrātyas in seven regions.[19]

Who the Vrātyas were is not entirely clear. According to A.L. Basham,

> [*vrātya*] in its later broad meaning, implied an Āryan who had fallen from the faith and no longer respected the Vedas; but the vrātya of the *Atharvaveda* was a priest of a non Vedic fertility cult, which involved ritual dancing and flagellation. He travelled from place to place in a cart, with a woman, whom he prostituted, and musician, who performed for him at his rites. The status and nature of the vrātyas are still not wholly clear, but it is evident that great efforts were made to convert them to the Āryan faith, and to find room for them in the orthodox cult, and they were probably one of the chief sources of the new doctrines and practices.[20]

To sum up Rudra's character as an outsider, we need only quote Gonda's condensation of these features: "He is the protector and patron of hunters and other people who kill because of occupation or inclination. But, he is also the patron of those who hide out in the forest — the lord of thieves and robbers (*Vājasaneyi-samhitā* 16:20-21), the leader of those who carry on their life outside the boundaries of Āryan culture, e.g., the *Vrātyas*. . . . Indeed, in *Ṛgveda* 10:136:7 we find the first trace of this god's intimate relationship with the wild ecstatic holy men."[21]

As might be presumed from the foregoing examples, Rudra is as much a ritual maverick as he is a social misfit. Indeed, in traditional Hindu society, as we know it from the texts we happen to have, social status is virtually synonymous with ritual status. In addition to his connections with those of questionable social repute and ritual practice, Rudra himself is treated rather unusually in 'orthodox' ritual situations. For one, offerings directed to him are frequently aimed not at gaining a boon but at bringing about his removal (e.g., *Ṛgveda* 1: 114: 10; 2: 33: 14). He is paid off, propitiated (*ava-√day*— e.g., *Ṛgveda* 2: 33: 5). One must be especially careful when worshipping him, lest a ritual mistake arouse his wrath (e.g., *Ṛgveda* 2: 33: 4).

In the later Veda, Rudra is seen as the recipient not of the sacrificial oblations proper but of the left-overs.[22] He is given what is injured in the sacrifice and the officiating priest is enjoined to perform special lustrations because of the connection with this unpredictable god (*Śatapatha-brāhmaṇa* 1:7:4:9).[23] Rudra's offering at other places in the same text is specified to be *gavedhukā* seed, because "gavedhukā grass is refuse"[24] (5:2:4:13; see also 5:3:1:10; 5:3:3:7; 9:1:1:9).

Rudra's ritually isolated position is further emphasized by his exclusion from the Soma cult; by the fact that he is seldom associated with the other gods; and by the kinds of offerings he receives: "Next to the left-overs from other sacrifices, uncultivated products not belonging to the village economy such as wild sesame, wild wheat, and doe's milk are frequently presented to him as offerings. . . . Besides, it befits his uncivilized nature that (according to *Taittirīya-saṃhitā* 2:6:3:4) he is called one who eats uncooked food: his sacrificial cakes are not baked. In addition, in the *Mahābhārata* (13: 161: 7), his name is brought into association with the eating of meat, blood, and marrow."[25] Rudra Śiva, as will be noted again, is certainly not the epitome of social-ritual orthodoxy.

The *Śvetāśvatara-upaniṣad* marks the culmination of Rudra-Śiva's development in the Vedas. The growing tendency in the later Saṃhitās and the Brāhmaṇas toward Rudra's assumption of a status befitting a supreme deity is brought to fruition in this text. In the *Śvetāśvatara* Rudra-Śiva achieves philosophical legitimacy, a crucial development for his later history in view of the increasing concern with philosophical speculation among the religious elite. Although, from a literary standpoint, the *Śvetāśvatara-upaniṣad* hardly matches the *Bhagavad Gītā* in power of expression and aesthetic appeal—and from a philosophical perspective is much less consistent and coherent, relatively speaking, than the *Gītā*—it accomplishes for Rudra-Śiva what the *Gītā* does for Kṛṣna-Viṣṇu: it legitimizes him in terms of the Upaniṣadic Brahman-Ātman philosophy and depicts him as the supreme god. Yet, one has the impression that the author(s) of this Upaniṣad would not have singled Rudra-Śiva out for such prominent attention unless something about his basic personality made him an appropriate recipient for the new significance ascribed to him.

The *Śvetāśvatara* is an important transitional text in the

history of Indian religion and is of great interest quite apart from its pivotal position in the ascendancy of Rudra-Śiva. The tension, a characteristic of much later Hindu philosophy, between monistic and theistic emphases is incipient here. Concepts, which later crystallized into the Sāṃkhya-Yoga and Vedānta *darśanas*, appear cheek by jowl. The terms for divine grace (*prasāda*) and devotion (*bhakti*) are tantalizingly mentioned without being expounded. To the last two elements we shall briefly return in the next section.

Although there are numerous inconsistencies in this Upaniṣad, one should not assume that its author(s) has naively made a facile identification of Rudra-Śiva with the all-pervading Brahman. He, in fact, quotes some of the early Vedic deprecations of this god's wrath (3:5-6; 5:21-22); so he is well aware of Rudra's terrifying abilities. Apparently, he senses no incongruity here. We might say he has penetrated to Rudra-Śiva's basic meaning, a meaning highly compatible with Upaniṣadic notions about the universal Brahman. Viewed as the sum of the features accumulated from his individual manifestations, the character of Rudra-Śiva appears to be exceedingly complex. However, the essential nature that is glimpsed between, as it were, the individual items in that series of his manifold forms, allows one to suggest that Rudra-Śiva is not so much complexity personified as the solvent of all complexity, the great leveller not simply of men but more notably of cosmic and temporal processes into an underlying unity which transcends all differentiation and complexity. Later representations of Śiva as Śiva-Śakti, as Ardhanārīśvara, and as the *līnga* combined with the *yoni* attempt to convey the same point through the graphic symbolism of human sexuality. In him all opposites coalesce.

This section has traced, in rather coarse outline, the features of the Vedic deity Rudra-Śiva. In the process, we have gained a sense of this god's basic form and meaning. As depicted in the *Śvetāśvatara-upaniṣad*, Śiva is at the threshold of the full flowering of his mythology and his attainment of the stature of a monotheistic deity in the Epic and Purāṇic literature. Only he and Viṣṇu evolve in this manner in India. It may seem strange that these two, rather minor, Vedic deities should achieve such exalted positions. But perhaps Rudra-Śiva's development is not surprising. In a sense his character was simultaneously both definite enough and vague enough for him to become the object of increasing attention—definite in the vividness of his terrifying power, but vague in the basic uncertainty and unpredictability his worshippers perceived in his conduct, thus making it possible for him to assimilate features of seemingly contrary meaning.

Rudra's character was sufficiently open to new influences that he was able to survive the transition from Vedic religion to Hinduism. He did not wither from a lack of attention as did so many of the Vedic deities who were closely identified with natural phenomena. On the other hand, his character had a degree of specificity lacking in a Varuṇa, a Prajapāti, or a Brahmā—supreme deities who became largely otiose. His figure became ever more fully delineated by the assimilation of a wide range of traits. But, the basic theme, that in him opposites cohere, is never completely submerged. In fact, the Epic and Purāṇic mythology accentuates this structure even more pointedly than the Vedas.

Rudra-Śiva symbolizes one prominent and persuasive way by which a man in India understands his environment and his own place in it. This section's point will have been made, if it has succeeded in bringing into focus an underlying structure in the mass of detail about Rudra-Śiva. It will be claimed below that Māṇikkavācakar's god displays much of this same fundamental form as his Vedic predecessor. For, Rudra-Śiva's many manifestations all vein in toward a common centre.

Bhakti in the Early Sanskrit Sources

While one can discern fairly strong parallels between the Vedic Rudra-Śiva and the god worshipped in the *Tiruvācakam*, there is far less continuity of structure in the response this god evokes. Indeed, ecstatic loving devotion to a personal deity as expressed by Māṇikkavācakar and his Tamil Śaiva and Vaiṣṇava predecessors of the Tamil bhakti movements in the seventh to ninth centuries is unprecedented in Indian religious history. Historical influences in this case are better sought in indigenous South Indian traditions of possession by a god than they are in the extant Brahmanical religious literature with its ritual, philosophical, or mythical focus. In chapter 7, an argument will be presented for the connection of Māṇikkavācakar's bhakti with more distinctively Tamil traditions. Nonetheless, a brief and selective exposition of bhakti, as it initially appears in the Sanskrit sources, is useful and justified to show that at least the philosophical underpinnings of bhakti were current for many centuries before Māṇikkavācakar's time. On the other hand, it will also help to show how misleading is the all too common tendency to overstate this philosophical kinship and conclude that the devotion of the Tamil bhaktas, including Māṇikkavācakar, was a natural outgrowth of, and hence deeply indebted to, the speculations found in the late Upaniṣads and *Bhagavad Gītā*.[26]

Bhakti is commonly translated as 'devotion' or 'love', the worshipful love of the bhakta (devotee) towards God, usually in the form of either Śiva or Viṣṇu, the latter especially in his *avatāras* as Kṛṣṇa and Rāma. While these translations are good ones and are widely serviceable when rendering Indian religious texts into English, we should note some of the more extensive connotations of the term.[27] Bhakti stems from the root *bhaj*, which, like many Sanskrit verbs of long history, has borne several shades of meaning at various times and in differing contexts. The earliest and most basic meaning of *bhaj*, already exemplified in the *Ṛgveda*, is the sense of dividing, sharing, partaking of, or participating in something.[28] The later idea of devotion can be seen as growing out of this concept of participation—the mutual participation of the worshipper and the deity in each other. Indeed, this meaning seems still to be intended in the first hemistich of *Bhagavad Gīta* 4:11: Kṛṣṇa says, "In whatever way men take refuge (*prapadyante*) in me, in that same way do I participate (*bhajāmi*) in them."[29] So, someone who participates in another person in the sense of being totally devoted to him manifests bhakti. The personal dimension of the imagery is quite important here and is crucial for the religious connotations of bhakti. While a type of participation of the devotee in his god, and vice versa, is very characteristic of Māṇikkavācakar's relationship with Śiva, the contention here will be that this relies little on a recovery of the basic meaning of *bhaj* but, rather, mainly reflects Tamil ideas extraneous to the early Sanskrit bhakti tradition.

If *bhaj* means to share or divide, it can also be taken in the sense of alloting portions, of distributing, of dealing out. This meaning could connect bhakti with the practice of presenting offerings, of 'sharing' one's possessions with the deity, particularly as he is enshrined at a temple or in the home—a very common feature of the later bhakti cults.[30] Whatever etymological history stands behind the use of the word in theistic texts which propagandize for devotion, it is clear that by the time of the late Upaniṣadas and the *Bhagavad Gītā*, bhakti had come to mean total devotion, love, and trust towards a personal deity. It had become a *terminus technicus* in Indian religious thought, capable of new nuances of meaning at the hands of various authors, but nonetheless always conveying a basic sense of personal relationship with and devotion to the deity. To be sure, the connotations of sexual participation and enjoyment, which *bhaj* and its derivatives can have, re-emerge in the later bhakti cults. This, one supposes, is so not because some enterprising *śāstrin* 'discovered' undetected shades of meaning in the ancient texts, but, because the impetus of a variety of non-linguistic influences brought eroticism into the bhakti tradition. Apart from the meanings of *bhaj*, it does not seem unnatural that the imagery of human sexuality should find a place in a tradition which, from the start, put great emphasis on a personal conception of the deity, an emphasis at least semantically encouraged, though not required by its principal term, bhakti.

We need pause only briefly over the use of *bhaj* and related words in the early Veda, since at this stage, though the terms were known, they suggest little of the sense they were later to acquire as labels for an important religious concept. Where they do occur in a religious context, *bhaj* and its derivatives indicate not a particular kind of inter-personal relationship but a participation in the sacrifice (e.g., *Ṛgveda* 10: 15: 3).[31] Moreover, apart from the presence or absence of particular terms, the early Veda breathes a religio-philosophical atmosphere uncongenial to the flourishing of devotional theism. There are various probable reasons why this is so. Among them are the great emphasis placed on the sacrifice and its potential for being viewed as a means of manipulating the deities, the widespread absence among the members of the Vedic pantheon of fully anthropomorphized figures of strong and definite personality, and perhaps the rather this-worldly character of early Vedic religion. Where a pleasant sojourn in the world of the fathers or a long life or the ownership of many cattle is the goal of religious activity rather than an ultimate transformation of life conceived as transcending ordinary existence (*mokṣa*, salvation), perhaps one should not expect men to be deeply involved in personal relationships with their gods.

Although here and there one or other of the Vedic deities briefly emerges as the object of affection and trust, these attitudes are exceptional in Vedic man's relationship to the gods. The kind of sustained intensity—even the rather austere intensity of the *Bhagavad Gītā*, not to mention the fervent emotion of the Tamil bhaktas—is simply absent in the Saṃhitās, Brāhmaṇas, and the early Upaniṣads. One frequently finds the *devas* addressed in terms of kinship or friendly affection, but the concomitant features of total, abiding trust, so characteristic of bhakti, are lacking.

With the unfolding in the later old Upaniṣads of an incipient theism, conditions favourable to the development of bhakti changed dramatically. The early Upaniṣads, with their emphasis on an ultimate transformation through intuitive realization of the identity of the individual self with the cosmic absolute, had, of course, marked a major departure from the cult of the sacrifice. But, these texts also prepared the ground for bhakti; for all that remained now in order for this new plant to thrive was for some Upaniṣadic seer to identify the supreme Brahman with a personal god, probably one of the old Vedic deities who had still not retreated into oblivion. Indeed, this is what happened. Why it should have occurred at this particular juncture, in the way that it did, is a good question. The once popular theory of Christian influence was discredited as it became increasingly clear that the appearance of bhakti in the Indian religious texts antedates Christianity by several centuries. A tempting explanation is to see the humanizing influence of Buddhism at work on the later Upaniṣadic authors. Although early Buddhism, at least what we reliably know of it, renounced worship of—and hence bhakti to—its founder, the tangible presence of personality at its origin must have sent ripples out across the religious world of northern India in the middle of the first millenium BC. And though the Buddhist *nirvāṇa* may seem even more abstract and austere than the Upaniṣadic Brahman, the human model of the Buddha, and the almost inevitable consequence that reverence to him would, for some, become worship, could well have been the proximate cause of devotional developments in the orthodox religion. After all, with the emphasis on the human self (*ātman*) already well established, it was not a long step to see the absolute as a personal reality.

As has already been noted, the *Śvetāśvatara-upaniṣad* identifies the absolute Brahman with Rudra-Śiva. The last verse of this Upaniṣad, although it, along with the immediately preceding one, may have been appended by a later hand, contains the earliest mention of bhakti, in Brahmanical literature, of bhakti in the sense of devotion to God:

> To one who has the highest devotion (*bhakti*) for
> God,
> And for his spiritual teacher (*guru*) even as for
> God,
> To him these matters which have been declared
> Become manifest [if he be] a great soul (*mahātman*)
> Yea, become manifest [if he be] a great soul![32]

Bhakti here appears to be the handmaiden of knowledge (a position to some extent repeated in the *Gītā*). It is a means to the clear understanding of the doctrine taught in the text, which essentially is that one can gain release by knowing God (1:8; 2:15; 4:16; 5:13; 6:13).

It is not inconsequential that the above verse also recommends devotion to one's guru. This is an extremely important aspect of Māṇikkavācakar's own experience (see chapter 7) and is a common feature of many of the later bhakti cults. *Guru bhakti* is fairly easily related to the complex of ideas that characterize Hindu devotionalism. The notion of God's accessibility to his devotees, a significant point in most bhakti teachings, often takes the concrete form of investing certain human personages, particularly the guru, with divine status.

Other important corollaries of bhakti also find mention in the *Śvetāśvatara*. The monotheistic conception of the deity is one factor. A total loving trust needs an appropriate object, and the Rudra-Śiva presented here as the supreme god meets those qualifications. A typical concomitant of bhakti is a sense of reliance on God's grace, on his gift rather than the devotee's own effort. Quite different from the members of the Vedic pantheon, bhakti's deity cannot be manipulated. He is in charge, a free agent who dispenses or withholds favor in accord with his own designs. The *Śvetāśvatara* is one of the earliest Indian texts to know a concept of grace. At 3:20, it is said that by means of the creator's (*dhātṛ*) grace (*prasāda*) one sees the Lord (*Īśa*) and is freed from sorrow. And 6:21 attributes the sage Śvetāśvatara's wisdom, which finds expression in the Upaniṣad, to his austerity and to God's grace (*devaprasāda*).

Although the word bhakti is new in the *Śvetāśvatara-upaniṣad*, the theistic ideas which make bhakti's appearance possible are to be found in two other Upaniṣadic texts. The *Kaṭha-upaniṣad* is often cited alongwith the *Śvetāśvatara* as one of the fountainheads of Indian theism. Here we find the forerunner of *Śvetāśvatara*, 3:20 in a less fully-evolved theistic context:

> More minute than the minute, greater than the great,
> Is the Soul (Ātman) that is set in the heart of a creature here.
> One who is without the active will (*a-kratu*) beholds Him, and becomes freed from sorrow—
> When through the grace (*prasāda*) of the Creator (*dhātṛ*) he beholds the greatness of the Soul (Ātman).[33]

In this case, the indwelling self (*ātman*) is beheld through the creator's grace rather than the Lord's (*Īś*). But, like the Śvetāśvatara, the *Kaṭha-upaniṣad* identifies the Brahman-Ātman with the Puruṣa (4:12-13; 5:8-9), and thus personalizes the concept of the indwelling Absolute. Of the other old Upaniṣads, only the short and rather enigmatic *Īśa*, mainly because of its first verse, exhibits a salient theistic inclination.

Related to *bhaj* and bhakti is the word *bhagavat*, another important term in the growing vocabulary of devotionalism. It already appears in the *Śvetāśvatara-upaniṣad* (3:11; 5:4) where it describes the one god, Rudra-Śiva, as the 'holy' or the 'blessed one'. It is one of the most common terms applied to the Buddha in the Pali Canon. And, of course, it appears as a part of the title of the *Bhagavad Gītā*. In addition, its derivative *bhāgavata* is the name given to worshippers of God as Bhagavat, who apparently were already active in North India in the centuries immediately preceding the beginning of the Christian era. The earliest inscriptional evidence of *Bhāgavata* worship is found on the second century BC. Garuḍadhvaja (a type of votive column to Viṣṇu) of Heliodorus at Besnagar.[34] The epigraph proclaims Vāsudeva god of gods (*dēvadēvasa*) and describes Heliodorus, a Greek resident of Takṣaśilā, who was the donor, as being a *bhāgavata*. Elsewhere, Vāsudeva is identified with Kṛṣṇa (*Bhagvad Gīta* 7:19), who in turn is identified with Viṣṇu (*Bhagavad Gītā* 11:24, 30), thus forming the other great Hindu deity besides Śiva.

The development of the *Bhāgavata* and other early similar theistic groups, about whom there is only a scant record, e.g., the Pañcarātra school of Vaiṣṇavism and the Śaiva Pāśupatas, will not be traced here. What is historically noteworthy for our purpose is that there is a strong suspicion that these groups, both Vaiṣṇava and Śaiva, represent the intrusion into history and into Hindu orthodoxy of non-Brahmanical elements. The evidence is not conclusive, but the apparent monotheism (which among the *Bhāgavatas* and other ancillary groups appears to be more than merely a philosophical conviction, as is the case in the theistic Upaniṣads) and indicators of a nascent temple cult and image worship do attest the extra-orthodox influences.[35] As is so often true of Brahmanical thought and practice in India's history, orthodoxy stoops to conquer. In the Hindu tradition, even more so than in the other so-called 'world religions', orthodoxy is a shifting form, a moving point, constantly assimilating new features and adjusting old emphases. In an historical sense, no orthodoxy is pure and in India this is particularly true.

The *Bhagavad Gītā*, of course, establishes the philosophical basis of the later Vaiṣṇava bhakti. Nor can its influence on non-Vaiṣṇava traditions be discounted. Here, however, notice will simply be made of the *Gītā's* basically philosophical character. It is a text quite far removed in atmosphere from the Tamil devotional lyrics. It recommends a rather intellectualized form of bhakti. Franklin Edgerton has stated this quite well, although his mention in the following quotation of "the emotionalism of popular religion" must be taken as a supposition with regard to the time of the *Gīta*; for there is no textual evidence from the centuries just prior to the Christian era that 'popular religion' in India was 'emotional':

> . . . the *Gītā's* religion is a compromise between the speculation of the intellectuals and the emotionalism of popular religion. So the notion of *bhakti*, devotion, enters into its scheme of salvation by a side door, without at first displacing the old intellectual theory of salvation by knowledge. At least it is rationalized in this way. It is represented that by devoted love of God one can attain knowledge (of God), and so indirectly the salvation which comes through this knowledge: "By devotion one comes to know Me, what My measure is and what I am in very truth; then, knowing Me in very truth, he straightway enters into me" (18:55). So after the mystic revelation of his true form to Arjuna, Krishna declares that such a revelation can come to a man through no other means than devoted love: "But by unswerving devotion it is possible to know Me in this form, Arjuna, and to behold Me in very truth, and (so) to enter into Me" (11:54). Thus it is possible logically to reconcile the theory of devotion with the theory so often expressed that knowledge of God is what brings man to union with Him, that is, to salvation. Devotion to God is an auxillary means of gaining knowledge of Him.[36]

Undoubtedly, bhakti had established a strong hold on the Hindu imagination centuries before the appearance of the Nāyaṉmārs and Āḻvārs of Tamilnad in the seventh century. But, the hymns of the Tamil bhakti poets move in a very different milieu from that of the late Upaniṣads, the *Bhagavad*

Gītā, or even the Epics and early Purāṇas. The roots of the surging emotionalism prevalent in their lyrics are to be found elsewhere. The early literary tradition of South India written in Tamil, the Indian vernacular with the oldest literature, will offer a number of clues as to where these roots lie. Although the argument for understanding certain significant aspects of Māṇikkavācakar's bhakti as outgrowths of Tamil traditions will be developed in later chapters, a sketch of Tamil literature and religion prior to his time will conclude this chapter.

The Tamil Background of the *Tiruvācakam*

To catch the spirit of a rich and varied literary tradition is, of course, impossible in the scope of a few pages devoted to the eight centuries of Tamil literature prior to Māṇikkavācakar. The goal here is far more modest; for, it is the aim of this section to provide a rough chronology of Tamil literature preceding our poet and to sketch in very general lines the nature of the more important works and some of the religious views they reflect. This section is primarily one of orientation. Matters of substance relating Māṇikkavācakar's thought and expression to particular forms and ideas attested in early Tamil literature will be dealt with when the *Tiruvācakam* itself comes under consideration in subsequent chapters.

The earliest stratum of Tamil literature is referred to as Caṅkam poetry, because this body of texts, according to legend, is the product of an assembly or academy of poets who met in Madurai under the patronage of the Pāṇṭiyan kings.[37] Whatever the historical value of such legendary accounts, the Caṅkam literary corpus which constitutes 'eight anthologies' (*Eṭṭuttokai*), 'ten songs' (*Pattuppāṭṭu*), and a grammar (*Tolkāppiyam*), representing the work of no less than 473 different authors, is characterized by a pervasive common tone and spirit. Indeed, the single most distinctive feature of Caṅkam poetry is that all its authors share a set of sophisticated symbolic conventions which enable these poets to achieve considerable semantic richness and depth within the confines of what at first sight may appear to be simple, rather straightforward, lyric poetry.

Caṅkam poetry, the bulk of which stems from the second and third centuries AD,[38] is classified according to the theme into two types, *akam* (the "inner part" or interior) poems and *puram* (the "outer part" or exterior) poems. A.K. Ramanujan aptly sums up the major differences between *akam* and *puram*:

> *Akam* poems are love poems; *puram* poems are all other kinds of poems, usually about good and evil, action, community, kingdom; it is the "public" poetry of the ancient Tamils, celebrating the ferocity and glory of kings, lamenting the death of heroes, the poverty of poets. Elegies, panegyrics, invectives, poems on wars and tragic events are *puram* poems.
>
> Unlike *akam* poems, *puram* poems may mention explicitly the names of kings and poets and places. The poem is placed in a real society and given a context of real history. *Akam* poems tend to focus attention on a spare single image; in *puram* poems, the images rush and tumble over one another.[39]

The system of symbolism used by the Caṅkam authors is developed around the natural features of the South Indian countryside. In Caṅkam poetry, the landscape is divided into five well-defined regions (*tiṇai*), each containing a set of natural details appropriate to it. In *akam* poetry, these five regions are named by the type of the flower considered to be most characteristic of each, viz. *kuṟiñci* (hills), *mullai* (forest and pastureland), *marutam* (agricultural area), *neytal* (sea coast), and *pālai* (desert).[40] Each area has its own distinctive set of spatial and temporal features, e.g., birds, animals, trees and plants, people, occupations, times of day, seasons, etc. Most importantly, each landscape is symbolically associated with a particular phase of love. Thus, the poems set in the hill region treat of lovers' union; the pastureland is the scene of patient waiting; the agricultural region is the setting for lovers' unfaithfulness; the seashore symbolizes anxiety and separation; and the desert provides the backdrop for elopement, hardship, and long separation. Thus, without mentioning any human emotions at all it is possible for a poem to symbolize on emotional state:

> What Her Girl-Friend Said
>
> In the seaside grove
> where he drove back in his chariot
> the *neytal* flowers are on the ground,
> some of their thick petals plowed in
> and their stalks broken
> by the knife-edge of his wheels' golden rims
> furrowing the earth.[41]

Although no reference is made to the heroine's condition, we know from the imagery of the sea coast and *neytal* flowers that this is a poem about the separation of lovers. After the joy of union, the hero's departure is marked by harsh and violent images of knife-edged chariot wheels and broken flowers, suggesting the fragile nature of love and its liability to sudden rupture, thus increasing the heroine's and her friend's anxiety about eventual reunion with the hero.

It is noteworthy that each *tiṇai* also correlates with a particular deity: *kuṟiñci* with Murukaṉ, *mullai* with *Māyōṉ* (Viṣṇu), *marutam* with Indra, *neytal* with Varuṇa, and *pālai* with the goddess Koṟṟavai. Except for Murukaṉ and Koṟṟavai, these deities, however, receive very scant attention in Caṅkam works. If Caṅkam poetry is any indication of the prominence of these various gods in ancient Tamilnad, the premier position clearly belongs to Murukaṉ, a god who later is identified with Śiva's son, Skanda, and incorporated into Tamil Śaivism. Distinctive features of Murukaṉ's cult will be discussed in later chapters where parallels suggest themselves between his worship as depicted in the Caṅkam texts and certain aspects of Māṇikkavācakar's thought and practice. Koṟṟavai is a rather ferocious goddess to whom gruesome sacrifices were made following a battle.[42] Although, probably an indigenous Tamil deity, by Caṅkam times, she is already identified with Durgā.[43]

Caṅkam poetry, except for the rather late *Paripāṭal* and *Tirumurukāṟṟuppaṭai* which give evidence of Brahmanical influences and reveal a nascent kind of bhakti, displays little overt interest in 'religion'. Unlike early Sanskrit literature, this poetry is not cultic or philosophical, nor does it narrate myths about the gods. To conclude, however, that Caṅkam literature is therefore 'secular' or that the early Tamils had no concern with religious matters would be quite misleading. Recent publications by George Hart have especially advanced the argument that Caṅkam poetry is deeply imbued with concern about the sacred, although contrasting markedly with Āryan religious ideas.[44] Hart is convinced that the Caṅkam Tamils experienced a kind of immanent impersonal sacred power inherent particularly in women and kings. Since early Tamil poetry focuses principally on love (*akam*), where the female role is highlighted, and in *puram* poems on the exploits of heroes, who are usually kings or chiefs, Hart is claiming that this literary corpus is centrally concerned with those very factors which most characterized a decidedly religious *Weltanschauung* of early Tamil society. Hart's argument will not be summarized here, although there will be occasion to refer to his ideas again, particularly in chapter 5, when Māṇikkavācakar's attitude toward women and the goddess will come under discussion.

Moving to the centuries immediately after the earliest Caṅkam poetry, one notes an increasing 'Āryanization' of Tamil literature and religion.[45] The lyric poem gives way to the production of gnomic verse and large scale narrative works. Jainism and Buddhism make their appearance in Tamil literature and become influential religio-cultural forces from the fourth through seventh centuries. The principal Tamil literary works of the period between the 'classical age' of the early Caṅkam collections and the rise of bhakti in the seventh century are, in addition to the above mentioned late Caṅkam texts (see note 38), the 'twin epics' *Cilappatikāram* and *Maṇimēkalai*, and the 'eighteen shorter texts' (*Patiṉeṇkiḻkkaṇakku*). The last mentioned is a rather motely grouping of works including "a war-poem developing the *puram* genre and heralding later war-poetry, six poems which may be considered as echoes of the vanishing tradition of the *akam* genre (the *tiṇai* poems), and eleven collections of maxims on ethical and social conventions, dealing with rules of private and public conduct."[46] Most of these eighteen works stem from the period in question and the one of most lasting significance, the *Tirukkuṟaḷ*, a book of maxims, is definitely prior to the seventh century.

The *Cilappatikāram* (The Story about the Anklet) is the first epic poem in Tamil. (It also contains several short prose passages, the first examples of Tamil narrative prose.) The authorship of the epic is ascribed to a Cēra prince named Iḷaṅkōvaṭikaḷ, and the text, as we have it, probably stems from about the middle of the fifth century. The theme of the epic is wifely fidelity. The heroine Kaṇṇaki is faithfully submissive to her husband Kōvalaṉ despite his relations with the courtesan Madhavi upon whom he squanders his wealth. When Kōvalaṉ is unjustly accused of theft and murdered, Kaṇṇaki's feminine power assumes terrifying proportions. The epic concludes with her consecration as the goddess Pattiṉikkaṭavuḷ (25:113). The *Cilappatikāram* is designed in such a way so that each of its three major subdivisions is set in a different place, representing the capital cities of the three royal houses of ancient Tamilnad: the Cōḷas in Pukār, the Pāṇṭiyas in Madurai, and the Cēras in Vañci. The author of the epic does not propagandize for a particular religious point of view, although various religious practices of considerable interest are pictured in this text, to which reference will be made later. Principally because of his name ending in *aṭikaḷ*, and the prominence in the epic of a Jain nun named Kavunti, the author is believed to have been a Jain. The Kōvalaṉ-Kaṇṇaki story is still quite popular in Tamilnad.

The second of the twin epics, *Maṇimēkalai* by Cāttaṉār, is the story of Kōvalaṉ and Madhavi's daughter Māṇimēkalai. Unlike the *Cilappatikāram*, its author presents a decidedly Buddhist point of view and in this epic the heroine Māṇimēkalai becomes a Buddhist nun. There are highly philosophical, polemical passages on Buddhist doctrine (cf. *kātais* 27-29), and the twenty-ninth *kātai* in particular is an abstract discourse on Buddhist logic.[47] This work was probably written about AD 550 and shows the influence of Buddhism in South India at this time.

The foremost work of the 'eighteen shorter texts'—and certainly the one most highly touted (largely for political reasons) in present-day Tamilnad—is the *Tirukkuṟaḷ* (The

Sacred Kuṟaḷ) by Tiruvaḷḷuvar, who probably lived in the latter half of the fifth century and may have been a Jain. The *Tirukkuṟaḷ* contains 1,330 pithy couplets (*kuṟaḷs*) divided into sections on moral order (*aṟam*, cf. Skt. *dharma*), politics and property (*poruḷ*, cf. Skt. *artha*), and love (*kāmam*). The last section is more in the spirit, although not the form, of *akam* poetry than it is in any sense similar to Sanskrit erotic manuals such as Vātsyāyana's *Kāmasūtra*.

In turning to the bhakti movements of the seventh through ninth centuries, which dominate the next period of Tamil literature and religion, a word should be said about the political situation in South India during the centuries just before the efflorescence of Tamil devotionalism. Apparently, the prowess of the Cōḻas, Pāṇṭiyas, and Cēras went into eclipse several centuries before the rise of Pallava power at the end of the sixth century. This intervening 'dark period' of South Indian political history is marked by the appearance of "a mysterious and ubiquitous enemy of civilization, the evil rulers called Kalabhras (Kaḷappāḷar)."[48] Despite the political instability, this was the time when the above-mentioned post-Caṅkam works were written. The inclination of these texts toward Buddhism or Jainism is more understandable if Nilakanta Sastri's suggestion is correct that the Kalabhras were probably Buddhists and that their rise to power may have been motivated by religion.[49] There is certainly evidence of religious antagonism in the bhakti movements themselves, and perhaps it, at least partially, stems from persecutions suffered at the hands of the Kalabhras. As will be argued with regard to particular aspects of Māṇikkavācakar's bhakti, (and this could be claimed generally of Tamil devotionalism in the seventh through ninth centuries), there are indicators of a revival, a reassertion of distinctively Tamil elements that may have been suppressed during a period of Jain and Buddhist cultural hegemony. Of course, if Tamil bhakti is a revival of sorts, it does not simply reproduce the *status quo ante*. Far from it. The longing for a transcendent goal is a feature shared with Jainism and Buddhism, not with what is known of Caṅkam religion. The deities to whom devotion is directed are mainly Brahmanical gods who came to the Tamil country from the north. But the expression of Tamil bhakti is, as we shall see, in many respects quite peculiarly Tamil.

One of the important factors which allows one to speak of a revivalistic aspect of the Tamil bhakti movements is the popular flavor of much of the poetry. Most of the poems were obviously intended to be sung. Many of the hymns were set to particular melodies (*paṇ*) for congregational singing. The language is frequently simple and direct, accessible to ordinary people. It is also noteworthy that although a number of the most prominent bhakti poets were Brahmins, a not insignificant percentage of the leading bhaktas were non-Brahmins, a fact which does not give evidence of "class struggle"[50] so much as it supports the view that even in social origins, Tamil bhakti bespeaks a surfacing of indigenous Tamil traditions, within, to be sure, the wider context of Brahmanical theism. Thus, among the Śaivas, of the sixty-three Nāyaṉmārs at least thirty were from non-twice-born castes, and one was even a pariah and two others women. Among the twelve Vaiṣṇava Ālvārs, several were of low caste and Āṇṭāḷ, one of the leading Vaiṣṇava poets, was a woman.

While ideologically caste did not determine who could become a bhakta, neither was Tamil bhakti presented as something that would only appeal to a few religious virtuosi, unlike the markedly monastic tendencies of Jainism and Buddhism. Bhakti was compatible with the everyday tasks of the common villager. Pilgrimage, the practice of austerities, and the learning of sacred texts were not necessary. The only requirement was a mind at all times fixed on God. Perhaps this is nowhere better expressed than in the following verses by Appar, a prominent Śaiva of the early seventh century:

Why bathe in Gaṅga's stream, or Kāviri?
  Why go to Comorin in Koṅgu's land?
Why seek the waters of the sounding sea?
  Release is theirs, and theirs alone, who call
  In every place upon the Lord of all.

Why chant the Vedas, hear the Śāstras' lore?
  Why daily teach the books of righteousness?
Why the Vēdāṅgas six say o'er and o'er?
  Release is theirs, and theirs alone, whose heart

From thinking of its Lord shall ne'er depart.

Why roam the jungle, wander cities through?
Why plague life with unstinting penance hard?
Why eat no flesh, and gaze into the blue?
Release is theirs, and theirs alone, who cry
Unceasing to the Lord of wisdom high.

Why fast and starve, why suffer pains austere?
Why climb the mountains, doing penance harsh?
Why go to bathe in waters far and near?
Release is theirs, and theirs alone, who call
At every time upon the Lord of all.[51]

The major Tamil Śaiva poets preceding Māṇikkavācakar are the three authors whose devotional lyrics are referred to as the *Tēvāram*, which constitutes the first seven sections of the twelve-part *Tirumuṟai*, Tamil Śaivism's canon of mainly devotional, non-philosophical works preceding the later Śaiva Siddhānta *śāstras*. These poets and their dates are Tirunāvukkaracu (better known as Appar), who lived from the end of the sixth until after the middle of the seventh century; Tiruñāṉacampantar (usually simply called Campantar), a younger contemporary of Appar; and Nampiyārūrār alias Cuntaramūrtti (or simply Cuntarar) who was active at the end of the seventh and the beginning of the eighth century. Along with Māṇikkavācakar, they are the four (*nālvar*), the premier poets of Tamil Śaivism.

The controversy with non-Hindu traditions is quite sharp in the hymns of the *Tēvāram* authors.[52] Both Appar and Campantar make frequent disparaging references to the Jains (Campantar also often condemns Buddhists), and each is credited with effecting the conversion of a king from Jainism to the Śaiva point of view. Appar converted the Pallava monarch Mahendravarman I (580–630) and Campantar, a Pāṇṭiyan king, who if we can believe the legends about Campantar's life, upon his conversion ordered the impalement of 8,000 Jain ascetics. The stories about the lives of other Nāyaṉmārs and also about the Vaiṣṇava Āḻvārs evidence the intensity of the struggle with Jainism and Buddhism. As Zvelebil has pointed out, the rise of Tamil bhakti parallels political reassertion:

> The anti-Buddhist and anti-Jain *bhakti* movement coincides in Tamilnad in time and content with the establishment and spread of a strong Tamil national feeling and with the political expression of this fact—the origin and spread of the powerful Tamil kingdom of the Pallavas under Mahendravarman I (580–630 AD) and his son Narasiṃhavarman I (630–668 AD). In the second half of the first millennium, Buddhism and Jainism are regarded as something alien, something which is inimical to this national self-identification of the Tamils.[53]

What Śaṃkara was able to do philosophically vis-à-vis 'heterodoxy', the Tamil bhakti poets accomplished at a popular, emotional level. They sang Buddhism and Jainism out of South India. The bhakti movements mark the beginning of a period not merely of Hindu but also of Tamil resurgence, political, cultural, and religious, a renaissance which culminates in the age of the imperial Cōḻas in the tenth through twelfth centuries. The Cōḻas not only extended Tamil political power to an unprecedented degree but also built the great temples and patronized the now renowned works of art whose inspiration is rooted in the bhakti hymns of the Śaiva poets and the Āḻvārs.

The renaissance initiated by the Tamil bhakti movements had implications upon Indian religious life beyond the Tamil country itself. In the centuries following the rise of popular devotional religion in the South, a series of similar bhakti movements swept over other regions of the subcontinent. The significance of Tamilnad ("Drāviḍa country") is clearly recognized in a passage from the *Bhāgavatamāhātmya* where personified bhakti says, "Born in Drāviḍa country, I grew up in Karnāṭaka. In Mahārāṣṭra and Gujarat I became old. There, owing to the terrible *kali* age, I had been mutilated by the heretics. . . . Having arrived then at Vrindāvan, renewed and all beautiful, I have become young now with the most perfect and lovable charm."[54] Indeed, the "flood" (*veḷḷam*) of Tamil bhakti overspilled the boundaries of Tamilnad.

Notes

1. According to tradition there are sixty-three Nāyaṉmārs ('masters'), who were first enumerated in the "Tiruttoṇṭattokai" by Cuntaramūrtti, a Tamil Śaiva poet who flourished around the end of the seventh and the beginning of the eight centuries. On this point, with regard to Māṇikkavāçakar's date, see Chapter 3.

2. The "Proto-Śiva" hypothesis was formulated by Sir John Marshall, who was director of the Archaeological Survey of India when the principal sites of the Harappa Culture were first unearthed. This theory continues to be favourably mentioned in well-known survey works on early Indian history and pre-history, e.g., A.L. Basham, *The Wonder That Was India*, rev. ed. (New York: Hawthorn Books, 1963), p. 23; and Bridget and Raymond Allchin, *The Birth of Indian Civilization* (Baltimore: Penguin Books, 1968), pp. 311-312.

3. For a counter-view criticizing the theory that the Harappans venerated a god who was the forerunner of the later Śiva, see Herbert P. Sullivan, "A Re-Examination of the Religion of the Indus Civilization," *History of Religions* 4, no. 1 (Summer 1964): 115–125. Sullivan, who is not the only scholar to disagree with the "Proto-Śiva" theory, thinks that the figure is not really a male at all but probably represents the Great Goddess; see especially pp. 118–122.

4. The following description of the development of Rudra-Śiva and his characteristics relies on a number of sources which summarize the Vedic features of the deity. The principal works consulted in this regard have been: Jan Gonda, *Die Religionen Indiens I: Veda und älterer Hinduismus* (Stuttgart: W. Kohlhammer Verlag, 1960), pp. 85–89 and 254–262; Arthur Berriedale Keith, *The Religion and Philosophy of the Veda and Upanishads*, 2 vols. (1925; reprint ed., Delhi: Motilal Banarsidass, 1970), 1: 142–150; and R.G. Bhandarkar, *Vaiṣṇavism, Śaivism and Minor Religious Systems* (Strassburg: Karl J. Trübner, 1913), pp. 102–115. Only direct quotations and references to other sources will be noted.

5. Maurice Bloomfield, trans., *Hymns of the Atharva Veda*, The Sacred Books of the East, vol. 42 (1897; reprint ed., Delhi: Motilal Banarsidass, 1964), p. 157.

6. F. Max Müller, trans., *Vedic Hymns*, Part I, The Sacred Books of the East, vol. 32 (1891; reprint ed., Delhi: Motilal Banarsidass, 1964), p. 422.

7. Hermann Oldenberg, trans., *Vedic Hymns*, Part II, The Sacred Books of the East, vol. 46 (1897; reprint ed., Delhi: Motilal Banarsidass, 1964), p. 187.

8. Gonda, op. cit., 1: 86.

9. Müller, op. cit., Part I, p. 436.

10. See Rudolf Otto, *The Idea of the Holy*, trans., John W. Harvey (New York: Oxford University Press, 1958). With regard to Rudra, this point is also made by Joe Bruce Long, "Visions of Terror and Bliss: A Study of Rudra-Śiva in Pre-Purāṇic Hinduism" (Ph.D. diss., University

of Chicago, 1970), p. 35.

11. Ernst Arbman, *Rudra, Untersuchungen zum altindischen Glauben und Kultus*, in *Uppsala Universitiets Ärsskrift*, 1922 (Uppsala: A.—B. Akademiska Bokhandeln, 1922).

12. Long uses this term both in his dissertation, "Visions of Terror and Bliss," p. 386, and in an article partially based upon it: J. Bruce Long, "Śiva and Dionysos—Visions of Terror and Bliss," *Numen* 18, fasc. 3 (December 1971): 207–209.

13. Ibid., p. 182.

14. Gonda, op. cit., 1: 86.

15. Ibid.

16. This follows the translation of *Ṛgveda* 10: 136 found in Jeanine Miller, "Forerunners of Yoga: The *Keśin* Hymn," in George Feuerstein and Jeanine Miller, *Yoga and Beyond: Essays in Indian Philosophy* (New York: Schocken Books, 1972), pp. 95-120.

17. This verse is quite problematic, and there is no intention to sort out its difficulties here. With regard to Rudra, mention is made that the *keśin* along with Rudra drank poison from a cup. Apparently, this refers to the myth, later extensively elaborated in the *Mahābhārata* and Purāṇas, of Rudra's drinking the poison churned up by the *devas* and *asuras* from the ocean of milk in their attempt to produce the nectar of immortality. If this interpretation of the poison-drinking is correct, it meshes well with the above-cited references in the hymn to a type of possession by the gods; for the *muni* in his inspiration evidently becomes so completely absorbed in the deity that he senses that he even participates in the god's individual acts. Whether the *muni* interprets his identification with Rudra in such poison-drinking as evidence of his own participation in the god's gracious concern for a world threatened by "poison" or simply as another manifestation of his supernatural power, another *siddhi*, we have no way of knowing. Whatever the case may be regarding the interpretation of the *keśin's* and Rudra's swallowing the poison, the connection between Rudra and these rather extraordinary inhabitants of the early Vedic landscape is clear.

18. Monier Monier-Williams, *A Sanskrit-English Dictionary*, rev. ed. (Oxford: Clarendon Press, 1899), p. 561.

19. William Dwight Whitney, trans., *Atharva-Veda Saṃhitā*, 2 vols., ed. Charles Rockwell Lanman, Harvard Oriental Series, vols. 7-8 (Cambridge, Mass.: Harvard University, 1905), 2: 778-780. The same list of names with an eighth added (Aśani—'the thunderbolt'), without, however the association with the Vrātyas, appears in the *Kauṣītaki-brāhmaṇa* 6: 2–9. Here, Rudra is the offspring of Prajāpati's children and the names are given by Prajāpati. See Arthur Berriedale Keith, trans., *Rigveda Brahmanas: The Aitareya and Kauṣītaki Brahmaṇas of the Rigveda*, Harvard Oriental Series, vol. 25 (Cambridge, Mass.: Harvard University Press, 1920), pp. 377-379.

20. Basham, op. cit., pp. 245-246. Lanman's notes on the meaning of *vrātya* are interesting: "The *Mahābhārata*, at 5: 35: 46,

classes the *vrātya* with offscourings of society, such as incendiaries, poisoners, pimps, adulterers, abortionists, drunkards, and so on. . . . Böhtlingk and Roth express the opinion that the praise of the *vrātya* in this book [i.e., *Atharvaveda* 15] is an idealization of the pious vagrant or wandering religious mendicant" (Whitney, ibid., p. 769).

21. Gonda, op. cit., 1: 85.

22. See the myth related in *Śatapatha-brāhmaṇa* 1: 7: 3: 1-7 which explains why Rudra is given only the remains of the offering. This myth seems to prefigure the epic and Purāṇic story of Śiva's destruction of Dakṣa's sacrifice, a myth known to Māṇikkavācakar. See Julius Eggeling, trans., *The Satapatha-brāhmaṇa*, Part I, The Sacred Books of the East, vol. 12 (1882; reprint ed., Delhi: Motilal Banarsidass, 1963), pp. 199-201.

23. Ibid., p. 211.

24. Julius Eggeling, trans., op. cit., Part III, The Sacred Books of the East, vol. 41 (1894; reprint ed., Delhi: Motilal Banarsidass, 1963), p. 51.

25. Gonda, op. cit., 1: 87.

26. A good example of this sort of assumption, in this case linking the *Bhagavad Gītā* and the *Tiruvācakam* (although it is pointed out that "Śiva takes the place of Krishna" in the latter), is found in a recent encyclopedia of Hinduism; see the entry for "Māṇikkavāśagar" in Benjamin Walker, *The Hindu World*, 2 vols. (New York: Frederick A. Praeger, 1968), 2: 24.

27. For a detailed discussion of the etymology and semantics of bhakti and related terms, see Mariasusai Dhavamony, *Love of God according to Śaiva Siddhānta: A Study in the Mysticism and Theology of Śaivism* (Oxford: Clarendon Press, 1971), pp. 11-44.

28. For example, see *Ṛgveda* 10: 15: 3, which uses *bhaj* in the sense of participation in the sacrifice (cited by Dhavamony, ibid., p. 56).

29. My translation, although I have been influenced by R.C. Zaehner, trans. and commentator, *The Bhagvad Gītā* (Oxford: Clarendon Press, 1969), pp. 185-186.

30. For this suggestion I am indebted to Professor Charles S.J. White.

31. Dhavamony, op. cit. p. 56.

32. *Śvetāśvatara-upaniṣad* 6: 23 in Robert Ernest Hume, trans., *The Thirteen Principal Upanishads*, 2d ed. rev. (New York: Oxford University Press, 1931), p. 411.

33. *Kaṭha-upaniṣad* 2: 20 in ibid., pp. 349-350. There is an important variant translation of this verse, which Hume discusses in a note. Dhavamony considers the problem even more fully (*Love of God according to Śiva Siddhānta*, pp. 63-66) and adopts the same reading as Hume. Müller and Zaehner in their translations likewise follow the same interpretation reflected in Hume's translation; see F. Max Müller, trans., *The Upaniṣads* (1884; reprint ed., New York: Dover Publications, 1972), part 2, p. 11; and R.C. Zaehner, trans., *Hindu Scriptures* (London: J.M. Dent & Sons, 1966), p. 175.

34. Ted J. Solomon, "Early Vaiṣṇava Bhakti and its Autochthonous Heritage", *History of Religions* 10, no. 1 (August 1970): 42, A full translation and the text of the inscription are given.

35. See Solomon, ibid., for some far-reaching and not always convincing claims about the autochthonous origins of early Vaiṣṇava bhakti. This position is also that of George Grierson in his now somewhat dated entry on "Bhakti-Marga" in the *Encyclopedia of Religion and Ethics*, ed. James Hastings (Edinburgh: T. & T. Clark, 1909), 2: 539–551.

36. Franklin Edgerton, trans. and commentator, *The Bhagavad Gītā*, 2 vols. (Cambridge, Mass.: Harvard University Press, 1964), 2: 71.

37. In the last ten years, several excellent studies of early Tamil literature, particularly Caṅkam poetry, have appeared. Unless otherwise noted, the summary presented in this section will rely on the works listed below. Questions of dating reflect the positions stated in Zvelebil, *Tamil Literature*. Other particularly useful works are: A.K. Ramanujan, trans., *The Interior Landscape: Love Poems from a Classical Tamil Anthology* (Bloomington, Indiana: Indiana University Press, 1967); K. Kailasapathy, *Tamil Heroic Poetry* (Oxford: Clarendon Press, 1968); George L. Hart, III, *The Poems of Ancient Tamil: Their Milieu and Their Sanskrit Counterparts* (Berkeley: University of California Press, 1975); and Zvelebil, *Smile of Murugan*.

38. Two of the anthologies (*Kalittokai* and *Paripāṭal*) and one of the songs (*Tirumurukāṟṟuppaṭai*), while incorporating old elements, in their final forms are usually attributed to the period spanning the fourth through sixth centuries (i.e., after the Caṅkam period proper). See Zvelebil, *Tamil Literature*, pp. 99-106.

39. Ramanujan, op. cit., p. 101.

40. The terms used to designate the various regions differ for *puṟam* poems, but the same general format is followed; see Zvelebil, *Smile of Murugan*, pp. 103-105.

41. *Kuṟuntokai* 227 as translated in Ramanujan, op. cit., p. 73.

42. See *Puranāṉūṟu* 369, 372-373 and Kailasapathy's discussion op. cit., pp. 241-243.

43. Hart, *Poems of Ancient Tamil*, pp. 23–24.

44. Ibid., pp. 13-137 and the following articles also by Hart: "Women and the Sacred in Ancient Tamilnad", *Journal of Asian Studies* 32, no. 2 (February 1973): 233-250; "Some Related Literary Conventions in Tamil and Indo-Aryan and their Significance", *Journal of the American Oriental Society* 94, no. 2 (April-June 1974): 156-167; "Some Aspects of Kinship in Ancient Tamil Literature", *Kinship and History in South Asia*, Michigan Papers on South and Southeast Asia, no. 7, ed. Thomas T. Trautmann (Ann Arbor; Center for South and Southeast Asian Studies, The University of Michigan, 1974), pp. 29–60; and "Ancient Tamil Literature: Its Scholarly Past and Future", *Essays on South India*, Asian Studies at Hawaii, no. 15 (Honolulu: The University Press of Hawaii, 1975), pp. 41-63.

45. The term "Āryanization" is used here for want of a better word. One cannot properly speak of "Sanskritization" or "Brāhmanization" at this stage of Tamil history, since much of the influence flowing into Tamilnad from the north in this period entered through the Jain and Buddhist traditions. Even so, it should be stressed that Tamil literature, mainly due to a seminal period preceding such influences, is even in its later stages not so nearly beholden to "Āryan" or "Sanskritic" ideals as are the other Dravidian literatures of South India.

46. Zvelebil, *Tamil Literature*, p. 117. Zvelebil comments on each of these works on pp. 117-127.

47. See S. Krishnaswami Aiyangar, *Manimekhalāi in its Historical Setting* (London: Luzac & Co., 1928), pp. 204-221.

48. K.A. Nilkanta Sastri, *A History of South India from Prehistoric Times to the Fall of Vijayanagar*, 3rd ed. (Madras; Oxford University Press, 1966), pp. 144-145.

49. Ibid.

50. For a good discussion of the social origins of Tamil bhakti and a critique of the "class-struggle" interpretations of these movements by Soviet and Marxist-oriented Indian scholars, see Zvelebil, *Smile of Murugan*, pp. 190-195.

51. F. Kingsbury and G.E. Phillips, trans., *Hymns of the Tamil Śaivite Saints* (Calcutta: Association Press, 1921), p. 57. The translated passage comprises verses 2, 4, 6, and 8 of *patikam* 99 in the fifth *Tirumuṟai*. The above translation despite its somewhat outdated English style captures well the rhythm of the original.

52. On the Tamil bhakti movements' struggle with Jainism and Buddhism, see especially Zvelebil, *Smile of Murugan*, pp. 195-199; and Arno Lehmann, *Die sivaitische Frömmigkeit der tamulischen Erbauungsliteratur* (Berlin-Hermsdorf: Heimatdienstverlag, 1947), pp. 54-58.

53. Zvelebil, *Smile of Murugan*, p. 197.

54. *Bhāgavatamāhātmya* 1; 45: 50 (cf. *Padma Purāṇa*, *Uttarakhaṇḍa* 189: 51) as quoted in Dhavamony, op. cit., p. 102.

3

The Author and His Work

Before examining the ideas presented in the *Tiruvācakam* and their historical environment, it is necessary to fix the author's date, to recount briefly the traditional story of his life, and to describe the form and arrangement of his devotional hymns. These three items will be treated separately in this chapter.

Māṇikkavācakar's Date

While there is no unanimity among scholars as to when Māṇikkavācakar lived, a majority of modern scholars who use critical methods tend to locate him around the middle of the ninth century AD.[1] Arguments for his date range from as early as the end of the fourth century to as late as the second half of the tenth century.[2] But, there is no disagreement about where he flourished, namely, that his early years were spent in Madurai and its vicinity and that in the latter part of his life he lived in Cidambaram. Tradition assigns him a life span of thirty-two years.[3]

The procedure followed here, in examining the issue of Māṇikkavācakar's date, will be to present a summary of the evidence for assigning him to the ninth century and then two arguments countering this date. Epigraphy firmly establishes the *terminus a quo* for Māṇikkavācakar's life. An inscription from the Viraṭṭāṉēcuvara temple at Kīḻūr (Tirukōvilūr) dated in the fifth year of the reign of the Cōḻa king Parakēcarivarman Rājarājendradeva (1052-1062/63) mentions the "Tiruvempāvai", the seventh hymn of the *Tiruvācakam*.[4] There is further inscriptional evidence from the eleventh and twelfth centuries regarding the recital of hymns from the *Tiruvācakam* and also about land that had been set aside for support of *pūjā* to Māṇikkavācakar and several of the Śaiva Nāyaṉmars. Thus, by the mid-twelfth century, there is indisputable evidence that Māṇikkavācakar was the object of a cult. As previously noted, it is not uncommon to see his image enshrined in Śaiva temples in Tamilnad today.

There are six key reasons supporting a ninth-century date for Māṇikkavācakar. First, he is not counted as one of the sixty-three Nāyaṉmārs, the basis for which list is Cuntarar's "Tirruttoṇṭattokai", a hymn praising the major Tamil Śaiva bhaktas known to him. Thus, it is claimed that Māṇikkavācakar must come later than Cuntarar who can fairly reliably be dated around the end of the seventh and the beginning of the eighth centuries.[5]

Second, Māṇikkavācakar makes deprecating reference to "Māyāvāda" (*Tiruvācakam* 4: 54-55; see Chapter 5, especially n. 2), which indicates he was familiar with Śaṃkara's philosophy. Śaṃkara died about 820 AD; so, Māṇikkavācakar must come later.

The third reason for placing Māṇikkavācakar in the ninth century is that twice in his other extant work, the *Tirukkōvaiyār*, he refers to a Pāṇṭiyan king named Varaguṇa.[6] There are two Varaguṇas, both of whom lived in the ninth century: Varaguṇa I, also called Jaṭila Parāntaka Neḍunjaḍaiyan (756–815), and Varaguṇa II, also called Varaguṇavarman (862–880).[7] Most scholars think that Māṇikkavācakar meant Varaguṇa II, and that the poet and this king were contemporaries.

Fourth, Māṇikkavācakar explicitly refers to two of the Nāyaṉmārs, Caṇṭēcuvarar and Kaṇṇappaṉ,[8] and might have had Campantar and Cuntarar in mind in his mention of Kaḻumalam (i.e., Cīkāḻi) (2:88) and Tiruvārūr (2: 73-74), places respectively prominent in the lives of these two *Tēvāram* poets.[9] *Tiruvācakam* 5: 30, where Māṇikkavācakar says, "*yām ārkkum kuṭi allōm yātum añcōm*", appears to rely on Appar's *Tēvāram*: "*nāmārkkum kuṭi allōm namaṉai añcōm.*"[10] With regard to this quotation, one could, of course, claim that the direction of influence is the reverse of that indicated here. But, in view of the other evidence presented for a ninth-century date, this seems highly improbable.

Fifth, Māṇikkavācakar's "Tiruvempāvai" and the *Tiruppāvai*

of Āṇṭāḷ, a female Vaiṣṇava Āḻvār poet who lived in the mid-ninth century, bear remarkable resemblance to each other. Because these *pāvai* songs are "an exceptional form in Tamil literature", Jean Filliozat has said that the two poets were probably contemporaries.[11]

Finally, there is evidence from a Sinhalese chronicle, the *Nikāyasangrahaya*, that the Sinhalese king Sena I (833–853) was converted to Śaivism in Cidambaram and that his daughter was cured there of dumbness by "an ascetic clad in the robes of a priest."[12] This story clearly correlates with events related in the sixth *carukkam* of the *Tiruvātavūrar Purāṇam*, a late Tamil hagiography of Māṇikkavācakar, which tells how the poet defeated Buddhists from Ceylon in a debate, converted an unnamed Sinhalese king, and miraculously cured his daughter.

Of the arguments advanced against assigning Māṇikkavācakar to the ninth century, there are two items of evidence which deserve attention here, the first of which deals with the poet's attitude toward Buddhism. Not only the legendary accounts of Māṇikkavācakar's life mention Buddhism, there is also an unfavorable reference to Buddhists in the *Tiruvācakam* itself (15: 6). *Tiruvātavūrar Purāṇam* 499 also claims that hymn 12 of the *Tiruvācakam*, "Tiruccāḻal", stems from Māṇikkavācakar's encounter with the Buddhists in Cidambaram. While this hymn is in a question-and-answer form suggesting a debate, there is nothing to suggest that the questioner argues from a Buddhist point of view. By the ninth century, Buddhism was in decline in the Tamil country. The Chinese pilgrim, Hiuen Tsang, had already noted the plight of Buddhism in India two centuries previously.[13]

It is surprising then that Māṇikkavācakar takes note of Buddhists but fails to mention Jains who were probably more numerous in ninth century South India than were the adherents of Buddhism. But, if there is a historical core to the story of Māṇikkavācakar's encounter with Buddhists from Ceylon, his reference to Buddhism is more understandable. Certainly, the South Indian and Sinhalese kings' plundering of each other's territories makes an encounter with foreign Buddhists possible.[14] Indeed, Sena II sacked Madurai in the 850's, which could place this event very close to the time

Māṇikkavācakar lived there (depending on which Varaguṇa is associated with the poet). Perhaps it is more surprising that there are so few disparaging remarks about Buddhism. In this regard, it should be noted that for someone supposed to have been a high-ranking civil servant at the Pāṇṭiyan court, Māṇikkavācakar tells us singularly little—in fact, nothing at all—about the politics of his day.

A fact less easily reconciled to the conclusion that our poet lived in the ninth century than his mention of Buddhists is Appar's single reference to Śiva's changing jackals into horses, an event described in the hagiographical literature about Māṇikkavācakar. But more significantly, this 'sport' of Śiva's is also mentioned rather frequently in the *Tiruvācakam* itself (see chapter 6, especially n. 45). Appar's *Tēvāram* 4: 4: 2 says Śiva is the "One who made jackals into horses" (*naraiyaik kutirai ceyvāṉ*),[15] which is virtually identical to some of the *Tiruvācakam's* language about the incident (2: 36; 38: 1; 50: 7). Appar's mention of this event is cited as a proof by those claiming a date for Māṇikkavācakar in the seventh century or before that he lived contemporaneous with or prior to Appar.[16] However, in view of the overwhelming evidence which would locate Māṇikkavācakar after Appar, the only plausible explanation, although admittedly one based on conjecture, is that of Schomerus, who correctly noted that there is nothing in the *Tiruvācakam* itself which suggests Māṇikkavācakar is relating an autobiographical incident when he refers to Śiva's changing the jackals into horses: "Probably because Māṇikkavācakar alludes to this story more than the other poets, it was later very closely connected with his person. Therefore, the source of the reference to the story of the transformed jackals in Tirunāvukkaracunāyaṉār [i.e., Appar] and in the *Tiruvācakam* is not a miraculous experience of Māṇikkavācakar's but an older tale. Like so many others, it is used by both."[17]

Although some questions linger, the case for claiming that Māṇikkavācakar lived in the ninth century is substantial. Like most problems of chronology relating to pre-modern Hindu India, there probably never will be absolute certainty about our poet's date. For purposes of the present essay, it is, in fact, relatively immaterial whether he lived in the ninth or the seventh or the tenth century. The *Tiruvācakam* clearly is a part of the literature spawned by the Tamil bhakti movements. In any case, it comes later than the Caṅkam classics and prior to the philosophical texts of Śaiva Siddhānta; and these are the two major bodies of Tamil literature in which clues for a better understanding of the *Tiruvācakam* are to be sought.

TRADITIONAL BIOGRAPHY OF THE POET

There are two major sources relating to Māṇikkavācakar's life. Both stem from a period at least several centuries after the poet lived. Both are chock full of miracle and edifying incidents. In short, these are not 'histories' but hagiographies. The principal text for Māṇikkavācakar's legendary biography is the *Tiruvātavūrar Purāṇam* by Kaṭavuḷmāmuṉivar, who probably lived in the fifteenth century.[18] This work, in seven *carukkams* (Skt. *sarga*), contains 544 four-line verses and deals exclusively with the life history of our poet.[19] The title refers to Māṇikkavācakar's birth-place, Tiruvātavūr, near Madurai; hence, the title, "The Story of the One from Tiruvātavūr." There are several summaries of this text in English and a complete German translation.[20]

The other text is the *Tiruviḷaiyāṭal Purāṇam* (The Sacred Sports [of Śiva]), which is the *sthalapurāṇa* of the Mīṉāṭci-Cuntarēcuvarar temple in Madurai. Of the sixty-four 'sports' related in this text, four are about Māṇikkavācakar (chaps. 58–61 in Parañcōti's version), specifically about his relations with the Pāṇṭiyan king at Madurai. The text exists in three versions, the earliest of which is thought to stem from the twelfth century.[21] However, the oldest version is obviously based on previous traditions, since, for example the *Tiruvācakam* itself alludes to eighteen of the sixty-four sports related in the *Tiruviḷaiyāṭal Purāṇam* (see chapter 6). The stories about Māṇikkavācakar in this text are basically the same as those sections of the *Tiruvātavūrar Purāṇam* which recount the poet's trials and tribulations with the Pāṇṭiyan king before leaving Madurai. Various events in Māṇikkavācakar's life are also related in several later, less well-known *sthalapurāṇas*.[22]

The following is a brief summary of Māṇikkavācakar's life as presented in the *Tiruvātavūrar Purāṇam.*[23] The text opens with an invocation of Vināyaka and a seven-verse preface containing praises of Śiva, Umā, and Murukaṉ, a brief synopsis of the text (4-5), an expression of the author's modesty (*avaiyaṭakkam*) (6), and a verse on the benefits to be gained from the encounter with Māṇikkavācakar's story (7).

Carukkam 1 — The chapter about the minister (8-47). Māṇikkavācakar was born in the town of Tiruvātavūr to Brahmin parents of the Āmāttiyar *kulam* (11), who served as ministers of the Pāṇṭiyan king at Madurai. He was given the name Tiruvātavūrar (13). The precocious youngster was invested with the sacred thread and, by the time he was sixteen, had mastered all the various branches of knowledge. The Pāṇṭiyan king learned of the boy's reputation, summoned him to Madurai, and made him his prime minister, bestowing on him the title 'Teṉṉavaṉ Piramarāyaṉ, (the Pāṇṭiyaṉ's king of Brahmins) (22). Tiruvātavūrar was an exemplary prime minister, but his concern with religious matters deepened. Particularly, he desired to meet a guru who could teach him the highest truths of Śaivism. When news arrived in Madurai that foreign merchants with fine horses had landed on the coast, the king dispatched Māṇikkavācakar to the east (46), to the port of Peruntuṟai, in order to buy the horses. Māṇikkavacakar, prescient about his forthcoming encounter with a guru in Peruntuṟai, departed from Madurai with great pomp and pageantry, taking with him a huge sum of money and a large retinue.

Carukkam 2 — The chapter about holy Peruntuṟai (48–182). Śiva, surrounded on Mt. Kailasa by his various hosts, decided to take on the form of a guru in Peruntuṟai. His heavenly followers became human devotees. He seated himself with his multitude of disciples under a *kuruntam* tree. The beauty of Peruntuṟai is extensively described as nature itself appears to anticipate the meeting of Māṇikkavācakar and the guru. Māṇikkavācakar approached the guru who was surrounded by 999 bhaktas (*aṭiyār*) (81). The guru held in his hand a book, the "falsehood-free *Civañāṉapōtam*" (82).[24] Upon receiving answers to his questions about Śiva, *ñāṉam*, and *pōtam*, Māṇikkavācakar pleaded with Śiva to accept him as a devotee. The guru consented and a temple was quickly erected for the initiation ceremony. After Māṇikkavācakar was formally inducted into Śiva's company of followers, the guru instructed him at greater length on the principles of Śaiva philosophy (111-121). Thereupon, Māṇikkavācakar surrendered to the guru all his belongings, including the treasure entrusted to him for purchasing the horses.[25] The prime minister was completely transformed, adopting the garb of Śaiva ascetic and oblivious to anything not connected with Śiva. Unable to communicate with Māṇikkavācakar, his aides returned to Madurai and reported the incident to the king. The king was enraged and immediately dictated a letter ordering his prime minister back to Madurai. Māṇikkavācakar told the letter's contents to the guru, who advised him to return, saying that he himself would bring horses to Madurai. Greatly saddened at having to leave his new-found master, Māṇikkavācakar obeyed. Although Māṇikkavācakar was able, momentarily, to forestall the king's anger, the Pāṇṭiyan verified what had happened in Peruntuṟai and had his former minister imprisoned. In an attempt to force Māṇikkavācakar to return the misappropriated funds, he was made to stand in the hot sun, where he is pictured as addressing heart-felt appeals to Śiva.

Carukkam 3 — The chapter about the horses (183-248). Māṇikkavācakar's prayers did not go unanswered; for Śiva arrived in Madurai disguised as a horse-groom leading a herd of beautiful mounts, which he had produced by transforming all the jackals in the region into horses. The Pāṇṭiyan king was delighted and reinstituted Māṇikkavācakar to his former status. When the horse-groom failed to show proper deference to the king, Māṇikkavācakar, who recognized that he was really Śiva, assuaged the king's anger by attributing the apparent affront to his foreign customs (213).[26] That night, however, the horses reverted to their former nature and the entire city was awakened by a frightful howling in the royal stables. The king again had Māṇikkavācakar taken into custody and tortured in the hot sun in an attempt to regain his lost treasure. The chapter closes in the same vein as the previous one with Māṇikkavācakar imploring Śiva to come to his rescue.

Carukkam 4 — The chapter about carrying earth (249-343). (Since the incident in this chapter will be discussed more elaborately in chapter 6, the following summary is very cursory.) Śiva caused the river Vaikai to flood, threatening Madurai. The king ordered the dikes reinforced. Śiva, in the guise of a laborer, helped carry earth to strengthen the levees. Since this laborer, however, did not perform his job well, he was beaten. At this, Śiva's true identity was revealed, and Māṇikkavācakar was released from the king's service, enabling him to return to his guru in Perunturai. Not long after Māṇikkavācakar's arrival in Perunturai, Śiva told him that he would soon return to Kailāsa, to be followed shortly thereafter by his retinue of bhaktas. However, after these things had happened, he ordered Māṇikkavācakar to go to Uttarakōcamaṅkai (341), Kaḻukkuṉṟam, and Cidambaram, where he would achieve final union with the god after defeating Buddhists in a debate (342).

Carukkam 5 — The chapter about the Tiruvambalam (i.e., the golden hall in Naṭarāja temple at Cidambaram) (344-413) After Śiva departed, Māṇikkavācakar began to sing the hymns which form the *Tiruvācakam*. When the other devotees joined. Śiva, the poet set out for Cidambaram, visiting *en route* Uttarakōcamaṅkai, Tiruvārūr, Tiruvaṇṇāmalai, Kaḻukkuṉṟam, and other temples, composing hymns at several of these places. When he first saw the golden hall of the temple in Cidambaram, his ecstasy was so great that the temple guard thought he was crazy. It was in Cidambaram that most of his hymns were composed, many of them to be sung by women.

Carukkam 6 — The chapter about defeating the Buddhists in a debate (414-509). The Buddhist king of Ceylon learned of Śiva's temple in Cidambaram from a wandering ascetic. When the Buddhist monks heard Śiva praised, one of them accompanied by several of his colleagues, decided to travel to Cidambaram in order to assert the superiority of Buddhism. The Ceylonese king also went to Cidambaram in hopes of finding a cure for his daughter who was dumb. When the Buddhists arrived, insults were traded with the Śaivas and a great debate was scheduled for the next day. The Cōḻa king was invited to this event. That night Śiva instructed the proponents of

Śaivism, in a dream, to enlist the help of Māṇikkavācakar who would defeat the Buddhists. The debate itself is pictured as a momentous occasion which even the gods attended (456). The ensuing disputation was more or less a philosophical one, interspersed, however, with many contemptuous remarks about the opponent's position.[27] Māṇikkavācakar completely vanquished the Buddhists, invoking Sarasvatī to strike them dumb. At this, the Ceylonese king said that if his daughter's speech would be restored, he would become a worshipper of Śiva. The daughter was brought and promptly answered all Māṇikkavācakar's questions to which the dumb-struck Buddhists were unable to respond. The king and the other Buddhists then all became devotees of Śiva, putting on the holy ashes and *rudrākṣa* beads. They remained in Cidambaram in order to worship the god.

Carukkam 7 — The chapter on attaining the Sacred Feet (510-544). After the debate with the Buddhists, Māṇikkavācakar continued to compose hymns in praise of Śiva. One day, the god himself took the form of a guru and visited him, requesting him to sing all of the hymns which he had composed. This the poet did, while the guru wrote down the entire *Tiruvācakam* and *Tirukkōvaiyār*, disappearing as soon as he had finished. Śiva now assembled the gods and sang Māṇikkavācakar's hymns to them. Then, he took the copy of the hymns, which he had made with his own hand, and placed it at the entrance of the Ampalam so that the whole world would know how Māṇikkavācakar gained salvation (525). When the text was discovered and the contents read, the devotees went to Māṇikkavācakar and asked him to explain the hymns. The poet led them to the golden hall in order to give his explanation. There, pointing to the god, he said, "This One alone is the meaning of this garland of Tamil songs", and at that he disappeared, having united with Śiva (537-538). This led to a great outpouring of devotion not only by those present but by the denizens of heaven as well. The Purāṇa closes with a verse capsulizing the benefits of reading and hearing the story (543) and a verse of praises (544).

Form and Style of the *Tiruvācakam*

The *Tiruvācakam* is Māṇikkavācakar's major work. Although he also wrote the *Tirukkōvaiyār*, a love poem which follows the model of Caṅkam *akam* poetry, and which traditionally has been interpreted as an allegory on the relationship between the soul and Śiva,[28] it is on the collection of devotional poems which constitute his 'Sacred Utterances' (*Tiruvācakam*), that Māṇikkavācakar's reputation as the premier poet of Tamil Śaivism rests. The *Tiruvācakam* contains fifty-one hymns comprising a total of 3,414 lines. The hymns range in length from the eight lines of "Tiruppaṭai Eḻucci" (hymn 46) to the 400-line "Tiruccatakam" (hymn 5). A complete list of the hymns along with their traditional places of composition and brief comments of the distinctive features of each hymn is found in the Appendix.

Four major kinds of meter are employed in the *Tiruvācakam: veṇpā, kalippā, āciriyappā* (*akaval*), and *viruttam*. Pope analyzes these meters into fourteen subvarieties.[29] Of the four principal metrical forms found in the text, all except *viruttam* are prominently used in Caṅkam poetry.[30] Other elements of Tamil prosody such as rhyme (particularly on the second syllable of a line), assonance. and alliteration are frequently encountered in Māṇikkavācakar's poetry. Many hymns feature a refrain-like word or phrase that is repeated in every stanza (e.g., hymns 7-18, 20, 23-31, 35, 37, 40-43, 51). These qualities of the *Tiruvācakam's* poetry give these hymns an unusual musicality, and indeed among Tamil speakers they are typically recited or sung rather than read or simply spoken in a normal voice, although unlike the *patikams* of the *Tēvāram* authors, the *Tiruvācakam* has not been set to specific tunes for congregational singing.[31] While there is much that the *Tiruvācakam* shares with the *Tēvāram* in language and symbols, Māṇikkavācakar's hymns are a more personal, autobiographical form of poetry than the lyrics of Appar, Campantar, and Cuntarar.

Regarding Māṇikkavācakar's vocabulary, it is certainly more highly Sanskritized than that of the Caṅkam poets. A word count from one of the shorter hymns indicates that about 14 per cent of the vocabulary represents lexical borrowing from Indo-Aryan.[32] Yet, the borrowed words are not intrusive. Many technical terms, for which there are well-known Sanskrit equivalents, are given their indigenous Dravidian counterparts, e.g., *aṉpu* far more frequeutly than *bhakti*, *viṉai* rather than *karman*, *vīṭu* rather than *mokṣa*, *aruḷ* more frequently than *karuṇā*, *maṟai* more frequently than Veda, etc. When one remembers that Māṇikkavācakar was a Brahmin and, according to his traditional biography, was highly educated and almost certainly acquainted with Sanskrit, the impression arises that he consciously avoids certain Sanskrit terminology. In all the examples just cited, there are Sanskrit-derived equivalents in Tamil. Yet Māṇikkavācakar uses Dravidian words, presumably because of this usage being already established in Tamil bhakti lyrics and also quite conceivably since he wants to avoid the semantic overtones of some of the Sanskrit terms. In vocabulary as well as prosody (and to a noteworthey extent in ideology too, as will be noted later), the *Tiruvācakam* bears the distinctive stamp of the Tamil literary tradition.

The arrangement of the fifty-one hymns in the *Tiruvācakam*, while not completely arbitrary, does not warrant some of the theories about a hierarchy of mystical assent which modern interpreters of the text would have us see.[33] Basically, the kinds of themes mentioned at the beginning of the text are not much different from those to which the poet is giving voice in hymn 51. Clearly, individual hymns differ in tone and format from other hymns. Certain motifs are more evident in some hymns than others, but no obvious overarching pattern to the collection emerges. Apart from hymn 1, in their present arrangement, the poems of the *Tiruvācakam* do not follow the chronology of composition set forth in the *Tiruvātavūrar Purāṇam*. The hymns composed at Tillai (Cidambaram) are interspersed with others said to have been first recited at Peruntuṟai and other places (see Appendix).

It is possible, however, to speak of several distinct groups of poems. After the opening hymn, the "Civapurāṇam", there follow three hymns in varieties of the *akaval* meter. The first four hymns are not arranged in stanzas and are not as autobiographical in tone as the remainder of the *Tiruvācakam*. They tend to be summaries of Śaiva ideas, of epithets of Śiva, and of places sacred to the god. In this, Vanmikanathan is right, hymns 1 through 4 are a kind of 'prologue."[34] The fifth hymn is the longest in the text and is arranged in ten decads of four-line stanzas. The meter varies from decad to decad and there is a sense of spiritual progress from the first decad to the last, the tone having become much more personal in this hymn than in the preceding four. Both the hymns, 5 and 6, are *antāti* poems, in which the last word or foot of each verse becomes the first word or foot of the succeeding verse and the last word of the entire poem is also the initial word of the verse 1. This fairly typical device of post-Caṅkam Tamil poetry probably originated as an aid to memorization and in the *Tiruvācakam* is indicative of the decidedly oral nature of the hymns. Hymns 20, 21, 32, and 33 are also in the *antāti* form.

Hymns 7 to 19 comprise those poems which are formally the most intriguing in the collection. Their interest lies not so much in meter, rhyme, or vocabulary, but in the setting presupposed by these hymns. Most of these poems are intended to be sung by women while performing various domestic activities or in accompaniment to village games which were at one time popular in the Tamil country. All presuppose that those singing the hymns have psychologically/spiritually cast themselves in the role of females devoted to Śiva, their beloved or husband. Thus, hymn 7 is to be sung by young women taking their morning bath.[35] The next poem is meant for singing while playing a village game (cf. *Cilappatikāram* 29 : 16-19).

The ninth hymn pictures the devotees as singing praises of Śiva while they prepare an aromatic bathing compound with mortar and pestle. There are references in Caṅkam literature to verses sung by women at times of grinding grain with a pestle. In *Kuṟuntokai* 89, a girl sings of her lover as she pounds paddy, probably a discreet means of announcing her love to her parents so that a speedy marriage will be arranged. In *Malaipaṭukaṭam* 342 references to this kind of a song (called *vaḷḷaippaṭṭu)* occurs in the context of praises sung about King Naṉṉāṉ.[36] And *Cilappatikāram* 29:26-29 mentions 'pestle songs' *(vaḷḷaippaṭṭu)* praising the monarchs of the three kingdoms of ancient Tamilnad. All these references indicate an original non-cultic, non-religious context for such pestle songs, as is the case with other work and game songs attested in both the *Tiruvācakam* and in pre-bhakti Tamil literature.

Hymn 10's setting is that of a woman addressing a

humming bee who will carry her message to Śiva. Likewise the eighteenth hymn has a cuckoo for a messenger. Both these poems are of the *tūtu* (Skt. *dūta*) genre, a form known in other Indian literatures. The bee (*tumpi*) is already pictured as a messenger between lovers in several Caṅkam poems.[37] Somewhat similar in form is hymn 19, in which a parrot and a female devotee of Śiva carry on a dialogue about Śiva's ten special features, hence, the hymn's title, "Tiruttacāṅkam" (Skt. *daśāṅga*).

The eleventh and twelfth poems are both meant to accompany the playing of girls' games. Hymn 12, "Tiruccāḻal", is the dialogue supposed to have taken place between Māṇikkavācakar and the formerly dumb daughter of the Ceylonese king. A *cāḻal* is a question and answer type of game still played by young women in North Arcot and South Arcot districts.[38] Two sides, each accompanied by drums, trade questions and answers all night. The game begins with patterned responses and then becomes spontaneous. A similar game is also played in the river beds around Madurai during the hot season, particularly in the month of Cittirai.

Hymn 13 is a flower-picking poem, to be sung while gathering flowers for Śiva. The next two hymns are again conceived as accompaniments to female games. The sixteenth hymn is for singing while gliding on a swing. Again, this is a form of composition known to pre-bhakti authors (*Cilappatikāram* 29:23-25), although, as before, the context there is not a religious one. And hymn 17 has the young woman confessing her love for Śiva to her mother.

This remarkable series of hymns reveals something about the social context of Tamil bhakti. Devotion is related to the daily routine. It is popular, intended for the majority of people for whom renunciation of the world is not a live option. Bhakti is non-esoteric, not limited to an elite of religious virtuosi. Although many of the major bhakti poets, including Māṇikkavācakar, altered their life styles rather drastically when they became devotees of Śiva, the forms of many hymns show that they did not expect most people who became bhaktas to follow their example in this regard. In the same vein, one can find a modern Tamil "saint", Ramana Maharshi, (whose philosophical position is, to be sure, quite different from our poet's) writing a lyric based on making *pappaṭams*.[39] The adaptation of devotional hymn-singing to the playing of games is also known to the Marathi-speaking Vārkarīs who make the annual pilgrimage to Pandharpur in Maharashtra.[40]

The remaining hymns of the *Tiruvācakam* do not fall into any distinctive groupings. Many are poems of ten stanzas and bear titles indicating this (e.g., hymns 23-29, 31, 33-35, 37, 40-42, 45 all of which are called *pattu*, and hymns 21, 22, 36 which are ten-verse *patikams*). Most do not presuppose a special context, such as hymns 7 through 19. One of the more distinctive poems in these remaining hymns is "Tiruppaḷḷiyeḻucci", which is to be sung to the deity in order to awaken him in the morning. This poem presupposes a cultic setting. There is also a poem of the same title by Toṇṭaraṭippoṭi Āḻvār, who probably lived in the early ninth century.[41] Again, there is a "secular" reference to the same practice in Caṅkam literature; for one of the *puṟam* situations is that in which poets awaken the king in the morning by singing his praises (*tuyileṭai nilai—Tolkāppiyam Poruḷatikāram* 91:2).[42]

The *Tiruvācakam* was not the subject of formal commentary until modern times. Along with other Śaiva devotional hymns, it was considered too sacred for commentary.[43] Interestingly enough, however, Māṇikkavācakar's *Tirukkōvaiyār*, which also gained admission to the Śaiva canon, was extensively commented upon by Pēräciriyar in the thirteenth century. For fairly obvious reasons, the *Tirukkōvaiyār* was evidently not accorded the same exalted status as the *Tiruvācakam* and the *Tēvāram* hymns. The absence of old commentaries has not had the effect of encouraging nineteenth and twentieth-century interpreters of the text to attempt to understand the *Tiruvācakam* on its own terms. Rather, there has developed what can almost be labelled a modern commentarial tradition of interpreting the text in accordance with Śaiva Siddhānta notions which had not crystallized until several centuries after Māṇikkavācakar's time. One also notes in some quarters frequent comparative comment claiming similarities with the Upaniṣads and Western literature (e.g., Shakespeare, Dante, Plato, and even Walt Whitman). Much of the modern commentary tells us more about the intellectual milieu of the "Hindu Renaissance" than it does about the *Tiruvācakam*. In turning to the text itself, there is no relying upon a longstanding, venerable commentarial tradition.

NOTES

1. Among those authors who, in one way or another, argue for or accept a ninth-century date for the poet are Zvelebil, *Tamil Literature* pp. 143-144; K.A. Nilakanta Sastri in the following three books: *A History of South India*, pp. 175, 425; *Development of Religion in South India*, (Bombay: Orient Longmans, 1963), p. 44; *The Culture and History of the Tamils* (Calcutta: K.L. Mukhopadhyay, 1963), p. 111; S. Vaiyapuri Pillai, *History of Tamil Language and Literature (Beginning to 1000 AD)* (Madras: New Century Book House, 1956), pp. 114-115; T.P. Meenakshisundaran, *A History of Tamil Literature* (Annamalainagar: Annamalai University, 1965), p. 81; C. and Hephzibah Jesudasan, *A History of Tamil Literature* (Calcutta: YMCA Publishing House, 1961), pp. 85-86; K.K. Pillay, *South India and Ceylon* (Madras: University of Madras: 1963), pp. 57-58. Less recent authorities who also claim the poet lived in the ninth century include Schomerus, *Die Hymen des Māṇikka-vāśaga*, pp. xxviii-xxx; M. Srinivasa Aiyangar, *Tamil Studies* (Madras: Guardian Press, 1914), pp. 392, 396. Of the above scholars, it is interesting that K.A. Nilkanta Sastri apparently changed his mind on this issue, for in an earlier book he had argued that Māṇikkavācakar preceded the authors of the *Tēvāram: The Pāṇḍyan Kingdom: From the Earliest Times to the Sixteenth Century* (1929; reprint ed., Madras: Swathi Publications, 1972), pp. 59-60.

2. For the earlier date, see Navaratnam, *A New Approach to Tiruvacagam*, p. 45. For dating Māṇikkavācakar in the tenth century, see P. Graefe, "Legends as Mile-Stones in the History of Tamil Literature", *Professor P.K. Gode Commemoration Volume*, ed. H.L. Hariyappa and M.M. Patakar, Poona Oriental Series, no. 93 (Poona: Oriental Book Agency, 1960), p. 144. The work by Mrs. Navaratnam is, as noted above in the Introduction, rather uncritical. Graefe's argument for Māṇikkavācakar's date rests on allusions in the *Tiruvācakam* to stories related in the *Cidambaramāhātmya*, which Graefe thinks is of tenth-century origin. However, the fact that Māṇikkavācakar is aware of some traditions relating to Cidambaram which do not find an expression in Sanskrit literature until the tenth century, does not of itself constitute a cogent argument for assigning a particular temporal sequence to these works.

3. C.V. Narayana Ayyar, *Origin and Early History of Śaivism in South India*, Madras University Historical Series, no. 6 (Madras: University of Madras, 1936), p. 419. Narayana Ayyar states a very long, convoluted argument for Māṇikkavācakar's having been a contemporary of Appar and Campantar, and by a series of ingenious

but unpersuasive reasonings arrives at the conclusion that our poet "must have lived between AD 660 and 692" (p. 431; see pp. 398-431 for the entire argument).

4. Zvelebil, op. cit., p. 143 (n. 92). This book is without doubt the most responsible and up-to-date work on the chronology of Tamil literature currently available. Unless otherwise noted, the argument for Māṇikkavācakar's date presented here relies on Zvelebil, pp. 143-144. The king mentioned in connection with the above inscription is the Rajendra II of K.A. Nilakanta Sastri's standard work on the Cōḻa dynasty: *The Cōḻas*, 2d ed., Madras University Historical Series, no. 9 (Madras: University of Madras, 1955), pp. 260-266.

5. Ibid., pp. 141-142.

6. *Tirukkōvaiyār* 306 (*varakuṇāṉ eṉṉavaṉ*) and 327 (*varakuṇāṉ*). For the text, see Po. Ve. Cōmacuntaraṉ, ed. and commentator, *Tirukkōvaiyār* (Madras: South India Saiva Siddhanta Works Publishing Society, 1970), pp. 490, 523.

7. Nilakanta Sastri, *History of South India*, pp. 156-157, 172, 174-175.

8. On Caṇṭēcuvarar, see 15: 7 translated and discussed in chapter 7; and on Kaṇṇappaṉ, see 10: 4 and 15: 3 and the translations and discussion of these verses in chapter 7.

9. V.R. Ramachandra Dikshitar, *Studies in Tamil Literature and History* (Madras: University of Madras, 1936), p. 99.

10. *Tēvāram* 6: 98: 1 in *Tēvārappatikaṅkaḷ* (*Aṟāntirumuṟai*) (Madras: Āṟumukavilāca Accukkūṭam, 1898), p. 117. For translation of 5: 30, see chapter 7.

11. J. Filliozat, *Tiruppāvai d'Āṇṭāḷ* (1972), p. xiii, quoted in Zvelebil, *Tamil Literature*, p. 114 (n. 95). Both the "Tiruvempāvai" and the *Tiruppāvai* have the same setting, on which see n. 35 below.

12. Pillay, *South India and Ceylon*, p. 57. The *Nikāyasangrahaya*, probably written about the beginning of the fifteenth century, is mainly concerned with the various difficulties which the Buddhist Saṃgha overcame in the course of its history in India and Ceylon; see C.E. Godakumbura, *Sinhalese Literature* (Colombo: Colombo Apothecaries' Co., 1955), pp. 122-124.

13. Nilakanta Sastri, *Development of Religion in South India*, p. 68.

14. George W. Spencer, "The Politics of Plunder: The Cholas in Eleventh-Century Ceylon", *Journal of Asian Studies* 35, no. 3 (May 1976): 405-419, esp. 407-408.

15. *Tēvārappatikaṅkaḷ* (*Nāṉkāntirumuṟai*) (Madras: Āṟumukavilāca Accukūṭam, 1898), p. 5.

16. For example, Navaratnam, *A New Approach to Tiruvacagam*, p. 44; Narayana Ayyar, *Śaivism in South India*, pp. 401-403; Nilakanta Sastri, *The Pāṇḍyan Kingdom*, pp. 59-60.

17. Schomerus, *Die Hymnen des Māṇikka-vāśaga*, p. xxx. Srinivasa Pillai (in *Tamil Varalāṟu*) attempts to discount Appar's mention of this incident on grammatical grounds, stating that Appar was merely saying that Śiva was capable of accomplishing such a transformation—

an argument recounted and refuted by Narayana Ayyar, *Śaivism in South India*, pp. 401:403.

18. Zvelebil, op. cit., p. 221.

19. Kaṭavuḷmāmuinvar, *Tiruvātavūraṭikaḷ Purāṇam*, ed. and commentator Pu. Ci. Puṉṉaivaṉanāta Mutaliyār (Madras: South India Saiva Siddhanta Works Publishing Society, 1967).

20. Pope summarizes the text in the introduction to his translation of the *Tiruvācakam*, pp. xvii-xxxii. Also see T.M.P. Mahadevan, *Ten Saints of India* (Bombay: Bharatiya Vidya Bhavan, 1965), pp. 61-73. The German translation is by H.W. Schomerus, trans., *Śivaitische Heilegenlegenden* (*Periyapurāṇa und Tiruvātavūrar-purāna*) (Jena: Eugen Diederichs, 1925), pp. 193-286.

21. The earliest version is by Perumpaṟṟappuliyūr Nampi. There is a second Tamil version by Parañcōtimuṉivar, probably of the sixteenth or seventeenth century. A Sanskrit text relating the same material and probably originating sometime between the two Tamil versions is the *Hālāsyamāhātmya*. See Zevlebil, *Tamil Literature*, pp. 220-221; and R. Dessigane, P.Z. Pattabiramin, and J. Filliozat, *La Legende des Jeux de çiva a Madurai: D'aprés les textes et les peintures* (Pondichery: Institut français d'indologie, 1960), vol. 1, pp. ii-ix. The last-mentioned work contains an extensive prose summary in French of Parañcōti's version (pp. 1-114).

22. Zvelebil, op. cit., p. 221 (n. 112).

23. Verse numbers in parentheses are those given in Puṉṉaivaṉanāta Mutaliyār's edition.

24. From the perspective of critical history, this is a glaring anachronism, since this basic Śaiva Siddhānta text by Meykaṇṭa Tēvar was not written until the thirteenth century.

25. Cf. a similar incident regarding misappropriated funds in the legends about the Vīraśaiva poet and reformer Basava; see *Basava Purāṇa* 11: 9-15 (a Kannada text of the fourteenth century) translated in Edward P. Rice, *A History of Kanarese Literature*, 2d ed., (Calcutta: Association Press, 1921), pp. 65-67.

26. Charlotte Vaudeville has speculated that Māṇikkavācakar was influenced by Sufi ideas which reached South India through Arab traders. She sees confirmation of this in the fact that the horse traders and the horse-groom in the hagiography are presented as foreigners. While the horse traders may well have been Arabs (at one place the *Tiruvācakam* refers this incident to the "western region" [*kuṭanāṭu*—2: 27], but the *Tiruvātavūrar Purāṇam* specifically locates Peruntuṟai on the east coast), the themes in Māṇikkavācakar's poems which Vaudeville attributes to Sufi influence can more cogently be explained by comparison with early Tamil literary traditions. There is no indication in the *Tiruvācakam* that Māṇikkavācakar met or had even heard of Muslims. See Charlotte Vaudeville, "Evalution of Love-Symbolism in Bhagavatism", *Journal of the American Oriental Society* 82 (1962); 35-36. More far-fetched still is the suggestion of "some writers", un-

named but mentioned by Nilakanta Sastri, that Māṇikkavācakar may have been influenced by Christian theology (*Culture and History of the Tamils*, p. 111).

27. Pope gives a detailed summary of the debate, although he has little admiration for the level of reasoning displayed: *Tiruvāçagam*, pp. lxvii-lxxii.

28. The *Tirrukkōvaiyār* is included alongwith the *Tiruvācakam* in the eighth *Tirumuṟai* of the Tamil Śaiva canon, although overtly it is not a religious poem at all. It is commonly interpreted as reversing the erotic symbolism of the *Tiruvācakam* and most other mystical poetry by seeing God as female and the soul as male. See Ramachandra Dikshitar, *Studies in Tamil Literature*, pp. 101-103; Meenakshisundaran, *History of Tamil Literature*, p. 138. On the *kōvai* form, see Zvelebil, *Tamil Literature*, p. 166 (n. 2).

29. Pope, *Tiruvāçagam*, pp. lxxxvii-xcii. A list of the meters used in the individual hymns is also found in Zvelebil, *Tamil Literature*, pp. 144-145 (n. 98).

30. Hart, *Poems of Ancient Tamil*, pp. 198-200.

31. Jesudasan, *History of Tamil Literature*, p. 90.

32. Based on hymn 48, which has twenty-eight lines and a total of 156 words. The *Tamil Lexicon*, 6 vols. (Madras: University of Madras, 1924–36), was used to determine whether a term was of Dravidian or Indo-Aryan origin.

33. In this regard, see Vanmikanathan, *Pathway to God through Tamil Literature: I—Through the Thiruvaachakam*, pp. xii-xxiii, 28–100. Vanmikanathan understands the text as a "manual of mystical theology" with four sections, the last three corresponding to well-known stages in Western mystical literature: prologue (hymns 1-4), purgation (5-6), illumination (7-22), and union (23-51). Apart from the difficulties inherent in trying to apply a Western mystical paradigm to a Hindu text, the argument is unpersuasive. For an essay which follows Vanmikanathan's interpretation, see M. Lucetta Mowry, "The Structure of Love in Māṇikkavācakar's *Tiruvācakam*", *Structural Approaches to South India Studies*, ed. Harry M. Buck and Glenn E. Yocum (Chambersburg, Penna.: Wilson Books, 1974), pp. 207-224.

34. Vanmikanathan, ibid., p. 29.

35. Hymn 7, "Tiruvempāvai", is one of the most popular hymns of the text. Along with Āṇṭāḷ's *Tiruppāvai* it is especially sung by young unmarried women performing a vow during Mārkaḻi month at the beginning of the marriage season in hopes of getting married to good husbands. Some verses of "Tiruvempāvai" are problematic because they seem to presuppose a dialogue between one female and a group of her friends without any clear indication, however, as to who is speaking at what time. This has opened the doors to a number of ingenious but philosophically anachronistic interpretations, some of which assume a rather elaborate Śaiva Siddhānta framework, e.g., Schomerus *Die Hymen des Mānikkavāśaga*, p. 57; and Vanmikanathan, ibid., pp. 223-229. A more restrained, descriptive account is that of K.M. Balasubramaniam,

"Saint Manickavachakar's Tiruvembavai", *Madurai Sri Meenakshi Sundareswarar Mahakumbabishekam Souvenir*, ed. P.T. Rajan (Madurai: Thiruppani Committee Sri Meenakshi Devasthanam, 1963), pp. x-xiii. On Āṇṭāḷ's *Tiruppāvai*, see D. Ramaswamy Iyengar, trans., *Thiruppavai*, 2d ed. (Madras: Sri Vishishtadvaita Pracharini Sabha, 1967).

36. On *vaḷḷaippāṭṭu*, see Kailasapathy, *Tamil Heroic Poetry*, p. 234.

37. *Kuṟuntokai* 392, *Naṟṟiṇai* 271 (cf. *Kuṟuntokai* 2), as cited in M. Varadarajan, *The Treatment of Nature in Sangam Literature* (Madras: South India Śaiva Siddhanta Works Publishing Society, 1969), pp. 359-360.

38. I am indebted to Professor M. Shanmugam Pillai for information on the contemporary performance of *cāḻal*.

39. *The Collected Works of Ramana Maharshi*, ed. Arthur Osborne (New York: Samuel Weiser, 1972), pp. 86-88.

40. I. Karve, "On the Road: A Maharashtrian Pilgrimage", *Journal of Asian Studies* 22, no. 1 (November 1962): 23-24. On the function of singing hymns among the Vārkarīs, also see G.A. Deleury, *The Cult of Viṭhobā* (Poona: Deccan College, 1960), pp. 88-89.

41. Zvelebil, op. cit., p. 156.

42. Ibid. See also N. Subrahmaniam *Pre-Pallavan Tamil Index* (Madras: University of Madras, 1966), p. 443.

43. Zvelebil, *Smile of Murugan*, p. 248 (n. 1). Mrs. Ratna Navaratnam says the first commentary on the *Tiruvācakam* was that of Kā-[illegible] Tantavarāyar in the second half of the nineteenth century (personal communication).

4

The Human Problem

At a personal level, religion is basically a dynamic process which aims to transform human existence from its ordinary problematic and unsatisfactory state to a condition of perfection and ultimate satisfaction, from the profane to the sacred. Thus, it is necessary to define the poles of this transformation in Māṇikkavācakar's case.[1] Accordingly, the next four chapters will examine the *Tiruvācakam* in terms of the way in which it presents the problem of human existence and its solution, of what is wrong with man and how this unsatisfactoriness can be overcome. The movement of these chapters will be from problem, to mediating categories between the sacred and profane, to answer (viz., Śiva), to the means by which the transformation is practically achieved (viz., through bhakti).

The present chapter will focus on Māṇikkavācakar's understanding of ordinary existence, in a sense his preconversion, pre-Peruntuṟai condition, although in the *Tiruvācakam*, which stems entirely from the period after his conversion, there is still considerable oscillation between 'ordinariness' and exaltation. The problems persist, although they are now recognized as such. From what does Māṇikkavācakar desire release? Why is ordinary existence unsatisfactory? These are the questions to be addressed in this chapter.

While the *Tiruvācakam* features much standard Hindu terminology in stating the *terminus a quo* and *terminus ad quem* of the desired transformation, such vocabulary assumes, as indeed one would expect, distinctive shades of meaning in Māṇikkavācakar's usage. Thus, it would be easy (and, in fact, accurate) to claim that Māṇikkavācakar seeks freedom *(mokṣa)* from karma-saṃsāra by means of bhakti; but this only serves to locate him in a very broad current of the Hindu tradition, namely, the path of bhakti. It tells one very little about the significance these words acquire when used by Māṇikkavācakar; for there is much that sets the *Tiruvācakam* apart from many of the other works which use the same terminology. How, then, does Māṇikkavācakar view unregenerate humanity?

Karma and Rebirth

Undoubtedly, that which weighs most heavily on Māṇikkavācakar's consciousness is the twin burden of karma and rebirth, or *viṉai* (deed) and *piṟappu* (birth) as his most commonly mentioned Tamil equivalents put the problem. Clearly, Māṇikkavācakar is not simply mouthing received tradition when he laments his bondage to karma-saṃsāra. The frequency and intensity of his reference to this most insidious human malady show that to do karmically potent "deeds" and to suffer their consequences is a very immediate threat to his psychological/spiritual well-being. In short, this is not a 'doctrine' kept at intellectual arm's length, an interesting but ultimately 'safe' philosophical issue. Although the content is very different from most Christian formulations of man's predicament, comparison with Luther's throwing inkpots at the devil is not entirely inappropriate; for Māṇikkavācakar too experienced the terrible crush of a force which menaced, pursued, indeed clung, to him at every turn.

Viṉai is a literal Tamil rendering of the Sanskrit *karman*, indicating both the deed and its effect.[2] Thus, Māṇikkavācakar speaks of his collection or accumulation (*tokuti*) of *viṉai* (6:6). Karma is a burden from the past; it is "former karma" (*muntai viṉai*–1:20; *muṉṉai viṉai*–47:4), "old karma" (*tollai viṉai*–14:13), or "ancient karma" (*paḻa viṉai*–13:8; 30:7; 51:1). *Viṉai* is twofold, for it encompasses both good and evil action (*iru viṉai*–3:87; 40:3: 41:8; *viṉa irantu*–47:1,4). The poet desires release from both the types of karma.

Although karma is always depicted as something baleful in the *Tiruvācakam*, it must be stressed that 'good' deeds with 'good' effects are also included in this category. Usually Māṇikkavācakar simply praises Śiva for "severing" (*aṟu*) or "destroying" (*keṭu*) his karma, but in 30:1 he speaks of Śiva's "obliterating future affliction, balancing my karma (*eṉ viṉai ottu*) so that no unwithering seed could mature thereafter." A likely interpretation of what it means to have balanced karma is that for such a person no karmic fruit will ripen because he acts with equanimity and detachment. While Māṇikkavācakar never explicitly states that only actions performed without egoistic desire are free of ensuing karmic consequences, this implication seems clear, if not from the reference just cited, from passages where he describes the transformation in his behavior effected by Śiva's bestowal of grace upon him. He becomes free of ego and desire.

Sometimes Māṇikkavācakar uses the unadorned term *viṉai* (e.g., 5:22,93; 6:39; 8:14). More typically, however, *viṉai* is qualified by one of a number of revealing adjectives. In the *Tiruvācakam*, the most common attribute of karma is its strength or potency; for this is not a problem lightly dismissed. Hence, reference is often made to "strong karma" (*val viṉai* – e.g., 1:50; 5:8; 6:37; 13:3; 26:3; 30:7; 48:4). In his frequent use of this adjective, Māṇikkavācakar emphasizes the stubbornness of the problem. In combating karma, one is up against a formidable opponent, as it were. Indeed, the imagery of warfare is found in the text itself. "Strong karma" shows "enmity" (*pakai*) towards Māṇikkavācakar, but this adversary is "destroyed" (*māy*) by Śiva (42:9)—significantly not by the comparatively weak and powerless Māṇikkavācakar. His meager resources are clearly no match for karma's strength. In a sense, man appears in the *Tiruvāckam* as a rather passive, impotent entity caught in a cosmic battle between karma and its consequences, on the one hand, and Śiva, on the other — a battle, however, the outcome of which literally makes all the difference in the world. Māṇikkavācakar, while not an active combatant, is hardly a disinterested observer of the fray.

Karma is also "cruel" (*kaṭu*–32:2; *koṭu*–33:1), "fierce" (*veyya*–47:1), "evil" (*pollā*–1:25), "wicked" (*tī*/*tīya*–5:21; 19:9; 36:9; 42:6), and "difficult" (*aru*–5:5; 11:11). Karma clings, cannot be gotten rid of (*piriyā viṉai*–34·1). It "destroys" (*keṭu* –5:22; 30:3). It is a "disease" (*nōy*–33:1), a "pain" (*vētaṉai*–31:2) and is referred to as a "sea" (*kaṭal*) in which one is liable to drown (35:2). But Śiva "makes ancient, tormenting (*utaṟṟu*) karma into a lie (*kiṟi cey*)" (13:8). In effect, God cheats karma.

Given the popularly held view that karma is a kind of impersonal cosmic law which operates in the sphere of moral events, akin to the laws of physics which govern the material environment, one is struck by the difference in tone, if not substance, of Māṇikkavācakar's expression. Here, karma appears not so much as an ineluctable law to which individuals are encouraged to conform, thus establishing a metaphysical basis for personal moral responsibility, as for example, in Pāli Buddhism.[3] Rather, in the *Tiruvācakam*, the deterministic side of the 'doctrine' is given great prominence. Māṇikkavācakar views karma almost entirely as a burden from the *past*, never suggesting that it might also present an opportunity for improving one's *future*. Karmic fruit rather than karmic seed is uppermost in his mind.

Where Māṇikkavācakar deviates even more strikingly from the common, more philosophical understanding of karma is in his tone, which makes karma appear to be a quasi-personal force imposed from without, indeed a sinister force. How else shall we interpret the vivid, highly personal adjectives mentioned in the previous paragraphs? One could say that, being a poet, Māṇikkavācakar was quite skilled in the use of metaphors. But, the total impression which I gain from the *Tiruvācakam* is that Māṇikkavācakar *experienced* karma as something strong, cruel, fierce, evil, destructive, indeed experienced it as an enemy which would yield only to a more powerful person. To be sure, karma is a mode of action, is the effect of such action, and is a principle of order regulating human affairs. But, the reality of that principle in Māṇikkavācakar's experience assumes haunting proportions. Just as many cultures have seen fit to personify death and evil, Māṇikkavācakar speaks of his basic problem in personal terms.

It is interesting that the operation of karma is personified, or rather partially personified, in the Tamil Śaiva Siddhānta philosophical system of which Māṇikkavācakar is considered a forerunner. The manner of personification, however, is totally different from that just noted in the *Tiruvācakam;* for in Śaiva Siddhānta, karma is set in motion by an aspect of Śiva's *śakti,* his female energy which is constantly guiding souls toward perfection. Whereas in the *Tiruvācakam* we have no suggestion that karma operates at Śiva's behest, the Śaiva Siddhānta *śāstras* systematize and rationalize the basically monotheistic impulse of the Tamil Śiva bhakti poets. What results is a kind of Indian variant on the classical western problem of theodicy. That is, if God is both omnipotent and benevolent, then there must be no force controlling human destiny apart from God himself, certainly not a morally ambiguous force. For the Siddhānta philosophers, however, karma was self-evident. How can both Śiva and karma be accommodated in the same philosophical system? The Siddhānta solution states that while karma is essentially something of Śiva's nature, it remains only potentially real until Śiva, through his *aruḷśakti*,[4] allows it to operate according to *his* rules (*Civañāṉacittiyār* 3:2:40).[5] Thus, although karma is independent of Śiva, it is also subordinate to him. Hc is the one who matches each soul with the karma appropriate to it (*Civañāṉacittiyār* 3:2:46), all of which is a function of his love for the souls (*Civañāṉacittiyār* 3:2:14-16). Śiva's joining of the soul to karma is consequenetly understood to be an aspect of the process of the soul's liberation, of the operation of Śiva's grace. Karma merely provides an orderly process by which souls eventually are released from bondage (*pācam*, Skt. *pāśa*).

How different is the mind of the poet from that of the philosopher. Although divergence in ideology between Māṇikkavācakar and the later Siddhāntins on the order of that just noted is quite unusual, their differing inflections demonstrate distinct modes of experience and expression, one mainly intellectual and rational, the other affective and aesthetic. And Indian terminology would probably state the difference as basically that between *jñānin* and *bhakta*. It is a difference which we shall meet again.

If karma seems to spin a confining web around Māṇikkavācakar, it is karma's result in rebirth that evokes even more frequent expressions of distress from the poet. Karma definitely is the root of the problem, but one has the impression that the situation would be far more tolerable if not for rebirth. Māṇikkavācakar accepts the pan-Hindu idea of transmigration regulated by karma. The prospect of virtually endless birth and death is anything but attractive. It is enervating, deadening. Māṇikkavācakar's view that a long chain of previous births lies behind his present existence is clearly stated in the first hymn of the *Tiruvācakam*. This passage is also of interest because it allows a glimpse of the extent of the realm in which rebirth is thought to occur.

> O boundless One
> who transcends my thoughts,
> I with my evil karma [*pollā vi<u>n</u>ai*]
> don't know any way to praise Your great glory.
> As grass, shrub, worm, tree,
> As many sorts of animals, birds, snakes,
> As stone, man, demon [*pēy*], *gaṇas*,
> As mighty *asuras*, ascetics [*mu<u>n</u>ivar*], gods [*tēvar*]—
> among these immobile and mobile forms,
> in every kind of birth [*pi<u>r</u>appu*],
> I was born [*pi<u>r</u>a*] and grew weary
> O great Lord!
> O Truth!
> Today I saw Your golden feet and was released [*vīṭu<u>r</u>u*].
> (1:24–32)

In this passage, one first notices the juxtaposition of karma and rebirth. "Evil karma" leads to a wearying rebirth. Elsewhere, the two are mentioned in the same breath as *vi<u>n</u>aippi<u>r</u>avi* (1:87; 31:2), the Tamil equivalent of karma-saṃsāra. Also noteworthy is the range of saṃsāra, including vegetable and even inanimate forms, an extension of the domain of 'life' that is rare for the Hindu tradition. Supernatural beings, including the *devas* (see also 8:14), share this unsatisfactory condition. Only Śiva, and those devotees whom he has released, are outside the cycle of rebirth. At the head of this passage, detailing the many forms of existence experienced by Māṇikkavācakar, Śiva is addressed as "the boundless One" (*ellai ilāta<u>n</u>*). Here is the expression of an opposition whose appearance will be noted again and again in the *Tiruvācakam*, viz. the polarity between Śiva and release, on the one side, and the state of ordinary reality, on the other. Śiva is without limit as contrasted with the innumerable forms of birth, which are confined and conditioned by space and time. He transcends the discriminating nature of thoughts. Birth and thought are egoizing, atomizing, are expressions of finite form. As the poet says at another place, "(Śiva) severed (*aṟu*) the creaturely affliction (*paricu turicu*) so that this birth (*ippiṟavi*) which is attached to name (*pēr*) and attribute (*kuṇam*) may be extinguished" (40:5). Śiva has no such boundaries. He is qualitatively different from "this birth attached to name and attribute" and from "these immobile and mobile forms." To be released is to experience this difference.

In this vein, the basic problem with regard to rebirth is that it involves one in "mundane form" (*pār uru āya piṟappu*–44:1). There are "many forms of earthly birth" (*pavam*, Skt. *bhava*) (49:5). Birth is peculiarly suited to the earth (*maṇ ārnta piṟappu:* 38:2). It is deceptive, false, produces illusion (*māyap piṟappu*/*piṟavi*–1:14;13:3;33:8). Consequently, Māṇikkavācakar begs Śiva to "destroy the affliction of binding births (*piṟavi*)" (7:12, cf. 49:3). Births are therefore called a "chain" (*tol*–16:6), an image which connects well with the Siddhānta description of the human problem under the rubric of *pācam* (noose, bondage), a term not unknown to Māṇikkavācakar (see below). *Piṟappu*/*piṟavi* is furthermore said to be a "misfortune" (*allal*–1:91), (along with karma) a "pain" (*vētaṉai*–31:2), "a disease" (*piṇi*-6:18; 27:9), a "jungle" (*kāṭu*–48:2; *poccai*–41:9), and a "five-mouthed snake" which "fights against" Māṇikkavācakar (*aivāy aravam poru*–6:35). Birth is useless, barren, desolate (*paḻtta*–5:16).

Rebirth has a root which Śiva pulls out (15:13) or cuts off (*piṟavi vēr aṟu*–24:2, 3; 37:16). The deity is also envisioned as destroying the germ (*karu*) of rebirth (14:12). This root or germ appears to be karma. The seeming endlessness of rebirth is often pointed out. Thus, birth follows birth in an unbroken succession (14:10), and Māṇikkavācakar praises Śiva for arresting the course of further births (36:2). Whenever we meet the term *piṟappiṟappu* (birth and death). It is this sense of inevitable continuity, numbing repetititon, and futility, which apart from Śiva's action knows no prospect of cessation, that is being evoked (e.g., 8:14; 10:9; 26:2, 6; 35:5; 37:10; 41:4, 6, 10; 51:8). Several of these ideas are brought together in a graphic image in hymn 11.

This twofold dread [*accam*]
of good deeds [*aṟam*] and bad [*pāvam*]
which cause the birth and death [*piṟappoṭu iṟappu*] of this body,
like a whirling pinwheel made of palm leaves,
He did away with
and enslaved [*āṇṭukoḷ*] me.

(11: 8)

Besides the skillful simile likening saṃsāra to a spinning pinwheel, the verse makes the point that karma and rebirth cause fear. This seems more than just an amorphous existential *Angst.* The fear has rather specific dimensions, which have already been touched upon. One is reminded of karma and rebirth as pursuing, ensnaring entities by which a person is buffeted willy-nilly and from which escape seems impossible. But interestingly, these forces only touch the body (*kāyam*). Śiva is able to destroy them by appealing to, in fact forcibly enslaving (*āṇṭukoḷ*), the poet at a deeper, more fundamental level.

The imagery of water appears several times when Māṇikkavācakar mentions rebirth. There is a reference to "this sea called birth" across which Śiva's grace enables Māṇikkavācakar to swim (42: 7). Verse 36: 9 speaks of "the sea (lit., three waters) of birth which originated from accumulated wicked karma (*tī viṉai*)."[6] More notable are two further passages, one which likens rebirth to a whirlpool, the other to a rough sea. In the next to last verse of the *Tiruvācakam*, Māṇikkavācakar says that before Śiva bestowed grace on him, "I was tossed about in the wide whirlpool called death (*cātal*) and birth" (51: 8). The image of being overpowered by water is more extensive in 5: 27:

Alone,
dashed by afflicting huge waves
in the great sea of births,
Without anything to hold on to,
agitated by the winds
of lips red like sweet ripe fruit,
caught in the jaws

of the big shark called lust [*kāma*],
Pondering, pondering,
"How shall I escape now?"
I grasped the five-lettered raft,
And You, O God [*muṉaivaṉ*],
showed foolish me,
who was just (passively) lying there,
the abundant shore,
which has neither beginning nor end,
And You enslaved [*āṭkoḷ*] me.
(5: 27)

Again, we note man's passivity vis-à-vis his environment as well as in his relation to God. This passage, more so than most, pictures man as having at least some initiative, for Māṇikkavācakar says he "grasped the five-lettered raft," i.e., the *pañcākṣara*, the five-syllabled mantra of Tamil Śaivism — "*namaccivāya*" (Skt. *namaḥ śivāya*), the same words that begin the first verse of the *Tiruvācakam*.[7] In this sea of rebirth (*perum piṟavip peḷavam*), which reminds one of the Sanskrit *saṃsāra-sāgara*, desire, particularly sexual desire, is an important feature. As we shall see below, one of Māṇikkavācakar's most persistent problems is his susceptibility to female beauty. Assuming that for Māṇikkavācakar lust, perhaps more than any other single factor, fuels karma which in turn produces birth, it becomes somewhat easier to understand his sense of drivenness and helplessness in the face of karma-saṃsāra.

An image of philosophical interest in the above verse is the shore which Śiva shows to Māṇikkavācakar. It is characterized by *mallal* (abundance, fertility, beauty) and is without beginning or end. The shore, unlike the sea of rebirth, is abundant, so that karmic striving and desire have no place there. Furthermore, the shore's lack of spatial dimension shows it to be infinite, non-differentiated. Although in one sense the shore is a boundary, an end, it is also a beginning, stretching infinitely inland. This parallels the passage translated previously in which Śiva is invoked as "the boundless One". In the present verse, the shore represents that mystical state of awareness in which the distinctions of ordinary consciousness collapse.

It is surprising that the imagery of water and the sea are also commonly used to depict Śiva and his grace and the bhaktas' experience of devotion and release. Hence, there is a sea of bliss in which the devotees of Śiva do not wallow or struggle but rather frolic (5:30; 32:3; 49:5). The setting of one of the best known hymns of the *Tiruvācakam* has female devotees taking their morning bath in a tank while they sing songs in praise of Śiva (hymn 7: Tiruvempāvai). At one point, the natural features of the tank symbolize Śiva and Pārvatī themselves (7:13, also see chapter 5). Māṇikkavācakar often calls Śiva a great sea (*kaṭal*) of grace (*aruḷ* – e.g., 23:1; *karuṇai* – e.g., 10:9; 37:1), of bliss (*āṉanta* – e.g., 3:66; 22:9), or of *amṛta*, the nectar of immortality (Tamil *amutu* – e.g., 4:150; 5:26; 6:12). Unlike the sea of rebirth, in which Māṇikkavācakar is buffeted by winds and waves of lust, Śiva as the sea of ambrosia is devoid of dashing waves (22:3).[8] In 32:6 he is addressed as "the unchanging, unceasing, undifferentiated (*pirivu illā*), unforgetting, unthinking, immeasurable, undying great Sea of joy (*iṉpa mā kaṭal*)." Another, fairly common epithet of Śiva is that of a flood or deluge (*veḷḷam*) of grace or joy (e.g., 1:79; 5:91; 30:6; 45:1). The third hymn contains a very elaborate image of Śiva's activity and the soul's progress conceived in terms of a rain cloud which rises from the "ancient sea of highest bliss" (i.e., Śiva) and showers grace upon the earth (3:66-95). This passage will be examined in more details in the next chapter when the poet's attitude toward nature will be discussed. Suffice to note here that the sea is not a monochromatic symbol in the *Tiruvācakam*. It manifests symbolic as well as literal profundity.

Discussion of the various kinds of water imagery in the *Tiruvācakam* has led away from the immediate focus on karma-saṃsāra. But, this digression was undertaken in order to illuminate another side of the basic polarity which permeates the text, the dichotomy between Śiva's world and the ordinary world, between egolessness and egoistic desire, even though common imagery may be used to illuminate both sides of the opposition.

In concluding this section on karma and rebirth, it should be pointed out (although details will also be discussed in chapters 6 and 7) that there are modes of human action which are not problematic like karma. In the *Tiruvācakam viṉai* and its consequent *piṟappu* are opposed by other kinds of activity — primarily designated as *toṇṭu/toḻumpu* (service) or *aṉpu* (love) and *viḷaiyātal* (play, sport). Both service and play, unlike karma, are non-grasping, non-egoizing forms of action. Of course, Māṇikkavācakar sees service and play unfolding from his experience of Śiva's grace. They are impossible, unthinkable ways of being for the person still bound to karmic striving. In chapter 6, on Māṇikkavācakar's understanding of Śiva, we shall return to the idea of play; and service and love will receive their due attention in the seventh chapter when bhakti will be the focus of discussion.

Pācam AND *Malam*

Karma and rebirth may weigh most heavily and most immediately upon Māṇikkavācakar's spirit, but he also frequently uses two more general terms to describe his spiritual malaise: *pācam* (noose, bond, bondage) and *malam* (excrement, dirt, impurity).[9] Both the terms are very prominent in the Tamil Śaiva Siddhānta literature. Interestingly each word has both a concrete 'ordinary' denotation and a philosophical meaning, the kind of vocabulary to delight a metaphysical poet.

Pācam is the most common and most general Śaiva Siddhānta category designating what ails mankind. Along with *pati* (the supreme being Śiva) and *pacu* (the individual soul), it is one of the three *patārttams*, the three elements of reality which are eternal and uncreated. While there is no clear indication that Māṇikkavācakar shared this tripartite ontology, his use of *pācam* and *malam* shows that his understanding of these terms is similar in basic outline to Śaiva Siddhānta's. In the Siddhānta literature, *pācam* is often referred to as *malam*, and indeed the two terms seem interchangeable for Māṇikkavācakar as well. *Malam* is three-fold, a refinement also evidenced in the *Tiruvācakam*. But, where the Siddhāntins spell out in considerable detail what is involved in this threefold nature of *malam*, Māṇikkavācakar is silent. Briefly, in the Siddhānta texts, *malam* consists of these aspects: *āṇavamalam*, the first and most basic *malam* (*mūla-malam*), the root cause of ignorance, that which makes the soul limited, into an atom (*aṇu*), the egoizing factor; *kaṉma-malam* (Skt. *karmamala*); and *māyaimalam* (Skt. *māyāmala*), the material cause of the universe. None of these terms denoting the three types of *malam* is explicitly mentioned in the *Tiruvācakam*.

The *Tiruvācakam* contains eleven references to *pācam* as human bondage.[10] Practically half of these occur in conjunction with the verb *aṟu* — to cut off, sever (8:20; 18:9; 31:4, 7; 41:8). Māṇikkavācakar is extremely fond of this verb in describing an important aspect of Śiva's action towards him. Siva's action vis-à-vis Māṇikkavācakar can be capsulized in three of the poet's favorite verbs: *aruḷ* — to bestow grace; *āṭkoḷ* — to enslave, possess; and *aṟu*, which can have as its object karma, rebirth, *pācam*, *malam*, and even kinship ties (Māṇikkavācakar uses these terms to describe the problems of unregenerate humanity, and of the last named more will be said in the next section). In the case of *pācam*, however, the image is particularly apt. Thus, "He severed my creaturely bondage", literally, "He cut my noose". Māṇikkavācakar cleverly plays on this *double entendre* once or twice. In 31:7 he states that Siva "granted grace and cut the noose/bondage of a cow/soul (*pacu pācam*) like me. . . and tied me to His sacred feet with the strong rope called perfect certainty (*cittam*, Skt. *siddha*)."[11] The last verse of hymn 8 interweaves images of attachment and severance.[12]

Let us cling [*paṟṟu*]
 to the ancient fame
 of the One who cuts off [*aṟu*]
  the encircling connections with relatives.
Let us sing
 about the great bliss
  to which we cling [*paṟṟu*],
 the bliss of Him who clings [*paṟṟu*] to us
  in order to cut off [*aṟu*]
  the clinging hold [*paṟṟu*] of this bondage [*pācam*]
(8:20)

The severing of one kind of bondage must be replaced by the formation of new ties of attachment. But, these new ties are of an entirely different order from the old ones. The severance of Māṇikkavācakar's *pācam/viṉai/piṟappu* is simply the obverse of a coin whose other side is commonly described as enslavement (*āṭkoḷ*) to Śiva, a slavery, however, which is paradoxically liberating. In any case, man is not an independent entity. In the *Tiruvācakam* he is typically represented as a being who oscillates between two poles — *pācam* and Siva, not freely choosing the pole with which he is affiliated but rather coerced by one power or the other into a relationship with the constraining entity. There is a close parallel here between the *Tiruvācakam* and the basic dynamic of the Siddhānta system. According to Śaiva Siddhānta, the purpose of God's activity, indeed the purpose of the entire world process, is to bring souls (*pacu*) from an *advaita* relationship with *āṇavamalam*, the basic component to *pācam*, to an *advaita* relationship with God. To state the dynamic in a metaphor more befitting the *Tiruvācakam* than the Siddhānta *śāstras*, the combatants are Śiva and *pācam* and the battleground is man's soul. Māṇikka vācakar, of course, expresses this struggle with a freshness and verve quite foreign to the orderly logic of the Siddhāntins. But, in both cases, the view of man as a being defined by relationships over which he exercises little control prevails.

Two more of the eleven references to *pācam*, while not conjoined with the verb *aṟu*, occur in contexts mentioning Śiva's extirpation of this root evil. 9:4 states that Śiva "eradicated (lit. weeded or dug up) karmic bondage (*pācaviṉai*)." This passage shows that *viṉai* is at least an aspect of, if not synonymous with, *pācam*. In 51:7, the poet says, "He opened the latch called *pācam*."

The words which as used by Māṇikkavācakar have a virtually identical meaning to *pācam*, although not technical terms, in later Tamil Śaiva literature, are *pantam* (Skt. *bandha*) and its cognate *pantaṉai* (Skt. *bandhana*). In six of the twelve occurrences of these terms in our text, they are the object of the verb *aṟu* (5:32; 8:3; 13:2; 20:6; 22:9; 51:6), and four of these instances appear in conjunction with references to Śiva's enslaving (*āṭkoḷ*/*āṇṭukoḷ*/*āḷ*) his devotees (5:32; 8:3; 13:2; 51:6). A freedom from bondage and assertion of Śiva's lordship go together. Two of the remaining examples, while not using *aṟu*, also refer to Śiva's destruction of *pantam* (3:85; 43:5). 3:52 and 9:20 establish the opposition of *pantam* and *mokṣa*. Here, in series ascribing antithetical activities and characteristics to Śiva, he is extolled as the "Creator of bondage (*pantam*) and release (*vīṭu*)" (3:52) and "the One who is bondage (*pantam*) and release (*vīṭu*)" (9:20). In 3:70, *pantaṉai* is identified with the five senses represented as a snake which retreats in fear when the cloud of Śiva's grace appears in the sky.

Another synonym of *pācam* occurs in 5:49 where the common theme of severance and enslavement is sounded: "You cut (*aṟu*) my bonds (*kaṭṭu*) and ruled (*āḷ*) me." Similar, but slightly different, shades of meaning are expressed when Śiva is credited with serving bondage to sinful acts (*pāvaṅkaḷ paṟṟu aṟu*–16:7), cutting off faults (*iṭaṅkaḷ aṟu*–20:5), and putting an end to deceit (*kaḷavu aṟu*–5:35), all in contexts also praising his enslavement of the poet (*āṭkoḷ*–16:7; *āḷ*–20:5; *āṇṭamai*, a verbal noun derived from *āḷ*–5:06). Furthermore, Śiva appears as the destroyer (*nācaṉ* and variants) of sinful acts (*pāvam*, Skt. *pāpa*), at three other places in the text (2:57; 5:99; 28:9).

Pācam is sometimes called *pacu pācam*, another overlapping with the language of Śaiva Siddhānta. *Pacu* (Skt. *paśu*) is the second term of the Siddhānta ontology and designates the human being, or more specifically that indestructible, eternal part of him best captured by the English word 'soul'. The root meaning of the word is 'cow', which is extended to other animals to mean 'beast', and finally to creatures in general, hence, 'soul' in Śaiva thought. Three times in the *Tiruvācakam*, *pācam* is qualified as belonging to *pacu* (31:4, 7; 40:7), one instance occurring in an example translated above (31:7). *Pācam* is therefore a bondage peculiar to souls, particularly to humans but not excluding other forms in the transmigratory field also possessing souls. Remembering the soul's tendency to affiliate with either *pācam* or Śiva, it is to be expected that a parallel term expressing the contrasting relationship should also be found. Thus, *pacu pācam*, the soul's bondage, is opposed by *pacupati*, the lord of souls, although this well-known name of Śiva occurs only once in the entire *Tiruvācakam* (39:2).

Turning to the other *terminus technicus* widely used in the

Siddhānta canon to mark the problematic aspects of human existence, *malam* appears more frequently in our text than its twin term *pācam*.[13] As noted above, the base meaning of *malam* is 'excrement', which is generalized into 'dirt' or 'filth' and finally acquires a philosophical nuance indicating the soul's impurity, especially the basic impurity of *āṇavamalam*. Māṇikkavācakar, however, dose not restrict his usage to the philosophical meaning. Twice he clearly intends the word to designate bodily waste — at 1:54 where the reference is to the body "with nine gates oozing excreta (*malam*)",[14] and 4:28, where in the course of relating the life of the human soul, mention is made of "morning excrement (*kālai malam*)." A related, but not identical, use of the word occurs when Māṇikkavācakar bemoans his inability "to put an end to this big filthy body" (*mala māk kurampai itu māykka māṭṭēn*–5:54).

The meaning of *malam* as dirt is also present, for it provides a fitting metaphor for liberation from spiritual distress when used with verbs of washing or bathing. 7:13 depicts bhaktas bathing in a tank in order to "wash away their dirt/impurity" (*malam kaḻuvu*). *Malam* is again found as the object of the same verb: "Our Master's river is the bliss which drops down from heaven to wash away our minds' (*cintai*, Skt. *cintā*) impurity" (19:5). Elsewhere, another term for mind (*cittam*, Skt. *citta*) also serves as a qualifier of *malam* (51:1). In 48:2, *malam* is called the "inmost part's (*uḷḷam*) three *malams*." (*Uḷḷam*) can signify the heart, the mind, or the soul — literally, as translated above, "the interior", "the inside". Thus, we see *cintai malam*, *citta malam*, and *uḷḷa malam* as synoymous with *pacu pācam*. The imagery of exterior filth lines man's deepest inner affliction.

The last example cited in the previous paragraph mentions three *malams* (48:2). There are four other instances in the *Tiruvācakam* where *malam* is said to be three-fold (2:111; 19:7; 30:7; 51:9). As already noted, nowhere in the text are these three impurities named, although the commentarial tradition universally identifies them with the Siddhānta categories of *āṇavamalam*, *kaṉmamalam*, and *māyaimalam*. Māṇikkavācakar also employs the term *mūlam* in conjunction with *malam*, but he does this only once and in such a way that it is clear he is not using the word in the sense of the Siddhānta *mūlamalam*, the root impurity, viz. *āṇavamalam*. 2:111 lauds Śiva as the one who "severs (*aṟu*) the threefold impurity (*mummalam*) which is the root (*mūlam*)", presumably the root of karma-saṃsāra. Or perhaps *mūlam* could be translated adjectivally as a modifier of *mummalam*; thus, "the original three-fold impurity." Either way, however, the Siddhānta understanding of *āṇavamalam* cannot have been meant; for *āṇavamalam* is only one of the three *malams*. Parallel to our alternative translation of 2:111 is the designation of *malam* as ancient or primeval *malam* (*pāla malam*–36:8). Man has always been in bondage to *malam* nd will remain so until he becomes a devotee of Śiva.

Far more peculiar in terms of Tamil Śaiva thought is Māṇikkavācakar's single mention of five *malams* (*malaṅkaḷ aintu*) in 6:29 where he says, "I am whirled around by the five *malams* like the curd is agitated by the churning stick." Umāpati, one of the leading Siddhānta *ācāryas*, makes an anomalous reference to five *malams* rather than the usual three in his *Neñcuviṭutūtu* (90), a work of the early fourteenth century.[15] The *Tamil Lexicon* identifies these five impurities with the three standard *malams* supplemented by *māyēyamalam* and *tirōtaṉamalam*, citing as its source the *Piṅkalantai* (*Piṅkalanikaṭu*) by Piṅkalamuṉivar, an early Tamil dictionary probably stemming from the latter half of the ninth century, thus roughly contemporaneous with Māṇikkavācakar himself.[16] According to the Siddhānta commentarial tradition, *māyēyamalam* and *tirōtaṉamalam* are only subcategories of *māyaimalam* in the usual three-*malam* scheme, and thus the notion of five *malams* is seen to represent no real departure from the typical categorization of only three impurities.[17] Some modern-day commentators on the *Tirūvacakam*, however, do not think Maṇikkavācakar's use of *malaṅkaḷ aintu* refers to these five impurities at all. Rather they see in this phrase a reference to the five senses (*aimpulaṉkaḷ*), probably influenced in their interpretation by adjacent verses which portray the poet as confused, shaken, and fearful because of the five senses (6:28, 32).[18]

Śiva does to *malam* exactly the same thing he does to karma, rebirth, and *pācam*: he severs *(aṟu)* it or destroys (*keṭu)* it

(30:3). Five of the sixteen uses of *malam* in our text occur with *aṟu* (31:9; 34:6; 36:8; 51:1, 9). Again, several of these references to release are found in contexts also highlighting the over-powering effect Śiva exercises on his devotee (34:6; 36:8; 51:1,). Two of these references "to cutting off dirt" occur in the context of the sea imagery—in 34:6 a sea of problems and in 36:8 a flood of bliss (*āṉanta veḷḷam*). 34:6 is quite an interesting verse.

He put an end [*aṟu*]
  to the turbulent impurity [*malam*]
    which comes like waves of the sea,
entered and filled my body and soul [*uyir*]
  without leaving any space empty
Our God [*paraṉ*] who wears the light-giving lustrous moon,
  who dwells in holy Peruntuṟai,
  whose crown is his spreading matted locks—
O what a trick [*paṭiṟu*] He played! (34:6)

Here, after freeing Māṇikkavācakar from *malam*, Śiva is shown as not merely enslaving the poet but entering (*puku*) and filling (*niṟai*) him body and soul. And then the whole business is called a piece of Śiva's mischief, a trick — but more on this intriguing aspect of Śiva's character in chapter 6.

Finally, with regard to *malam*, one notes the expected opposition between this aspect of ordinary existence and the nature of the deity. This time, the opposition is expressed in the form of nouns based on negative adjectives. Hence, Śiva is called the spotless, or immaculate one (*nimalaṉ* and variants–1:13; 4:175; 29:2; *niṉmalaṉ* and variants–5:61, 78; 22:8; 34:8; and *vimalaṉ* and variants–1:34, 36,56; 4:106; 29:4). It is noteworthy that all of these usages but one (1:13) are vocatives. Thus, one of the more prevalent ways in which Māṇikkavācakar addresses Śiva in the *Tiruvācakam* — and he invokes him frequently in these hymns— is to call him the being who has no *malam*. These vocatives are instructive, because they give us an indication of the divine attributes most immediately impressive and most personally relevant to the poet. That Śiva is uniquely free of *malam* clearly attracts Māṇikkavācakar.

Before considering the problematic nature of Māṇikkavācakar's relations with other people, a few passages which sum up those attributes of life apart from Śiva, that are most troubling to the poet, will be examined. In this lies an opportunity to grasp the concrete dimensions of *pācam* and *malam*, even though these terms may not as such be mentioned. What exactly does it mean to be bound and to be impure? By translating several lengthier passages rather than just words, short phrases, or a few lines of a verse, one also gains a better sense of the vitality of Māṇikkavācakar's expression, a factor at least as important to understanding him as the ideology found in his poems.

The first example is a short verse from Tirukkōtumpi, "The Sacred (Song) about the Kingly Bee." The setting of this hymn depicts the devotee as a woman instructing a bee to carry a message to her beloved, namely, Śiva.

> In this mad world
> of hoarded wealth,
> of wives,
> of children,
> of family [*kulam*],
> of learning,
> where birth and death fluster the mind,
> Go to God [*tēvar*]
> whose enlightening wisdom dispels this perplexity
> And hum to Him, O Kingly bee!
> (10:6)

Here, we see Māṇikkavācakar oppressed not merely by birth and death, which set the mind reeling, but also by everyday social contacts and responsibilities. Not surprisingly, hoarded wealth is binding, because greed is a major factor in the creation of new karmic fruit and consequently leads to further birth and death. Wife, children and family involve one in a set of expectations and responsibilities which impinge upon one's social and psychic freedom. But, why should learning (*kalvi*) be condemned by an educated Brahmin, who at one time is reputed to have been a high-ranking civil servant? It is condemned because, throughout the *Tiruvācakam*, that which is shown to be most worth having is direct, affective experience of God rather than an intellectual theory about him— or about anything else, for that matter. In the fourth hymn, Māṇikkavācakar strongly rejects several Indian philosophical systems prevalent in his day (4:46-58). Moreover, at a deeper level, erudition leads to pride and makes one less likely to throw himself at Śiva's feet. And perhaps most basic of all, learning entails analysis and distinction-making, which from the standpoint of that "abundant shore which has neither beginning nor end" (5:27) is irrelevant and even misleading.

31:5 broadens and deepens the scope of what existence in bondage to *pācam* is like.

> A dog such as me [*nāyēṉ*]
> caught in the whirlpool of caste [*cāti*], family [*kulam*], and birth,
> floundering without support,
> He enslaved [*āṭkoḷ*],
> putting an end [*aṟu*] to my miserable condition.
> My foolishness,
> the forms of others,
> my thoughts of "I" and "mine",
> He destroyed.
> In shining Tillai I saw
> Him who is the faultless ambrosia.
>
> (31:5)

In commenting on this verse, mention should first be made of Māṇikkavācakar's tendency to call himself a dog *(nāy)*. He quite frequently disparages himself with this term.[19] In Hindu culture, 'dog' is a very opprobrious word when applied to humans. Dogs are not considered admirable animals, and for Māṇikkavācakar to describe himself in such language is demeaning himself to the extreme. This is part of a wider tendency he has toward self-denigration, for which there are at least two reasons. First, by such references to himself he emphasizes the great gulf which separates his own status from Śiva's, thus showing his total dependence on him and how little he deserves his grace. Secondly, by choosing to associate his own unregenerate nature with that of the dog he indicates how low he feels himself to have sunk, namely, to the level of a mangy, cringing, scavenging creature driven by no noble impulse.

By what impulses is Māṇikkavācakar driven in this abject state of bondage? "Caste, family, and birth", we are told. Society is like a whirlpool over which he has no control, a factor discussed in the next section. In addition, the forms of others and egoism are a problem. Here is another instance indicating the superiority of a mystical perspective transcending a sense of ego and the experience of differentiation. Thoughts of 'I' and 'mine', and "forms of others" stand in the way of that sense of integration and unity which union with Śiva affords. In a sense, the phrase "forms of others" is an abstract, more philosophical rendering of the social and psychological pressures suggested by "whirlpool of caste, family, and birth". Again we note the conjunction of "liberation from" (*aṟu*) with "enslavement to" *(āṭkoḷ)*, and the opposition between Māṇikkavācakar's dog-like estate and Śiva, the faultless ambrosia (*kōtu il amutu)*.

Similar themes along with several new ideas are present in 51:6.

I —
thinking that birth [*piṟavi*] in a body is real [*mey*],
a body which can be burned and destroyed,
multiplying my karma [*viṉai*],
falling upon the round breasts
of women with flower-adorned hair and
exquisite bangles,
He —
cut off [*aṟu*] my bondage [*pantam*],
ruled [*āḷ*] me,
cut off [*aṟu*] my faults
in order to terminate [*aṟu*] my nature [*paricu*],
bestowed [*aruḷ*] on me the end.
O wonder! Who but I knows such grace?
(51:6)

Here are the familiar references to *viṉai*, *piṟavi*, and *pantam*, to severing, asserting lordship, and granting grace. In addition, this verse presents the idea that birth in a body is not true, not real, because the body is transitory. A widespread notion in Indian philosophy and religion holds that whatever is subject to change is not fully real, and what is not fully real is not worth having, not deserving of one's attachment to it. That which is real or true must be permanent, unchanging. Bondage to spatial differentiation (name and attribute — 40:5; forms of others — 31:5) is accompanied by bondage to temporal differentiation, i.e., change. In gaining release one achieves stasis. Māṇikkavācakar is liberated from that which is fleeting, here the transient body, and is enslaved by that which is not subject to change, namely, Śiva.

Again, in this passage, we see what already was noted once before (5:27) — that Māṇikkavācakar is sexually aroused by attractive women and considers this a form of bondage from which Śiva releases him. The poet's rather frequent condemnations of his lascivious fascination with female beauty will be examined when discussion focuses on the role of the feminine in the *Tiruvācakam* in the next chapter. A final point of interest in the above verse is the reference to cutting off Māṇikkavācakar's nature (*paricu aṟu*). We are reminded here of how Śiva "severs creaturely bondage" (*pacu pācam aṟu*— 31:4, 7). *Paricu* is probably a derivative of the Sanskrit *sparśa* (touch, sensation) and therefore quite likely here indicates the differentiation associated with sense experience, an element of ordinary consciousness transcended in the ecstatic experience of Śiva's grace.

The first hymn of the *Tiruvācakam* contains a passage which records many of the familiar major obstacles to spiritual fulfilment. Here Māṇikkavācakar contrasts his own undeserved good fortune with that of the *devas* to whom Śiva does not reveal himself, an important, frequently mentioned theme.

> O One who has five colors![20] O our great One!
> You stay hidden from those celestial beings who extol You.
> But to me full of potent karma [*val viṉai*],
> bound by a strong rope called good [*āṟam*] and evil [*pāvam*] deeds
> so that concealing, delusive ignorance [*iruḷ*] covered me,
> enveloped in skin,

covered everywhere by the filth of maggots,
bewildered in this hut with nine gates oozing excreta,
and deceived by the five senses due to my beastly mind,
to insignificant me, devoid of virtue,
O pure One [*vimalaṉ*],
You kindly granted
my inmost self [*uḷ*] to melt and become mixed with you in love.
You came upon this very earth,
granted grace [*aruḷ*],
and showed your great feet
to a devotee like me who lay around lower than a dog.
O One whose love surpasses a mother's!

(1:49-61)

Karma leads to spiritual darkness (*iruḷ*). It prevents one from seeing the truth. The body, which is the result of birth, receives disparaging comments, obviously not something fit to be indulged. Again, the poet emphasizes his passivity and worthlessness in referring to himself as a devotee who does not even compare with a dog (*nāyil kaṭaiyāyk kiṭanta āṭiyēn*). Also, the reference to his beastly mind (*vilaṅku maṉam*) is far from complimentary, for *vilaṅku* connotes a being whose body is horizontal to the ground rather than erect.[21] Finally, with regard to this passage, Māṇikkavācakar plays with words in quite an interesting way to express the basic dynamics of his experience. The poet's inmost self (*uḷ*) is like the middle term, the prize, in a tug-of-war between spiritual ignorance (*iruḷ*) and Śiva's grace (*aruḷ*).

In a lengthy section of the hymn 4, Māṇikkavācakar relates a stylized account of the soul's human embodiment, a passage which is helpful to understanding his view of human sorrow and futility apart from Śiva's intervention. A summary, including several translated excerpts, of this 'history', which altogether comprises over sixty lines (4:10-74), will conclude this section.

Of the first thirty-two lines of this passage, twenty end

with the verb *piḻai* (to escape). Māṇikkavācakar catalogs those dangers from which the soul must escape on its way to release. The section opens by suggesting the immensity of the saṃsāric round:

> On earth surrounded by the spreading sea,
> beginning with the elephant
> and ending with the ant,
> from these indestructible wombs one must escape
> according to his karma [*viṉai*].
>
> (4: 10-12)

Then follows a month-by-month account of pre-natal problems which need to be surmounted before a baby can be born[22]:

> Born in human form,
> one must escape from the battle
> with the indestructible maggots in his mother's body —
> in the first month escaping from splitting in two,
> in the second month escaping from growing alone,
> in the third month escaping from the fluid inside the mother,
> in the fourth month escaping from the great darkness,
> in the fifth month escaping from death,
> in the sixth month escaping from the fetus' being smothered,
> in the seventh month escaping from premature birth,
> in the eighth month escaping from affliction,
> in the ninth month escaping from the pain which exists then,
> in the fitting tenth month escaping from the sorrow of the sea of distress
> which a child and its mother endure.
>
> (4:13–25)

After birth there is a whole new list of dangers to be escaped:

> Through all the years one must
> escape from the many times of growth and loss,
> escape from morning evacuation,

the pain of noontime hunger,
midnight sleep,
and travel,
escape from the pestilence of women's piercing eyes,[23]

....

escape from the many seas called learning,
escape from the affliction called wealth,
escape from the old poison called poverty,
escape from many situations of base conduct.
(4:26-29, 38-41)

As soon as one starts to think about God (*teyva*m–4:42), another set of problems appear, such as sixty million delusive powers (4:42), friends and neighbors who talk atheism (*nāttikam*, Skt. *nāstika*–4:47), other sectarians including those who espouse Advaita Vedānta (*māyāvātam*, Skt. *māyāvāda*–4:54) and the Lokāyatas (*ulōkāyatan*–4:56). The passage culminates with a vivid description of the soul's conversion to devotion to Śiva and the dramatic effects of such a change, a description to which reference will be made in the discussion of bhakti in chapter 7.

In the light of the selections just translated, the scope of *pācam* and *malam* is seen to be quite broad. It includes aspects of ordinary experience which would not have become evident if only occurrences of the key terms themselves had been listed. To conclude this chapter, our focus will center more closely on one of these aspects of *pācam*, namely, that of social relations.

Social Relations

Māṇikkavācakar views the network of kinship ties and caste-bound relationships as part of the problem from which he gains release through Śiva's gracious action. In certain respects, it is typical of medieval and modern Hindu devotional movements to reject the ideology and hierarchy of the caste system.[24] Māṇikkavācakar is, however, definitely not a social reformer. He offers no agenda for changing society.[25]

For him, devotion to Śiva has no social implications beyond the transformation it effects in the social behavior of individual bhaktas. In the *Tiruvācakam*, bhakti is a personal, individualistic system of salvation which shifts one's focus of attention from structured human relationships conceived in terms of kinship and caste to dyadic relationships between devotee and Śiva and between devotee and devotee.[26]

Note has already been taken in passing of several references to Māṇikkavācakar's liberation from the established social order. This section will deal more systematically with the poet's social attitudes. As has been seen in the translation of 8:20 (p. 76), Śiva is said to sever ties of kinship (*cuṟṟat toṭarvu aṟu*). The same noun and verb appear together in the thirteenth hymn. Here the ties that are broken are described in somewhat more detail.

> The Lord of the Pāṇṭiyan land
> severed my bondage [*pantām aṟu*]
> to my father,
> to my mother,
> to all my relatives [*cuṟṟam*],
> and enslaved [*āṇṭukoḷ*] me.
>
> (13:2)

Not merely kinship ties in general, but the closest and dearest of those relationships are terminated when the poet becomes Śiva's devotee. In the verse prior to that just quoted, it is obvious that Māṇikkavācakar has a sense of social obligation, for he recognizes the help given him by his kinsmen. This apparently is not a rebellious son angrily rejecting his parents and family. The result is, however, in one sense the same. Devotion to Śiva takes precedence over socially dictated reciprocity.

> The moment He put His sacred feet on my head,
> I abandoned all my relatives [*cuṟṟam*],
> who were my help and support.
>
> (13:1)[27]

Although Māṇikkavācakar gives up human parents and

relatives, he gains a divine androgyne who functions as father, mother, and kinsmen. Śiva is experienced as both father and mother, these being ways in which Māṇikkavācakar sometimes addresses the god. As for Śiva's being called kinsman, this title is attested once, in the ejaculatory section of the fourth hymn where in one line the deity is hailed as "relative" (*uṟavu*) and "life" (*uyir*) (4:181).

In the eleventh hymn, Māṇikkavācakar enumerates several factors which died (*māḷ*) when he was united (*kala*) with and ruled by Śiva (11:11). Among the things listed are relatives (*cuṟṟam*). In the same line mentioning relatives, if we take the word *ayal* to mean that which is alien, Māṇikkavācakar is saying that, from the standpoint of devotion to Śiva, there is no difference between kin and non-kin.[28] The same point is made in the last line of 22:8: "Who are related (*uṟavu*) to me here? Who are strangers (*ayal*)? O my bliss-bringing Light!" This interpretation of these passages fits well with what has been previously learned about the effects of Śiva's grace. Distinctions collapse. This is not only a philosophical statement or a description of a new state of awareness; it has a social reference too.

The theme connecting devotion to Śiva with the termination of usual kinship relations is also found at 39:3.

> I don't want kinsmen [*uṟṟār*]!
> I don't want a home town!
> I don't want a name!
> I don't want learned men [*kaṟṟār*]!
> Studies will now come to an end!
> O Dancer who dwells at Kuṟṟalam,
>   like the mind of a cow with a young calf,
> I want to melt and ooze with love
>   for Your anklet-tinkling feet!

For the poet to compare himself to a cow who tenderly cares for her calf contrasts markedly with his self-belittling references to his dog-like nature. As is typical of the wider Hindu tradition, the cow here symbolizes desirable qualities which Māṇikkavācakar dare only apply to himself in the context of describing love and Śiva. The cow's natural, steadfast affection for its calf is the kind of devotion the poet wishes he had for Śiva.

Māṇikkavācakar occasionally celebrates his release from *kulam* (*Skt. kula)*, a term which covers a fairly wide range of related meanings, viz., family, high birth, caste, tribe, nation.[29] The term has already been met in two passages (10:6; 31:5), where it was rendered with 'family', although in 10:6 the meaning 'caste' is also possible. 6:29 credits Śiva with destroying the poet's family (*kulam kaḷai)*. Elsewhere, the word is used more figuratively. In 5:39, Māṇikkavācakar says he is lower than the *kualm* of dogs, and turning the tables, in 11:20 he sings about *the kulam*, Śiva's 'tribe' of devotees.

A word which occurs only three times in the *Tiruvācakam*, but nevertheless is quite significant to an understanding of Māṇikkavācakar's social attitudes, is *cāti* (Skt. *jāti)* — caste. Caste, along with family and relatives, is a hindrance to devotion, but it ceases to be operative after Śiva enslaves his devotee. The usage at 31:5, where Māṇikkavācakar depicts himself floundering in a whirlpool, one of whose characteristics is caste, has already been noted (p. 83). The last verse of the forty-ninth hymn states that when Śiva appears in order to rule *(āḷ)* the poet, the "qualities *(kuṇam)* which are inseparable from caste *(cāti)* will no longer distress us" (49:8). The third reference to *cāti* (15:7) is simply to the Brahmin caste, mentioned in an incident discussed in chapter 7.

If caste is no longer a significant factor in Māṇikkavācakar's social behavior, this does not mean he completely ignores caste status. On numerous occasions he mentions that Śiva appeared to him as a Brahmin guru at Perunturai. He quite commonly refers to Śiva as *antaṇaṉ* (e.g., 2:42; 8:1, 18; 10:14; 11:1; 18:10; 20:8), *pārppaṉ* (27:10; 42:3), *vētiyaṉ* (4:88; 8:5; 7, 10,13; 35:4), and *maṟaiyōṉ/maṟaiyāṉ* (1:45; 5:85; 8:9; 16:7; 33:10; 49:8) — all words designating a member of the Brahmin caste. Of course, the tendency to ascribe exalted titles to Śiva is pronounced, but it is also noteworthy that Māṇikkavācakar reminds us so often that the sage who sparked his conversion was a Brahmin. In any case, we shall see that the god known to Māṇikkavācakar does not always hew to what one would consider to be orthodox Brahmanical criteria of behavior. Śiva is a 'funny' Brahmin.

Not only do family, relatives, and caste come in for severe treatment in the *Tiruvācakam*, less binding social contacts are also negatively evaluated. Thus neighbors (*ayalār*) are a stumbling block when they mislead the poet with false philosophy (4:46); and countrymen (*nāṭṭār* and variants) generally come off in a rather bad light too, since they are typically pictured as uncomprehending (3:154), smiling at (8:6), or even ridiculing (4:69) the devotees. While not always labelled 'countrymen' the motif of the devotees' being surrounded by people unsympathetic to ecstatic bhakti recurs at various places throughout the *Tiruvācakam*. This is not at all surprising in view of the highly peculiar, 'mad' behavior which is brought on by the experience of Śiva's grace. Sometimes those people who do not understand or make fun of the devotees are designated "men of the world" (*ulakavar*—26:4) or "people on earth"(*pūtalattor* — 11:5). Elsewhere, disparaging language is used to describe those who stand outside the circle of bhaktas; hence, crazy people (*pittar* — 26:9); fools (*mūrkkar* — 51:1); false ones (*poyyar* — 5:52; 35:1); blind, ignorant people (*citaṭar* — 51:9); and groups of people who have no character, no rule, and no virtue (*kuṟiyum neṟiyum kuṇamum ilār kuḻāṅkaḷ*—40:4).

To conclude, there is a verse in the Aṟputappattu, "The Miracle Decad", which not only indicates Māṇikkavācakar's release from traditional social roles but also describes the wider dimensions of his liberation from every kind of bondage which stultifies devotion to Śiva. It vigorously expresses Māṇikkavācakar's dramatic transformation from one mode of existence to a new style of life radically different from the old in every respect.

To wandering me,
  possessed by and delighting in the company of
    wealth,
    relatives [*cuṟṟam*],
    women,
    and other sensual pleasures [*pōkam*, Skt. *bhoga*],
He gave release [*vīṭu*],
  revealed His foot which is like a tender flower
    so that my cruel karma might be completely
                destroyed [*vem toḻil vīṭṭiṭu*],

caused me to dance,
entered my inmost part [*akam*],
ruled [*āḷ*] me.
This singular miracle I do not comprehend.

(41:5)

NOTES

1. Frederick Streng has formulated a definition of religion which I find useful in conceptualizing phenomena to which I apply the label 'religious.' He states that religion is a "means toward ultimate transformation". See Frederick J. Streng, *Understanding Religious Life*, 2d ed. (Belmont, California: Dickenson Publishing Company, 1976), pp. 7-9; Frederick Streng, Charles L. Lloyd, Jr., and Jay T. Allen, *Ways of Being Religious* (Englewood Cliffs, N.J.: Prentice-Hall, 1973), pp. 6-12.

2. It is interesting in this regard that Māṇikkavācakar does not use either *karumam* or *kaṉmam*, the Tamilized forms of *karman*. The single appearance of *karumam* in the *Tiruvācakam* (15:7) refers to a ritual act (which, indeed, is the earliest meaning of the Sanskrit term) rather than to the moral nexus of cause and effect. This verse is translated below in the chapter 7.

3. For example, see the story from the *Añguttara Nikāya* (4:197:1) of the Buddha's conversation with Queen Mallikā in Henry Clarke Warren, trans., *Buddhism in Translations* (1896; reprint ed., New York: Atheneum, 1973), pp. 228-231.

4. For a clear brief description of the Śaiva Siddhānta position on Śiva's five *śaktis*, see John H. Piet, *A Logical Presentation of the Śaiva Siddhānta Philosophy*, (Madras: Christian Literature Society for India, 1952), pp. 72-74.

5. In my references to the *Civañāṉacittiyār*, I rely on the verse numbering system and translation of J.M. Nallaswami Pillai, trans., *Sivajnana Siddhiyar of Arunandi Sivacharya*, (Madras: Meykandan Press, 1913).

6. According to the *Tamil Lexicon* (vol. 6, p. 3268), the sea as *munnīr* could refer either to the sea's three qualities of forming, protecting, and destroying the earth, or to its consisting of river water, spring water, and rain water.

7. The script in which Tamil is commonly written is a syllabic script. Hence, the five letters are five syllables, viz. na-ma-ci-vā-ya.

8. In 20:2, however, Śiva is represented as a billowing sea (*alai kaṭal*), where the context stresses images of divine activity rather than repose. This is the Tiruppaḷḷiyeḻucci, "The Hymn of Waking (Śiva)

from His Bed".

9. Both *pācam* and *malam* are Sanskrit derivatives, from *pāśa* and *mala*. But in keeping with Māṇikkavācakar's perference for non-Sanskritic vocabulary to signify key concepts, he uses them less often to portray the human condition than he does terms like *viṉai* and *piṟappu*.

10. 8:20; 9:4; 18:9; 31:4, 7; 40,7; 41:8; 43:10; 45:3; 51:7. There is one other use of the word at 7:2 where the context requires it to be given one of its secondary meanings, in this instance 'devotion'.

11. *Cittam* in this passage is quite ambiguous, for it is the Tamilized form of both *siddha* (that which is established or attained, certainty, assurance) and *citta* (mind, will, determination, firm conviction). In this context, either Sanskrit term is plausible, although here it seems somewhat more likely that Māṇikkavācakar intends *cittam* to mean *siddha*, this in the sense that Śiva had answered his questions, given him certainty or assurance, which the poet then figuratively describes as Śiva's having tied him to the god's feet.

12. The following translation sacrifices easy flow to the consistent rendering of *paṟṟu* and *aṟu* by the same English words, in this case 'cling' and 'cut off'. This passage displays a rather remarkable euphony which the translation completely lacks. There is a rhyme on the second syllable of each line, the letters —*ṟṟ*— being reproduced in every line. Additionally, in two of the last three lines of the verse (the lines translated above), the prominence of the alveolar trill (*ṟ*), particularly in its doubled form, continues beyond the second syllable. The phonetic result is that of a rippling, skipping sound. The same kind of virtuosic play upon the word *paṟṟu* with similar meaning and phonetic effects occurs in the first line of 34:5. What is true of any poetry is particularly applicable to the *Tiruvācakam*—it should be recited (or better still, in this case, sung), not read.

13. *Malam* occurs sixteen times in the *Tiruvācakam*. Except for the uses of the word at 1:54 and 4:28, the remaining references to the term all bear its philosophical connotation: 2:111; 5:54; 6:29; 7:13; 19:4, 7; 30:3, 7; 31:9; 34:6; 36:8; 48;2; 51:1, 9. This differs from the count given for this term in Carl-A. Keller, "Some Aspects of Manikkavasagar's Theology", *Proceedings of the Second International Conference Seminar of Tamil Studies*, ed. R.E. Asher (Madras: International Association of Tamil Research, 1971), vol. 2, p. 60. Keller, without giving textual citations, says there are only twelve occurrences of *malam*, which is clearly a mistake. He also claims differing numbers of references to other key terms than my count has shown.

14. This is an Indian figure of speech designating the body (e.g., *Atharavaveda* 10:2:31; 10:8:43). The nine gates stand for the nine orifices of the body: two eyes, two ears, two nostrils, mouth, genitals, and anus. For the same image, but a far more negative view of the body than found in the *Tiruvācakam*, see the translations of the Tamil Siddha poet Paṭṭinātar in Zvelebil, *Poets of the Powers*, pp. 90-107 (p. 94 for the image in question).

15. *Love of God according to Śaiva Siddhānta*, p. 313.

16. The entry in the *Tamil Lexicon* is *pañcamalam* (vol. 4, p. 2409). In dating the *Piṅkalantai*, I rely on Zvelebil, *Tamil Literature*, pp. 194–195.

17. Dhavamony, *Love of God according to Śaiva Siddhānta*, p. 313 (n. 1).

18. For this interpretation, see Ka. Cu. Navanīta Kiruṣṇa Pāratiyār, ed. and commentator, *Tiruvācakam: Arāycci Perurai* (Māviṭṭapuram, Srī Lanka: Patmā Patippakam, 1954), pp. 430–431; and Cuvāmi Citpavāṉantar, *Tiruvācakam* (Tirupparāyturai: Śrīramakiruṣṇa Tapōvaṉam, 1970), p. 427.

19. The many references include instances when the poet calls himself a dog (*nāyēṉ*–4:219; 10:12; 33:3, 8, 10; *nāyiṉēṉ*–2:127; 5:23, 50; *nāyaṭiyēṉ*–16:1) and other cases where he compares himself, usually unfavorably, to the animal (e.g., 1:60; 5:56; 6:13; 33:8). 6:13 has Māṇikkavācakar lapping water like a dog from Śiva's sea of grace.

20. The five colors probably represent the five elements: earth—golden, water — white, fire — red, wind — black, ether — black, like smoke. Thus, this designation portrays Śiva as inherent in all reality. On the five elements and their colors, see Navanīta Kiruṣṇa Pāratiyār, *Tiruvācakam*, p. 46.

21. *Tamil Lexicon*, vol. 6, p. 3712.

22. This section on fetal life and the lines detailing the seductive features of women (4:30-35) were apparently offensive to G.U. Pope's Victorian sensibilities, since he refuses to translate them, although he does at least include the Tamil text. The tenth-month gestation period assumed in vv. 15-25 is attributable to a reckoning strictly based on lunar months. The Tamil words for 'month' in this passage are *mati* and *tiṅkaḷ*, both of which literally mean 'moon'.

23. 4:30–37 is translated in chapter 5 (on women and the goddess).

24. Recent works which are relevant to this issue include several of the essays in *Krishna: Myths, Rites, and Attitudes*, ed. Milton Singer (Chicago: University of Chicago Press, 1968), particularly Thomas J. Hopkins, "The Social Teaching of the *Bhāgavata Purāṇa*", pp. 3-22; Edward C. Dimock, Jr., "Doctrine and Practice among the Vaiṣṇavas of Bengal", pp. 41-63 (esp. pp. 52-55); and Milton Singer, "The Rādhā-Krishna *Bhajanas* of Madras City", pp. 90-138 (esp. pp. 121-128). Also, on the Śrī Vaiṣṇava sect, see Burton Stein, "Social Mobility and Medieval South Indian Hindu Sects", *Social Mobility in the Caste System in India*, ed. James Silverberg (The Hague: Mouton, 1968), pp, 78-94; and on the Vīraśaivas of Karnataka, see the introduction to A.K, Ramanujan, trans., *Speaking of Śiva* (Baltimore: Penguin Books, 1973), pp. 19–55.

25. For the same point made with regard to Tamil Śaiva bhakti generally, see Zvelebil, *Smile of Murugan*, pp. 194-195.

26. The individualistic nature of bhakti and its resultant emphasis on a dyadic relationship with God will be discussed in chapter 7. It

will be suggested there that in this respect Tamil bhakti may have been influenced by early Tamil religious practices featuring possession of the worshipper by a god.

27. Since this translation telescopes two Tamil verbs into only one in translation and expands one Tamil noun into two English nouns, the Tamil of the second line is given here: *tuṉai āṉa cuṟṟaṅkaḷ attaṉaiyum tuṟantu oḻintēṉ.*

28. This is the interpretation of Citpavāṉantar, *Tiruvācakam*, p. 555, and seems to be a feasible one, although not the only possibility. As will be seen below, *ayal*/*ayalār* also can mean 'neighborhood'/'neighbor', and this meaning is conceivable in 11:11 too. At 32:9 *ayalār* fairly clearly means 'stranger'. The line in question also contains a reference to karma, and the syntax is such that this could modify *cuṟṟam* (thus, "my relatives called karma died") or could be taken as one more item which ceases to be operative after Māṇikkavācakar becomes a devotee of Śiva. The problematic line reads as follows: *ayal māṇṭu aru viṉaic cuṟṟamum māṇṭu avaṉiyiṉ mēl*, The translation reflected by the comments above is: "On earth strangers, difficult karma, and relatives died."

29. The scope of the word's various meanings is considerably broader than indicated here, since in this context I am only concerned with the meanings relevant to social structure; see *Tamil Lexicon*, vol. 2, p. 1023.

5

Nature and Woman: Mediators between the Sacred and the Profane

Of those aspects of ordinary existence which Māṇikkavācakar sees as impediments to spiritual satisfaction there are two whose function in the text is ambiguous. These are, broadly conceived, the phenomenal world and woman, *das Weibliche*. The *Tiruvācakam* contains vehement condemnations of sensory experience and female beauty. But, just as frequently one observes the poet praising the same feminine characteristics he elsewhere so vigorously repudiates when they are perceived as belonging to Śiva's spouse. And the poet's railing against the five senses is accompanied by a finely-tuned sensitivity to his natural environment, which is sometimes viewed almost sacramentally as providing signs of Śiva's love and grace. Thus, it seems clear that the phenomenal world and women are not simply negative quantities on the order of karma, rebirth, *pācam*, and social relations.

In this chapter, both sides of these features will be considered. In addition to discussing Māṇikkavācakar's denouncement of his senses and his use of the term *māyai*, we shall also examine how nature appears in a positive light in the *Tiruvācakam*. Likewise with the feminine in the text, both the poet's problematic lust for human females and his affection for the goddess will be topics of discussion, the latter leading into the next chapter on the nature of Śiva. Nature and woman seem to mediate between the sacred and the profane in the *Tiruvācakam*. Likewise, this chapter will be a transition from our previous discussion of what is overcome in becoming a devotee of Śiva to chapter 6 and 7 which will focus on Śiva himself and the means to achieving union with him.

The Phenomenal World: Sense-Experience and Nature

There are certain frustrations in attempting a systematic presentation of the thought of a devotional poet who uses terminology to which a later scholastic tradition has assigned very precise meanings. This difficulty has already been encountered in Māṇikkavācakar's use of terms like *pācam*, *malam* and *viṉai*. Nowhere, however, is this problem more apparent than in the case of *māyam/māyai* (Skt. *māyā*); for here, as we shall see, there seems to be even less connection with the Śaiva Siddhānta understanding of the word than in previous instances. Nevertheless, since this term is so frequently associated with a theory of material reality, discussion of it has been postponed until this section, where the topic will be Māṇikkavācakar's understanding of the phenomenal world, of sense experience, and of nature — interrelated, if not identical, categories. After attending to Māṇikkavācakar's use of *māyam*, we shall examine his statements regarding sense experience in general and then his view of nature in particular. Since he is a poet whose images are frequently drawn from the natural environment, this last item to be discussed in this section will be the most important for understanding how Māṇikkavācakar reacts to the world around him.

Māyam/māyai in the *Tiruvācakam* bears less relation to Śaiva Siddhānta concepts than does most of the other vocabulary he shares with the later philosphical tradition. In fact, only three times does our poet use the noun form favored by the Siddhānta authors, viz. *māyai*, and in two of these instances (4:45, 58) the Tamil Śaiva philosophical understanding of *māyai* as "matter", *māyaimalam*, clearly could not apply. Often in the *Tiruvācakam*, *māyam* simply appears as a qualifier of other, already undesirable, entities; hence, "delusive birth" (*māyap piṟappu/piṟavi* — 1:14; 13:3; 33:8), "delusive darkness/ignorance" (*māya iruḷ* — 1:51; *māyā iruḷ* — 36:6), and "delusive powers" (*māyā cattikaḷ* — 4:44). Śiva grants to Māṇikkavācakar the ability not to confuse "delusive happiness" (*māya vā**l**kkai*) with something true or real (*mey*) (42:5).

In 45:3, *māyam* refers to a set of questions which had vexed Māṇikkavācakar before he became a devotee of Śiva; from his new-found perspective, these questions are "delusive" (*māyam*) (cf. 49:8). 41:3 pictures the poet caught "in the mouth (presumably a snake's mouth) of *māyam* called 'I' and 'mine'." Here *māyam* signifies the deceptive nature of egoizing thought and action (cf. 31:5, translated above on p. 83). On several occasions, *māyam* means a trick, something accomplished by sleight of hand, as it were (5:42; 36:7). Śiva himself is once invoked as "the conjurer" (*māyaṉ*–23:7), a reference to his unpredictable, sportive, and trick-loving nature.

Three of the remaining references to *māyam* could be construed in a way consistent with the Siddhānta understanding of the term. On the other hand, these three instances certainly do not force one to conclude that Māṇikkavācakar intends *māyam* to mean "matter" or that he is even aware of such a meaning. 46:1 mentions "the army of *māyam*" (*māyap paṭai*). The image evoked in this hymn is that of doing battle with *māyam*, probably best rendered here by "delusion" rather than "matter". Elsewhere, the poet says "the supreme Light guarded me from *pavamāyam* (Skt. *bhavamāyā*)" (11:4). Several translations are possible in this case, viz., "delusive birth, earthly life or existence", or "mundane matter". In view of other occurrences of these terms in the text, "delusive birth" seems the preferable reading.

Of all Māṇikkavācakar's uses of *māyam* that at 49:5, a very problematic verse is most easily translated by "matter". Here, reference is made to the "spiritual ignorance which *māyai* intentionally distributes on earth."[1] If this rendering is correct, then we could see in *māyai* a reference to the material cause of the world, which according to the Śaiva Siddhānta system, exercises its effect upon individual souls (*pacu*) due to the operation of Siva's *tirodhāna-śakti*. However, it is also possible to translate the passage: "the spiritual ignorance which leads to valuing illusory things (*māyai*) on earth." Even if all three of the above passages are translated according to a Siddhānta interpretation, it is still a slender basis for assuming that Māṇikkavācakar understands *māyam* along Siddhānta lines, particularly in view of the more numerous times he uses the term in a non-technical sense.

Māṇikkavācakar specifically rejects the Advaita Vedānta understanding of *māyā*; for he makes a slighting reference to the "vain hurricane of Māyāvāda" (i.e., Advaita Vedānta) which "whirled and blew and roared" (4:54-55).[2] A bit further on in the same passage he uses *māyai* to describe other teachings considered to be false and debilitating (4:58).

It is noteworthy that Māṇikkavācakar never says that Śiva 'severs' *māyam*. Why this should be so is not easy to explain in view of the poet's predilection for this verb. But, there are several possible reasons. First, *māyam* is usually used adjectivally and thus seldom has the opportunity to be the object of any verb in the *Tiruvācakam*. Second, it appears from the text that Māṇikkavācakar does not have as clear an image in mind when he uses this term as when he mentions *viṉai*, *piṟappu*, *pācam*, or *malam*.[3] And finally, *māyam* is associated with Śiva (*māyaṉ*–23:7) in his role as trickster and deceiver (see chapter 6) and consequently is not so unambiguously negative a term as the other items just mentioned. In any case, *māyam* seems to bear no special relation to the material world in the *Tiruvācakam* as it definitely does in Siddhānta thought.

Before considering Māṇikkavācakar's attitude toward sensory experience, this is a good point at which to note his acceptance of a doctrine widespread in the Indian religions: Whatever the problems inherent in mundane existence, the earth is the arena *par excellence* of release. Thus, Māṇikkavācakar has Brahmā and Viṣṇu, who are frequently presented in the text as incapable of knowing Śiva, lamenting their plight in the following way: "Without going to the earth and being born there, we're vainly wasting our days; for we've seen how Śiva saves (*uyyakkoḷ*) (those who live on) this earth" (20:10). As will be seen again, Māṇikkavācakar often mentions that Śiva came specifically to the earth in order to grant grace to his devotees. In this one important respect humans are superior to even the inhabitants of the celestial regions.

If the meaning of *māyam* is not entirely obvious in the *Tiruvācakam*, there is little chance of misconstruing Māṇikkavācakar's pronouncements condemning 'the five senses'. The poet mentions his problems with sensory experience quite frequently, and no less than twelve references are clustered in the fifty verses of the sixth hymn alone. The description of the havoc wreaked in his life by the senses is varied and striking and it is tempting to quote extensively from the text. To begin our summary of the *Tiruvācakam's* view of sensory experience, some of the verbs and adjectives which Māṇikkavācakar uses to delineate the effect which the senses exercise on him should be noted.

The senses "deceive" (*vañci* and variants) the poet (1:55; 6:11; 22:1). They also "bewilder" (*tikai*–6:28), "agitate" (*kalaṅku*–6:30) after and "hem him in" (*aṭar* 6:38). Furthermore, Māṇikkavācakar feels himself to be "dragged along" (*īr*–6:8) and "boiled" (*vetumpu*–6:36) by the burning senses. The senses are "worthless" (*cīril*–5:79) but "powerful" (*irum*–4:120), and are the "cause of death" (*iṟappataṟkē kāraṇam*–31:1) if one becomes intoxicated (*mayaṅku*) by them. They are a mire in which one can sink (*aimpulaṉ āya cēṟṟil aḻuntu*–27:2) and a river on whose bank one is liable to become rooted like a tree (6:3).

Also instructive with regard to Māṇikkavācakar's view of sensory experience are similies comparing the operation of the senses to certain animals. When discussing *pantam/pantaṉai* we saw one instance where the five senses are likened to a snake (3:70, p. 119). This image recurs at 6:35 where birth is called a "five-mouthed snake", almost certainly symbolizing the five senses (see p. 78). The senses are "like ants quietly swarming in a pot of ghee, not permitting me to go to You" (6:24). Since, hymn 6 is an *antāti* poem, in which the last word of each verse becomes the first word of the succeeding verse and the last word of the entire poem is also the initial word of its first verse, 6:25 begins with 'ant' just as verse 24 ended with this word. Again, the five senses are compared to ants, but in other respects the image is quite different: "Don't leave empty, lonely me, distressed and gnawed by the senses as an earthworm amid ants" (6:25).

At one point Māṇikkavācakar likens the senses to birds (*paṟavai*) who cannot get enough prey (*irai*), presumably vultures, and who are said to fly away when Śiva enters the poet's mind (*uḷam*) (15:14). Twice elephants characterize the activity of the senses. Māṇikkavācakar portrays himself as someone so harassed (*alai*) by the senses that he is like "a little bush (*tuṟu*) where elephants are in fierce struggle" (6:21). And 6:32 simply states that he fears the five senses which resemble a "murderous powerful elephant" (*aṭal kari*). This last example occurs at the beginning of a verse in the *antāti* sixth hymn. The previous verse ends by noting how Śiva defeated the *aṭal kari* (6:31), a reference to the myth of Śiva's slaying an elephant and wearing its skin (*gajāsurasaṃhāra mūrti*/*gajāha mūrti*). The juxtaposition of these two verses strongly implies that if Śiva can subdue the elephant demon he can do the same to Māṇikkavācakar's raging, elephant-like senses, an implication supported by other passages in the *Tiruvācakam*.

While not explicitly comparing the senses to a wild boar, the following verse subtly suggests such a simile and also indicates Śiva's role in this situation:

> The sacred foot which walked in the forest
> after the reckless black boar,
> which roots up (the earth),
> He placed on my head
> and tamed the powerful sport [*āṭṭu*],
> of those five cruel men [*aivar kaṇṭakar*, Skt. *kaṇṭaka*),
> who possess overwhelming strength.
> Is it not so that I acquired [*koḷ*] resplendent
> Tillai's Lord [*āṇṭāṉ*]?
> (40:8)

This verse assumes the story found in the *Mahābhārata* of Arjuna's *tapas* undertaken in order to acquire the *pāśupatāstra* from Śiva.[4] One incident in this myth relates how Śiva appeared in the form of a hunter and killed a boar who was really an *asura* in disguise intent on attacking Arjuna. There is a parallel in this verse between the savage boar and the poet's barbaric senses, "the five cruel men". In both instances, Śiva masters the situation, his foot symbolizing his lordship over both the boar *asura* and Māṇikkavācakar's rampant sensory life. Just as the Śiva of mythology conquers demonic wild beasts, he also subdues his devotee's senses.

It is significant that the animals with which the senses are associated are all wild creatures, unlike the dog or cow to which Māṇikkavācakar otherwise compares himself. The senses are not easily domesticated, particularly not by Māṇikkavācakar himself. However, Śiva appears as the subduer, the domesticator, of the senses. Never is he said to 'cut off' the senses as he does karma, rebirth, *pācam*, *malam*, and relatives. The senses are not destroyed; rather they are brought under control, reformed. Thus, Śiva is a warrior (*cēvakaṉ*) who "subdues the five kings" (i.e., the five senses) (*aivar kōkkaḷaiyum vel*–36:10). In a verse also proclaiming Śiva's forceful assertion of sovereignty over him, Māṇikkavācakar says, "I directed my thoughts (*eṇṇam*), body, mouth, nose, ears, and eyes on You alone" (28:5).[5] The senses have a proper function. They are to be used in the service of Śiva.

In the fifth hymn, Māṇikkavācakar describes the effect which Śiva's grace exercises on him, mentioning among other things the transformation of his senses.

My thoughts You caused
(to think) of You.
The eyes of dog-like me You caused
(to see) the flower of Your sacred foot.
My worship You caused
(to adore) that foot.
My tongue You caused
(to utter) Your gem-like phrases.
So that my five senses are satisfied [*ār*]
You (accepted) my worship and enslaved [*āṭkoḷ*] me.
(5:26)

The verse concludes with a series of vocatives further praising Śiva for entering the poet's mind (*uḷḷam*) and for giving himself to lonely, destitute Māṇikkavācakar. The point worth noting in the context of the present discussion is that when brought into contact with Śiva as part of his overall enslavement of Māṇikkavācakar, the senses are transformed into something worthwhile. Indeed their voracious appetite is satisfied.

Although the *Tiruvācakam* sometimes describes Śiva as being unavailable to the sense organs (3:113; 5:70, 76), which in one respect is not surprising, there are other passages in which the god is hailed as being in the senses. Thus, Śiva is the sole guiding cause (*muḻumutal*) of the senses (21:4). 15:5 states that he is united (*puṇar*) with eight different forms, one of which is "man who has sense organs" (*pulaṉ āya mainıaṉ*).[6] And elsewhere, Śiva is said to be both the sense organs and their objects (31:10).

Māṇikkavācakar's view of sensory experience has a dual focus. Unchecked, the senses wreak havoc on one's life. Probably subdued, however, they become agents of spiritual satisfaction rather than frustration. The subduing power, of course, is Śiva. In fact, in one respect the all-pervading god himself already inhabits man's senses. The senses are therefore not inherently bad. They need not be suppressed (no *pratyāhāra* here), only reformed. It is to the reformed senses' view of nature, nature as a source of images and insights into more than sensory reality, that our discussion now turns.

While Māṇikkavācakar sometimes speaks of the world in terms of a philosophical abstraction mentioning its five elements (earth, water, fire, air, and ether),[7] he generally seems quite uninterested in cosmological speculation. Rather his attitude toward his surroundings is best seen in the many poetic images found in the *Tiruvācakam* that are based upon the South Indian environment. The sea, the rain clouds, flowers, animals, and the like, all play a prominent role in his poetry.

Māṇikkavācakar's love of natural detail is at least partially attributable to the literary environment in which he flourished. Early Tamil poetry, as noted in chapter 2, displays a great fondness for natural description in order to illumine human emotions. While the rather elaborate system of conventions known to the Tamil Caṅkam poets was no longer in use in Māṇikkavācakar's time, he does share their sensitivity to nature. Māṇikkavācakar utilizes natural description to heighten his presentation of religious matters, a technique already evident in several passages of the *Paripāṭal* and *Tirumurukāṟ-ṟuppaṭai*, two late texts included in the Caṅkam corpus which will be discussed in due course.

Natural description serves Māṇikkavācakar quite well when he attempts to depict the manner in which Śiva overpowers his devotees. The very sensory experience of the phenomenal world which is elsewhere so problematic now becomes the means better to comprehend the workings of Śiva's grace. In this regard, the extended metaphor of the third hymn picturing Śiva as a rain cloud is an excellent example.

That ancient Sea of highest bliss
appeared as a great black cloud
ascending the hill of beautiful holy Peruntuṟai,
with sacred lightning gleaming,
unfolding in every direction,
so that the bright snake, the bondage [*pantaṉai*]
of the five senses,
slithered away in retreat,
so that the cruel afflicting intense heat of summer
goes into hiding,
so that the thriving beautiful *toṉṟi* flower
shines in gleaming splendor.

On account of our births its fury increased
and its great grace [*karuṇai*] thundered
like the beat of a war drum,
so that the *kāntaḷ* flowers showed flower-like
adoration [*añcali*],
and drops of undiminishing sweet grace [*aruḷ*], fell,
and the great deluge overflowed in every direction,
spreading to the pond of distress,
that mirage of the six religions
[*irumuc camayam*]
where a herd of long-eyed deer
had come desiring water,
had drunk with great mouthfuls
of *tapas* [*tavam*],
but went away
staggering,
(the draft) in vain,
their great burning thirst unslaked.

Into a great celestial river the deluge gushed,
rose up and whirled in great eddies of joy.
It thundered, beat, and dashed
against the high bank of our bondage [*pantam*],

rose up and uprooted the great tree of our twofold
deeds [*iru viṉai*]
which had flourished with fruit for birth
after birth [*uḻ uḻ*].

Guiding this water of beautiful grace [*aruḷ*]
to a juncture in the high hills,
a dam was built,
forming a tank full of fragrant flowers
dripping honey,
on whose banks the bees mingle
with a great cloud of *akil* smoke.
Rejoicing,
watching (the water) rise higher and higher in the tank,
the devoted ploughmen [*toṇṭa uḻavar*]
sowed (seeds) of love in the paddy field of worship.

Hail the Cloud
who is hard to reach on this earth,
who gave His ploughmen full satisfaction [*ār*]!
(3:66-95)

This is not the place for extensive commentary on the religious contents of the above passage, although several possibly obscure items are discussed in a note.[8] Our concern here is with Māṇikkavācakar's deft use of the various characteristics of the monsoon to enliven our understanding of Śiva's activity. One could read this passage along with some commentators as a detailed allegory, but Māṇikkavācakar gives enough clues within the poem itself for us to appreciate his point without having to seek correspondences for every detail. This metaphor seems a rather ingenious device, drawing a parallel between what by almost any account must be considered the central feature of the Indian ecosystem, the monsoon, and the key aspect of Māṇikkavācakar's spiritual experience, the bestowal of Śiva's grace. The coming of the rains, with all that it entails in anticipation, celebration, awe, and danger, is captured in this passage describing both the arrival of the monsoon and the descent of Śiva's grace. The awesome, irresistible, lifegiving monsoon's soaking of the parched earth is an apt image for the equally radical change brought about by Śiva's intervention in Māṇikkavācakar's life. While almost certainly not a conscious influence, it is worth noting that like the Vedic Rudra, Māṇikkavācakar's Śiva is also symbolized by the monsoon storm, albeit now transformed to exclude those malevolent features so prominent in Rudra's character.

In imagining Śiva's irresistible grace to be like a monsoon flood, the *Tiruvācakam* is reminiscent of the earlier *Tirumurukāṟṟuppaṭai*, "The Guide to Holy Murukaṉ", whose last section contains an account of the god's self-revelation to his devotees, concluding with a long description of the torrents that rush down the slopes of Murukaṉ's mountainous domain (288-317).[9] The raging stream parallels the god's powerful embrace (*aḷai*), granting his worshippers the gift (*paricil*) of escape from death and ruin (*viḻivu*) (292-295).[10] The *Tirumurukāṟṟuppaṭai*, which is counted as part of the Caṅkam anthology the *Pattuppāṭṭu* (although in its final form it must stem from at least the middle of the first millenium), is rich in natural description throughout. This text also delineates other aspects of the Murukaṉ cult which will later be seen to find an echo in Māṇikkavācakar's devotion. The point to note here is that the *Tiruvācakam's* expression of religious emotion to the accompaniment of natural description, even in its particulars, is not unprecedented in Tamil literature some centuries antecedent to Māṇikkavācakar.

The same image of the life-giving rain cloud also portrays certain features of the goddess, who is said to be inseparable from Śiva (7:12). And, in the next verse of the same hymn, both the god and goddess are likened to the features of a tank in which devotees bathe (7:13). Translations of both these verses will be given henceforth.

Tiruppaḷḷiyeḻucci, "The Sacred (Song) of Rising from Bed", is sung in the morning in order to awaken the god from his sleep. As might be expected, this hymn highlights features associated with the sunrise.

> The sun has reached Indra's quarter (i.e., the East),
> darkness [*iruḷ*] has fled,
> dawn is spreading.

As the sun,
which is like the mercy [*karuṇai*] of Your Holy
flower-like face,
rises higher and higher,
and the fragrant flowers,
which are like Your eyes
have begun to bloom,
the swarming beetles will crowd around the King
and hum.
Consider these things.
. . . .
Graciously [*aruḷ*] arise from Your bed.
The beautiful cuckoos are calling,
the cocks crowing,
the birds singing,
the conch shells sounding,
the stars have dimmed,
the sun has risen and is on its course.
With love show us
Your divine, good, ankleted pair of feet,
O Lord Śiva who dwells in holy Peruntuṟai.
You are difficult for all to know.
For us You are easy.
O our Lord, graciously [*aruḷ*] arise from Your bed.
(20:2-3)

Here the sunrise represents the dawning of Śiva's grace. It invigorates the birds and flowers, and also arouses the six-footed beetles (*aṟupatam*), whose humming parallels the praises sung to Śiva in the morning by his devotees.

Further examples of natural description from the *Tiruvācakam*, while perhaps not quite so elaborate as the above passages, could be considerably multiplied. But it will suffice to let most of these instances appear coincidentally in other contexts. We have already seen a number of cases where characteristics of animals, birds, and insects are used to depict human behavior. Flowers are a great favorite of Māṇikkavācakar, and there are very many references, particularly to the lotus (*kamalam*, *tāmarai*, *paṅkayam*)[11]; to the Indian laburnam or cassia (*koṉṟai*), which is part of Śiva's attire[12]: and simply to flowers in general (*malar, pōtu, pū*), often used to characterize Śiva's feet.[13] There is, however, one further item in Māṇikkavācakar's repertory of images drawn from the phenomenal world which should be dealt with systematically in the present context.

Māṇikkavācakar's image-making is not solely drawn from visual and auditory experience, or even from the sense of smell, flowers being mentioned as much for their fragrance as for their beauty of form and color. A highly preferred metaphor in the *Tiruvācakam* is based on the sense of taste. One is surprised to discover a high incidence of gustatory images in a collection of devotional poetry, but then most of us probably do not expect such poets to have a sweet tooth. In view of the abundance of references to sweetness in the *Tiruvācakam*, all positive images, our only surmise is that Māṇikkavācakar was blessed by such a liking for sweets. (We cannot say he was "bedevilled by a weakness" for sweet foods, since he never mentions this as a problem. In fact, references to gluttony of any sort are rare, 6:41 being one of the few, where he says he is a "two-trunked elephant" and that the only thing he can do is eat.)

There are a number of specific images which center on sweetness, but several of the more general descriptions of Śiva's grace also have overtones of sweetness. Thus, *iṉpam*, one of the common terms for bliss or delight, also connotes sweetness. It is a cognate of the noun *iṉimai* (sweetness), from which is derived a rather frequently used adjective *iṉ* (sweet). Siva's grace is sweet (*iṉ aruḷ*–e.g , 3:76; 5:30; 7:16; 8:12, 18; 20:4). Ambrosia is sweet (*iṉ amutu*–e.g., 7:7; 8:19; 42:2). Indeed, Śiva himself is called the sweet one (*tittikkummāṉ*–5:90). Ambrosia, even when not specifically said to be sweet still evokes such an image, and furthermore, *amutu* is one of the common ways in which Māṇikkavācakar addresses the deity.[14]

More fascinating are those images referring to a particular kind of sweet food. Śiva is not just the sweet one, he is the lord who is as delicious as honey and sweet ambrosia (*tēṉ āy iṉ amutamum āyt tittikkum civaperumāṉ*–38:10). He is honey (*tēṉ*–e.g., 5:58, 98; 20:9; 22:8; 34:8), milk (*pāl*–e.g., 5:58; 13:11), sugar-cane (*karumpu*–20:9), and the juice of the sugar-cane (*kaṉṉaliṉ teḷi*–5:58). To his worshippers he is sweet, ripe fruit (*maturak kaṉi*–32:10). Indeed, he is the taste of the fruit (*paḻac cuvai āyiṉāṉ*–9:15).

The foods to which Śiva is likened occur naturally. They are uncooked, unprepared substances—including the divine ambrosia. It is tempting to read philosophical significance into this common feature of these images, namely, that Śiva's grace is complete in itself, requiring no human modification or effort to render it digestible. While it is quite possible that a concept of this sort did influence Māṇikkavācakar's choice of images—and such a notion, to be sure, is consistent with the *Tiruvācakam's* general view of human effort and divine grace—it seems just as likely that other factors (e.g., considerations of the relative purity of the substances, literary-historical influences) may have determined which foods were deemed appropriate for mention.

Not only Śiva himself, but his action toward his devotees, is described in terms of sweet-tasting substances.

Like a sweet King
  resembling honey, milk, and sugar cane,
He came
and graciously took me into His service [*toḻumpu*].
(8:14)

O brilliant One!
You melted my flesh and bones
  making them like honey, milk, sugar-cane, and ambrosia.
(6:21)

Don't eat honey from a flower.
  That's only a trifle like a millet seed.
But go to the Dancer who pours forth the honey of bliss
  so that your very bones will melt
  whenever you think of Him, see Him, or speak of Him.
(10:3)

When shall I embrace,
when shall I be united with
  the ripe *nelli* Fruit,
  the Honey,

the Milk,
the copious Ambrosia,
the delicious Flavor of ambrosia [*amutin cuvai*]?
Ah, when shall I be united with my uncut Gem?
(27:4)

Several of these images will be encountered again in the discussion of bhakti in chapter 7. More sensuous, immediate ways of portraying God and his activity could hardly be imagined than to call him the savor of ripe fruit. In certain respects, the poets of the Tamil bhakti movements, both Śaiva and Vaiṣṇava,[15] achieved with sensuous language what the later North Indian miniature painters accomplished visually for Kṛṣṇaite devotion based on the *Bhāgavata Purāṇa* and the *Gītagovinda*. Certainly, comparable images in western religious poetry are not easy to find (Edward Taylor's earthy metaphors for God's grace come to mind as an exception[16]).

For someone who otherwise condemns the senses, Māṇikkavācakar put them to quite effective use in describing matters of the spirit. But the poet's censure of the 'five senses' and his simultaneous appreciation of sense-experience as a provider of images are not irreconcilable. Philosophically, as we have noted, Śiva subdues the senses, enabling them to become proper receptors of spiritual insight.

Historically, Māṇikkavācakar's sensitivity to the phenomenal world lies in a cultural tradition which in its literature and religion expressed a strong penchant for the natural environment. George Hart has argued that the earliest stratum of Tamil literature exhibits an understanding of the sacred fundamentally different from that of the Āryan civilization of North India. The deities of ancient Tamilnad, he claims, "were not transcendent beings, but rather immanent powers, present in objects encountered every day and involved in every aspect of ordinary life."[17] And even though the bhakti movements represent a great infusion of northern traditions into the South Indian cultural milieu, the old fascination with nature, with the idea of an immanent sacred, still finds a voice in Tamil bhakti literature.[18] While Hart sometimes tends to overstate his case, there is little doubt that the *Tiruvācakam*, particularly in its imagery and to some extent in its ideology too, reflects its Tamil literary and cultural provenance.

Alongwith the *Tirumurukāṟṟuppaṭai*, the *Paripāṭal* is another transitional text which combines elements of the nascent bhakti movement with the earlier Caṅkam tradition. There are several passages in this work where the universe is spoken of sacramentally as a manifestation of Tirumāl (i.e., Viṣṇu), echoes of which can be heard in Māṇikkavācakar's poetry. These passages portray nature as a series of theophanies. Here is a translation of one of them:

> In the sun are Your wrath and Your light.
> In the moon are Your coolness and Your tenderness.
> In the cloud are Your abundance and Your liberality.
> In the earth are Your protection and Your endurance.
> In the flower are Your scent and Your splendor.
> In the water are Your appearance and Your expanse.
> In the atmosphere [*ākāyam*, Skt. *ākāśa*] are Your form and Your speech.
> In the wind are Your coming and Your retreat.
> (Paripāṭal 4:25–32)[19]

This is a peculiarly Tamil appropriation of Brahmanical theism. It is not simply Upaniṣadic monism translated into another language, but rather marks the beginning of an acceptance of Sanskritic deities and their mythologies refracted through a Tamil literary and cultural tradition which prized the natural environment and the concrete manifestation of the sacred. Although medieval Tamil poetry was much influenced by Brahmanical mythology and Sanskrit literary techniques, "yet all Tamil poetry, including that of the medieval period, is very different from Sanskrit. Tamil writers always followed Tamil conventions and took most of their ideas from earlier Tamil literature."[20]

It would be easy to say that the Tamil poet in Māṇikkavācakar affirms the phenomenal world and the Brahmanical philosopher in him berates the senses, but the situation is more complex than that. What from one point of view may appear to be a kind of cultural schizophrenia about sense experience, at a deeper level is discerned to be a paradox widely attested in mystical literature. In one sense, the ordinary world of phenomena, of sensory experience, of differentiation, is abandoned, transcended, in the experience of union with the "uncut Gem". But seen from another angle, the same experience cleanses "the doors of perception" so that one may "see a world in a grain of sand/and a heaven in a wild flower/ hold infinity in the palm of your hand/and eternity in an hour."[21] Through the experience of union — in Māṇikkavāca-kar's case not just union with 'God' but also with the "ripe *nelli* Fruit, Honey, Milk, and the Taste of ambrosia" — the world as well as one's inner life can be transformed. Sight, hearing, taste, touch, and smell no longer need be impediments but become vehicles to perceive the rains, the sunrise, flowers, milk, honey, and sugar-cane as manifestations of the ultimate reality. Anyone who imagines that Indian religious traditions are characterized by a *Weltanschauung* of "world and life negation"[22] should read the *Tiruvācakam* as an antidote. Certainly in one respect, Māṇikkavācakar profoundly affirms the world.

Women and the Goddess

When Māṇikkavācakar's attitude toward woman is scrutinized, one is confronted by the same kind of ambivalence already noted with regard to sensory experience. In this case the distinction is quite sharp, despite the use of identical language for purposes of both praise and blame. The distinction between femininity worthy of esteem and femininity drawing censure is the difference between Śiva's spouse as goddess or human devotee, on the one hand, and human females, on the other. Again, Māṇikkavācakar's literary legacy from the Caṅkam poets helps make possible an affirmation of the feminine which might otherwise have been dismissed as totally inimical to the devotion to Śiva.

First, what does Māṇikkavācakar think of the women whom he sees around him? Since he only comments on voluptuous females, we must assume that sexual attractiveness was a prime factor in his attitude toward members of the opposite sex. He obviously was aroused by female beauty, otherwise he would not mention this 'problem' so frequently. Hence, the poet laments the allure of women, mentioning among other features their black hair (4:30; 41:4), red lips (4:30; 5:19, 27; 6:2, 41; 49:3), black eyes (6:3; 24:6; 41:7), white teeth (4:30; 6:27), full breasts (4:31–34; 6:2, 27, 46; 26:1; 41:2, 7; 51:3, 6), and narrow waists (24:7; 40:2; 49:6). The most extensive description of beautiful women occurs in the fourth hymn where Māṇikka-vācakar enumerates the various pitfalls which must be escaped before one can become a devotee.

> The black hair,
> the red mouths,
> the white teeth,
> the gracefulness like that of the peacock
> in the rainy season,
> the tender breasts which are
> pressed close together.
> flourishing,
> bodice bursting,
> shining,
> large,
> wearying (with the weight of carrying them),
> coming to the waist,
> rising,
> swelling,
> the rib of a palm leaf unable to go between them —
> From the pestilence of such women's piercing eyes
> one must escape.
> From the rutting elephant called desire,
> which (rages) in the great wide expanse of
> mad men of the world,
> one must escape.
>
> (4:30-37)

The fascination of twentieth-century American males with full-busted women is obviously not a unique cultural phenomenon. But, as will be seen below, in classical Tamilnad female breasts had more significance than either biology or male lechery would ascribe to them.

Women appear to Māṇikkavācakar as seductresses. Their glance is piercing, as in the passage above, or enticingly oblique (35:9; 38:6; 51:5). They have their designs (*karuttu*–51:9), are deceitful (*paṭiṟu*–5:40) and engage in trifling speech (*cil moḻi*–6:5). The poet speaks of their company as a net in which he becomes entangled (6:40; 24:7; 25:10) or a whirlpool engulfing him (41:1). Women bite him like crocodiles in the hot waters of lust (6:41). Consequently, the effect they exercise on Māṇikkavācakar is completely to immobilize him with lust. There are several telling images which depict this paralysis.

> Unmindful that when Kāma's arrow pierces me
> moonlight will burn,
> in the midst of those deceitful women
> with their fawn-like glances,
> I became like curds being churned by a churning stick.
> (5:40)

> Don't leave me
> who lusts after the breasts of those women
> with deer-like eyes,
> like a fly on a ripe jack fruit.
> (6:46)

> I was lying in this jungle of birth,
> and like a worm-infested dog,
> driven back and forth.
> I wandered about in the company of silly women [*ēḻai*],
> doing for them whatever they wished.
> (41:9)

Despite his consistent criticism of women, Māṇikkavācakar is not a misogynist, for he shows real affection for Śiva's spouse. While the *Tiruvācakam* is, of course, primarily concerned with the poet's relationship with Śiva, the goddess is frequently mentioned and the attention accorded her is not merely casual. In fact, her position is important enough to justify a close examination of the role she plays in the text. In the course of this discussion, we shall come to understand how Māṇikkavācakar, who wants to be repelled by the voluptuous appearance of human females, can simultaneously dote upon identical features of the goddess.

In the *Tiruvācakam*, the goddess invariably appears in conjunction with Śiva. She is not an independent figure in her own right, a point to be developed shortly. She is referred to by a variety of names, often words simply meaning "woman", "female" or "lady".[23] Māṇikkavācakar also uses terms reflecting her divine status, such as *tēvi* (Skt. *devī*)—"goddess" (36:10; 41:4), *uṭaiyāḷ*—"mistress" (5:85; 7:16; 21:1), and *pirāṭṭi*—"lady" or "mistress" (7:13,16). Sometimes, names related to the goddess's particular persona, are applied to her. For instance, we meet with *umai* (2:142; 34:1; 42:5; 43:8) and *umaiyāḷ* (5:55; 9:3; 33:1), both Tamil forms of the Sanskrit "Umā". And while Māṇikkavācakar only mentions the name Pārvatī (Tamil *pārpatti*) twice (9:1; 14:1), he is fond of the myth connecting Śiva's wife with the Himālaya.[24]

Frequently Śiva's spouse is pictured as a coparticipant in his acts of grace, both toward the universe in general and Māṇikkavācakar in particular. Thus, it is not just Śiva who comes into Māṇikkavācakar's life, enslaving, possessing, transforming the poet; rather it is Śiva along with the goddess.[25] Likewise, the goddess participates in some of Śiva's world-saving actions.[26] The *Tiruvācakam's* most elaborate description of the goddess's action toward mankind is found in the seventh hymn. In a familiar image, her benevolent workings are compared to the life-giving rain cloud. Although, in this example, she nearly achieves independent status, note that at the end of the verse she is inextricably linked with Śiva.

Our Mistress [*uṭaiyāḷ*] is like a rain cloud
  which diminishes the water of the sea
  and then rises up.
The lightning shines
  like the delicate waist
  of the Mistress [*uṭaiyāḷ*] who rules [*āḷ*] us.
It thunders
  like the beautiful golden anklets
  on our Lady's [*pirāṭṭi*] sacred feet.
The rainbow is bent
  like her blessed eyebrows.
O cloud,

pour down upon us
like the sweet grace [*aruḷ*]
which She gives to the devotees
of our King
who is not separate from our Mistress [*uṭaiyāḷ*].
(7:16)

It is noteworthy that Māṇikkavācakar does not associate the goddess with those of Śiva's more bizarre actions which find mention in the *Tiruvācakam* (e.g., his destruction of Dakṣa's sacrifice, his killing the elephant and tiger, and his dancing at night in the crematorium). Only once when he refers to Śiva's skinning the elephant does Māṇikkavācakar also mention the god's spouse in association with his odd actions, and then to say that such violent behavior frightened the goddess, who in this instance is likened to a delicate creeper, a simile further accentuating the inappropriateness of such action in her presence (6:19).

The goddess definitely appears to be a restraining influence on Śiva's eccentric behavior. But conversely, there are also instances where Śiva restrains the goddess. For example, the myth of Śiva's catching the falling Gaṅgā in order to save the world from ruin is cited several times by Māṇikkavācakar.[27] With regard to Gaṅgā, it is Śiva who holds the goddess in check, bearing her potentially destructive power in his hair. The story of Śiva's dance contest with the fearsome Kālī is also known to Māṇikkavācakar. In defeating Kālī at dancing, Śiva tames her, rescuing the universe from her devastating fury (12:14).[28] Although Māṇikkavācakar differentiates Gaṅgā from Pārvatī (12:7) and Kālī from Umā (2:142), he does view Gaṅgā and Kālī as Śiva's spouses. Moreover, at a deeper level, Māṇikkavācakar shares the Indian tendency to integrate all manifestations of the feminine sacred, indeed of the sacred generally (as we shall see), into one figure.

There are two instances where the goddess is designated by the peculiarly Tamil term *aṇaṅku* (13:7; 20:6), the first of which refers to Śiva's dance with Kālī just mentioned. In the early Tamil literature, *aṇaṅku* denotes the sacred power that resides in the mature female, particularly in her breasts and loins, an aspect of what George Hart has argued is the immanence of the sacred in ancient Tamilnad. Thus, it is apparent that the early Tamils sensed a numinous quality surrounding female fertility. Hart's publications have shown that *aṇaṅku* is potentially dangerous and that precautions need be taken in order to keep it under control.[29] Specifically, marriage and the wife's ensuing faithfulness to her husband are considered to be the best way of ensuring that *aṇaṅku* will not become a source of social destruction. Widows and unmarried post-pubescent women are especially dangerous, since chastity is assumed to be more difficult in such circumstances than in the marital state. Hence, *aṇaṅku* is controlled by marriage. Both the times that Māṇikkavācakar uses this word in relation to the goddess, he very pointedly associates her with Śiva. In 13:7, as already noted, the image is that of Śiva dancing with the goddess (*aṇaṅku*) in Tillai (i.e., Cidambaram); and in 20:6 the poet simply addresses Śiva as "O Bridegroom of *aṇaṅku*". Clearly, *aṇaṅku* is held in check and rendered beneficent by the marital bond requiring wifely submission which assists in securing the goddess's chastity.

An unexpected confirmation of the salutary results of marriage for Hindu goddesses comes from recent ethnographic research carried out by Lawrence Babb in the Chhatisgarh region of Madhya Pradesh.[30] Briefly stated, Babb's thesis is that the goddess, when not connected with a male deity or when clearly dominant over her husband, is a blood-thirsty, malevolent figure. But, in cases where her feminine power is domesticated by marriage, the goddess appears as benevolent. Consequently, the potentially sinister goddess when properly subordinated to her husband is the source of wealth and progeny. "An appetite for conflict and destruction is thus transformed into the most fundamental of social virtues, that of wifely submission, which, on the premises given in Hindu culture, makes the continuation of society possible."[31]

Māṇikkavācakar's depiction of the goddess confirms the positive consequences of her association with Śiva. With regard to Śiva himself, a few of his anti-social idiosyncracies have already been indicated, characteristics which will command our full attention in the next chapter. Apparently, however, these aspects of the god's character are not deemed appropriate for mention when Māṇikkavācakar visualizes the goddess at his side. Hence, it seems that we have to do here not merely with the transformation of dangerous feminine power into a benevolent quantum but with a mutual taming of god and goddess by each other. Śiva, the great unpredictable "madman" (*pittaṉ*, *piccaṉ*), as Māṇikkavācakar occasionally addresses him (e.g., 6:49; 11:16; 12:9), is rendered momentarily sane (i.e., behaves in a socially acceptable manner) when in the company of the goddess.

Hart claims that in early Tamil literature, man corresponds to nature, whereas woman corresponds to culture.[32] That is, women tend to be associated with the home and domestic life, while man's life typically revolves around the harvest and war, considered to be uncultured, natural activities. A woman's power, her *aṇaṅku*, must be domesticated, and indeed, not only her wifely duties but her attire and ornaments are artificial domesticating checks on her power. As Hart's translation of *Aiṅkuṟunūṟu* 405 and his commentary on this verse point out, a woman is like fire, fundamentally a natural thing, which if controlled, however, ceases to be dangerous, becoming in fact a source of great satisfaction. But, likewise in the case of Śiva himself, contact with his properly cultured spouse seems to connect him with ordinary social reality and temporarily domesticates him too. Nevertheless, his principal role vis-à-vis both the goddess and his devotees is that of a domesticator, a subduer of *aṇaṅku* and misguided human inclinations.

Even more significant for Māṇikkavācakar than the goddess's conjunction with Śiva in a partnership of benevolent action, is her paradigmatic role as a devoted wife and faithful servant of the god. Although he does not attempt to 'relive' Śaiva mythology by identifying himself with specific details in the myths about the deity, he does in a general sense see the goddess as a model for what a true bhakta of Śiva aspires to be, namely, a faithful wife. In short, he does not try to become Umā or Pārvatī in a particular aspect of her relationship to Śiva, but he longs for the intimacy and devotion vis-à-vis Śiva which her position and behavior epitomize.

While the *Tiruvācakam* does not approach Kṛṣṇaite devotional literature in either the prominence or explicitness of its erotic imagery, we nevertheless do meet with the typical elements of bridal mysticism in which the human self is understood to be a female desiring union with a male deity. Thus, we find Māṇikkavācakar addressing Śiva as his bridegroom and husband.[33] However, Māṇikkavācakar's use of erotic imagery is in some ways unique; for it is the context of a number of his poems even more than their specific content that allows us to speak of bridal mysticism in the *Tiruvācakam.* Especially relevant to this point is the series of hymns which we have seen (in chapter 3, p. 54) have as their setting various female activities, e.g., flower-picking, preparing a bathing compound with mortar and pestle, and several village games. Such verses are ostensibly intended to be sung while performing these distaff actions. Each stanza ends in a refrain which states the context of the hymn, e.g., "let us pound the golden powder" in hymn 9 and "may we pluck the creeper flowers" in the thirteenth hymn. The devotees singing the hymns are thus cast as young women devoted to Śiva.

That the devotees are being homologized with the goddess is evident from the initial verse of the ninth hymn, Tiruppoṟcuṇṇam (The Sacred [Song] or the Golden Powder), to be sung while pounding with a pestle. In this stanza, several female deities are invoked to come join the devotees in praising Śiva and in preparing an aromatic bath powder for him. The names mentioned include Śakti, Somi (Tamil *cōmi*), the goddess of earth (*pārmakaḷ*). Sarasvatī, Siddhi, Gaurī, Pārvatī, and Gaṅgā (9:1), all considered in this context to be manifestations of Śiva's spouse. Plainly, Māṇikkavācakar wants his own relationship with Śiva to parallel that of the goddess.

Interestingly, the women/devotees' physical appearance also matches that of the goddess. To continue with the ninth hymn as our example, the women praising Śiva refer to their own "wide bright eyes, jingling striped bangles (*vaḷai*),[34] and abundant swelling breasts" (9:8); their "eyes streaked like flowers, arms bearing golden bracelets, and Venus mounts resembling a cobra's hood" (9:12); their "waists like lightning,[35] red coral lips, black eyes, white teeth, soft melodious speech, and gold-ornamented breasts" (9:13). In order to give a sense of the context in which these descriptions occur, here is a complete stanza from Tiruppoṟcuṇṇam:

O you fair women

whose eyes are streaked with red as are flowers,
whose arms bear golden bracelets,
whose Venus mounts [*alkul*] are like a cobra's hood,
let us sing about Him
whose throat is black,
the Medicine for the inhabitants of heaven,
the ruby Dancer,
the Chief One,
the Chief of the chief ones,
a False One to the false,
Truth to the true,
who subdued [*akappaṭu*] us,
enslaved [*āṭkoḷ*] us,
showed His rareness to us,
and let us pound the golden powder! (9:12)

Elsewhere many of the same characteristics are ascribed to the goddess herself. Examples of Māṇikkavācakar's description of the goddess's features, which are sometimes virtually identical in vocabulary to the devotees' characteristics just listed, include her "bright eyes" (5:65), "wide eyes" (7;11; 24:5), "bangles" (*vaḷai*–10:18; 11:10, 20), "large breasts" (14:8; 29:1), "bangled arms" (11:10), "mount of Venus resembling a cobra's hood" (5:65; 34;1), "waist resembling an hour-glass drum" (29:5),[36] "red lips" (2:142; 5:65), "black eyes" (5:65; 6:37), "white teeth" (5:65; 6:37), "melodious speech" (28:5; 38:2; 48:5), and "bejewelled breasts" (6:3, 41). Thus, even in their physical appearance, the devotees are pictured as being like the goddess.

It is many of these same features, so attractive in Śiva's spouse and in the devotees likened to females in love with him, which cause such consternation when found in 'ordinary' human women. The vocabulary used to compliment the goddess and the devotees as women overlaps extensively with that found in passages disapproving the attractiveness of human females. There are several rather remarkable passages where Māṇikkavācakar's descriptions of the lust-inciting features of women are juxtaposed with parallel descriptions of the goddess. For example, in verses 5 through 8 of hymn 24, the devotee decries his desire for "women whose hair curls in ringlets" (v. 5), who have "collyrium-blackened eyes resembling a (split) young mango fruit" (v. 6), "flashing eyes and thin trembling waists" (v. 7). In verse 5, Māṇikkavācakar imagines the goddess as having "collyrium-blackened wide eyes and glances like a frightened fawn", and verse 8 mentions her "eyes like a split, tender mango." Although these verses exhibit a higher congruence of individual features within a narrow focus than any other passage in the *Tiruvācakam*, it is not unusual for Māṇikkavācakar to mix disapproval of female beauty with praise of the goddess in the same verse (e.g., 6:3, 10, 41; 24:5; 25:10; 41:4-6; 51:3, 8). One such verse is 6:41.

Down into the hot waters of lust I plunged,
  where the crocodiles, those red-lipped women,
    bite and devour me.

Look, don't leave me who trembles (in fear).
This diseased body full of rotting flesh
  I can't endure.
O Śiva!
Is it just? Is it just?
O Half [*paṅku*[of the Lady [*maṅkai*]
  whose breasts are adorned with jewels and yellow beauty spots [*titalai*]!
O my Salvation [*civakati*]!

(6:41)

It would be easy to dismiss Māṇikkavācakar's condemnation of human female beauty coupled with his simultaneous praise of identical features in the goddess as simply being a particularly conspicuous case of sublimated sexual energy. Or if Māṇikkavācakar shared the widespread Indian esteem for *tapas*, one could attribute his aversion toward human women to ascetical values.[37] But he clearly rejects *tapas* as an efficacious means for achieving release.[38] Taking into account the previous discussion of *aṇaṅku* and marriage, it is seen that there is more to Māṇikkavācakar's distrust of women and affection for the goddess than an individually accomplished resolution of sexual tension through sublimation. Māṇikkavācakar's weakness for good-looking women is potentially a threat to the social order; for to act upon such desires might set in motion the destructive force of *aṇaṅku*. In the Tamil tradition, to violate a woman's chastity risks grave consequences. On the other hand, to become a faithful wife—in this instance a wife of Śiva in the manner of the goddess—is to domesticate the feminine sacred, which for Māṇikkavācakar is achieved by a psychological/spiritual reversal of sex roles. Man becomes woman vis-à-vis God so that the sacred power of human women, who arouse man's passion, will not be unleashed upon society through a breach of chastity—a curious psychological dynamic, but apparently a successful one in Māṇikkavācakar's case.

In effect, we are faced again with the recurring theme of a change of subordination—or "enslavement", "possession" (*āṭkoḷ*), as Māṇikkavācakar most typically puts it. As a male, Māṇikkavācakar is "engulfed (*akappaṭu*) in the whirlpool called women" (41:1), "caught (*akappaṭu*) in hot passion's net of women with eyes like the red carp" (25:10), and "entangled (*akappaṭu*) in the difficulty of karma and birth" (31:2). As a female devoted to God, he/she is "subdued" (*akappaṭu*) by Śiva (9:12), which brings about his/her chastity, fidelity (*kaṟpu*) (30:6).[39] Whether human or divine, female sexuality must be subdued by marriage.

As was noted regarding images drawn from nature, the *Tiruvācakam* does not adopt the system of conventions known to Caṅkam *akam* poetry, although Māṇikkavācakar does share the Caṅkam poets' sensitivity to their natural surroundings. Likewise, with respect to erotic mysticism in the *Tiruvācakam*, the *akam* scheme is not appropriated in detail, but the tradition of Tamil erotics found in the early literature doubtless facilitates Māṇikkavācakar's conceptualization and expression of the relationship between Śiva and devotee as homologous to that between husband and wife. A particularly instructive example of this influence in our text is found in the eighth hymn.

> I shall wreathe my head with *koṉṟai* flowers.
>   Having wreathed myself,
> I shall embrace Śiva's mighty shoulders.
>   Having thus embraced Him,

I shall cling to him,
  lose my senses,
  sulk and feign aversion for him [*ūṭu*].
I shall melt (in love) for His red mouth.
  my mind [*uḷ*] having melted,
I shall seek Him.
  Having sought Him,
I shall think only about Śiva's foot.
I shall wither away (but then) bloom again.
Let us sing about the red foot
  of the Dancer who carries fire.

(8:17)

Here we recognize several typically *akam* motifs. The flowers are presumably those brought by the lover, especially in this case since *koṉṟai* flowers are associated with Śiva. The female wears these flowers as a sign of her acceptance of his love. In Caṅkam poetry, the wearing of flowers by the female indicates that love has been consummated and that thus the pair are married, even though the 'ceremony' may be a secret one.[40] Even clandestine union (*kaḷavu*) issues in *kaṟpu* (fidelity). The theme of feigned quarreling (*ūṭal*) as an important aspect of love is well-known in ancient Tamil literature. In fact, one of the five distinctive modes of love (*urripporuḷ*) in *akam* poetry is that of *ūṭal*, which is associated with *marutam* or the agricultural region where the hero's liaison with prostitutes often provides the dramatic impulse for the poems of this landscape (*tiṇai*). Such quarrels are felt to enhance the pleasure of union, as is apparent above. In the same vein, the final ten couplets of the *Tirukkuṟaḷ* (1321–1330) are concerned with the "delight of lovers' quarrels" (*ūṭal uvakai*).[41] Down to the present day, enactment of such lovers' quarrels between the god and his spouse continues to form a part of both Śaiva and Vaiṣṇava religious festivals in Tamilnad.[42]

Returning to specific references to the goddess in the *Tiruvācakam*, Māṇikkavācakar most frequently mentions her when he praises Śiva as Ardhanārīśvara (the lord who is half woman).[43] In view of the mutually beneficial effects that Śiva and the goddess exercise upon each other, and considering the exemplary devotion and intimacy of her relationship with the god, it is not surprising that the poet should find the androgynous form of the deity so appealing. Here the god and goddess are revealed as not merely bound to each other in marital relationship but as actually conjoined physically in one bisexual body. Indeed, many of the goddess's features to which reference has already been made occur when Māṇikkavācakar envisions Śiva and her as "parts", "shares", or "halves" of each other.[44]

The most extended description of Ardhanārīśvara in the *Tiruvācakam* is found in hymn 10.

> The (tiger) skin and fine cloth,
> the earring and curled leaf (for the ear),
> the milk-white ashes and yellow sandal paste along with the green parrot too,
> the trident and the linked bangles —
> Look at the ancient form of the Lord
> and hum pleasingly
> O Kingly Bee!
>
> (10:18)

Here, one finds a vivid visualization of Ardhanārīśvara, in which the male features are always listed first. Māṇikkavācakar quite conceivably had in mind a particular icon when he sang this hymn, since the androgynous deity is sometimes represented in South Indian Śaiva temples, Śiva's features appealing on the right side, the goddess's on the left (cf. 51:3). It is ierntesting that Māṇikkavācakar calls this "the Lord's ancient form" (*uṭait toṉmaik kōlamē*). Here, "ancient" seems to indicate that which is original, basic, or essential, a point to which we shall return below.

A particularly arresting verse employing the Ardhanārīśvara image, to which reference has previously been made, depicts a group of women devotees taking their morning bath in a tank. As they bathe, they sing hymns in the praise of Śiva and his consort. In this example, the natural features of the tank itself remind the devotees of the beauty of the hermaphroditic god and goddess.

> Plunge into the swelling pool

which resembles our Lady [*pirāṭṭi*] and our King
  with its fresh dark *kuvaḷai* flowers
    and its fresh red lotus blossoms,
  with its beautiful flock of birds
    and its entwined snakes,
  and with the coming of those people
    who wash away their impurity [*malam*].

With conch-shell bangles tinkling,
  the sounding of our anklets joining in,
  our breasts swelling,
  the water set foaming,
Plunge, and playfully bathe in the lotus-filled water.
(7:13)

The *kuvaḷai* flowers are associated with the goddess, the red lotuses with Śiva. Birds are reminiscent of Pārvatī's parrot, and Śiva typically adorns himself with snakes. The people coming to bathe are like devotees approaching Ardhanārīśvara to rid themselves of *malam*.

Apart from such graphic and unmistakable references to Ardhanārīśvara, Māṇikkavācakar also calls upon Śiva as both father and mother. The epithet 'father' occurs very frequently, as is to be expected.[45] But, the maternal aspect of the deity is also prominent in Māṇikkavācakar's lyrics. Sometimes, Śiva himself is addressed or described as mother.[46] In other instances the poet simply likens Śiva's actions to those of a mother.[47] Here emphasis is most typically on the tenderness of divine grace. Whereas elsewhere Śiva's grace appears as an overpowering, enslaving, subduing force, the awesomeness of the god's revelation is mitigated when Māṇikkavācakar asserts that Śiva's tenderness surpasses even a mother's (1:61; 13:3). At one point, the god is praised as "the one who gives the breast like a mother" (50:5). And like a mother he patiently puts up with Māṇikkavācakar's faults and accepts his trifling service.

The beloved Lord [*nāyakaṉ*]
  who caused a dog such as me
  to sing about His feet,
The great One
  who forgives the faults of this demon's mind,

The Lord like a mother
who without reproach
graciously [*aruḷ*] accepts my (worthless) services—

To Him go hum
O Kingly Bee! (10:12)

It is not far from Māṇikkavācakar's experience of God as mother to the Śaiva Siddhānta notion of *aruḷ-śakti*, i.e., God's grace conceived of as a feminine power. Indeed, there are a few passages in the *Tiruvācakam* where the goddess appears to be a personification of Śiva's grace and mercy, thus directly prefiguring the later philosophical idea. In 9:10, Māṇikkavācakar mentions the "Father accompanied by His Mercy" (*karuṇai*, Skt. *karuṇā*). And in the next hymn, even more strikingly, the poet describes how "Śiva came like a mother, and His Mercy (*karuṇai*) enslaved me (*āṇṭukoḷ*)" (10:10). The last verse of the twentieth hymn states that "You (Śiva) and Your blossoming true Mercy came upon the earth and enslaved (*āṭkoḷ*) us" (20:10). We also remember the passage translated above in which the goddess is likened to a rain cloud which dispenses grace (*aruḷ*) (7:16). But, as with other philosophical concepts, these few examples do not suggest that we read the *Tiruvācakam* as if it espoused the full-fledged Śaiva Siddhānta position on Śakti.

On several occasions, Māṇikkavācakar refers to Śiva as being simultaneously father and mother, a mother-father, an *ammai-appa<u>n</u>* (5:47; 27:9; 37:3). He is thus the androgynous origin of the universe and of individual human beings, another aspect of his Ardhanārīśvara form. Vis-à-vis his bhaktas, he combines the attitudes of both the parents and takes their place. He is complete in himself.

To conclude this chapter, I shall attempt to relate Māṇikkavācakar's understanding of the goddess, particularly his view of her as conjoined with Śiva-Ardhanārīśvara, to the central currents of his thought and experience. The goal of the religious life for Māṇikkavācakar is personal union with God, a fact we have already seen expressed in the paradigmatic role the goddess plays for him. Achieving union with God means a number of things for the bhakta. It brings about a release from karma-saṃsāra by replacing karmic striving and resulting rebirth with service and 'melting', selfless love.[48] The union effects a new state of consciousness which transcends thoughts of 'I' and 'mine'. The grasping, desiring ego is liquified, flowing into the divine reality. Yet, this clearly is a personal union, and what better image for such a joining than Ardhanārīśvara? Māṇikkavācakar sees the union of god and goddess as exemplary for the union of deity and devotee and for the communion of the bhaktas with each other.

> The Mistress [*uṭaiyāḷ*] dwells in the midst of You.
> You dwell in the midst of Her.
> If both of You dwell in the midst of me, Your servant,
> exercise Your grace [*aruḷ*]
> so that I may dwell in the midst of Your devotees.
> (21:1)

More basic than the paradigmatic and benevolent connotations of the Ardhanārīśvara form for Māṇikkavācakar's devotion and theology, are the androgyne's symbolic overtones suggesting the nature of the transformation experienced by the poet. It is almost commonplace to speak of Śiva as the one in whom all polarities co-inhere, the *coincidentia oppositorum par excellence*. Consequently, in the Epics and Purāṇas he is both horrible (*ghora*) and kind (*śiva*), both master *yogin* (*mahāyogin*) skilled in the practice of austerities and the archetypal family man of the Hindu pantheon, both destroyer and creator, both male and female. Thus, Māṇikkavācakar's verse:

> For Him who is
> both Veda and sacrifice,
> both truth and falsehood,
> both light and darkness,
> both sorrow and delight
> both half and whole,
> both bondage and release,
> both beginning and end,
> let us, dancing, pound the golden powder.
> (9:20)

As Ardhanārīśvara, Śiva integrates the basic human polarity, that of sexual differentiation. What this conception in particular, but also the other items just mentioned, indicate is that God is complete; he is whole, perfectly integrated. In himself he has no fragmention. He is a unity, an ultimate unity of infinite possibility. To use one of Māṇikkavācakar's most illuminating images, Śiva is an "uncut Gem" *(pollā maṇi* — 27:10).[49] His potentiality is always full. He is inexhaustible in finite forms (cf. 31:10). "Śiva embodies all of life, in all of its detail,at every minute. He alone need make no choice; through him all of the conflicting challenges are accepted at once."[50]

The nature of Śiva is not characterized by "either . . . or" but by "both . . . and". From Śiva's standpoint, the standpoint of absolute reality, antitheses, including the dichotomy into male and female sexes, are no longer opposed but rather are, in fact seen to be, two aspects of the same reality. Likewise, the experience of his devotees, who are "possessed" by him and enjoy mystical union with God, is that of reconciliation, wholeness, non-fragmentation.[51] It is in the Puṇarccippattu, "The Ten Verses on Union", that Māṇikkavācakar repeats at the end of every verse, "when shall I be united with my uncut Gem?" (27:1–10). To be united with the "uncut Gem" is to experience a world where there are no negations, limitations, or restrictions placed on human possibility, including the limitation of being either male or female. This is another way of speaking about the realm of mystical awareness transcending space and time. As will be claimed in the next two chapters, it is also the arena of play (*līlā*, Tamil *viḷaiyāṭal*) rather than work (*karman*, *viṉai*).[52] Some mystics would say (and I think this would also be a valid interpretation of Māṇikkavācakar's thought) that such is the experience of man's original nature, his essence, an essence which includes both masculine and feminine dimensions.

Ultimately, we see Māṇikkavācakar not as a critic of all things female. Rather, the feminine has very positive connotations for him, at least at a psychological and spiritual level, whatever his misgivings may be about physical, sexual activity. His imagining himself to be Śiva's faithful wife and seeing in God's nature a union of male and female elements are factors which need to be held alongside his denunciation of human females. Certainly, his decrial of women is not on a par with his condemnations of karma-saṃsāra, *pācam*, and *malam*. For, women are seen to have some very admirable qualities, qualities which anyone, male or female, must internalize if he is to be united with Śiva, that is, from Māṇikkavācakar's point of view, to become fully, essentially human.

Notes

1. The Tamil reads: *maṇṇiṉil māyai matittu vakutta mayakku.*

2. There is a probable *double entendre* in these lines which requires some explanation. *Māyāvātam* can mean not only "the teaching about *māyā*" (i.e., Advaita Vedānta) but also "the wind of *māyā*" or "delusive wind". As with the Tamil *cittam* for both Sanskrit *citta* and *siddha*, the Tamil *vātam* can be the transliteration of either the Sanskrit *vāta* (wind) or *vāda* (statement, proposition, argument). There is only one dental stop in the Tamil script (t), which covers both the unvoiced Sanskrit "t" and the voiced "d" (and also both of their aspirates) in Tamil words borrowed from Sanskrit. In this case it is not unlikely that Māṇikkavācakar intends the double meaning, since translated according to the second meaning of *māyāvātam*, the two lines read: "The vain hurricane (lit. violent wind) called the wind of delusion (*māyāvātam*) which whirled and blew and roared."

3. Contra Carl-A. Keller who assumes a definite and significant meaning for *māyam* in the *Tiruvācakam*, more important than the other terms we discussed in Chapter 4. While Keller does not argue that Māṇikkavācakar's use of the word reflects a Siddhānta understanding, he does make some highly questionable interpretations of several passages where *māyam* appears only adjectivally. This is unfortunate, for in other respects, Keller's essay is a competent, though brief, survey of several important ideas in the *Tiruvācakam*: "Some Aspects of Manikkavasagar's Theology", *Proceedings of Conference of Tamil Studies*, vol. 2, pp. 60-61.

4. On this myth in general and its appearance in Cuntarar's *Tēvāram* in particular, see M.A. Dorai Rangaswamy, *The Religion and Philosophy of Tēvāram: With Special Reference to Nampi Ārūrar (Sundarar)* (Madras: University of Madras, 1958), bk. 1, pp. 281-285.

5. One might see in this passage a reference to six senses, as is typical of some Indian religio-philosophical systems, e.g., Pāli Buddhism. Māṇikkavācakar, however, repeatedly refers specifically to five senses (*aimpulaṉ*), and to take *eṇṇam*, which in any case is not a technical term for 'mind', in this instance as indicative of a sixth sense would violate the pattern established by the other references. To my knowledge this is the only occasion in the text where the various senses are

enumerated.

6. An alternative translation is "man who has intellect", understanding *pulaṉ* to signify man's intelligence or intellect rather than the typical meaning in the *Tiruvācakam* of 'sense' or 'sense organ'.

7. In most cases where the five elements are mentioned they are associated with the all-pervading deity, who is said to be in each of the elements (e.g., 4:137-141; 5:63, 70; 6:20, 31; 15:5; 22:6; 27:7; 31:10), although apart from this context there are a few other times when the elements are listed (e.g., 5:8; 11:18). Unlike the senses, the names of the elements are almost always spelled out, the reference at 31:10 to *pūtaṅkaḷ aintu* being an exception (cf. 3:114; 20:5).

8. The reference to the "mirage of the six (lit. two times three) religions" is interesting, for it shows that Māṇikkavācakar was probably familiar with the Brahmanical concept of the *ṣaḍdarśana*, the six systems of philosophy (Nyāya, Vaiśeṣika, Sāṃkhya, Yoga, Mīmāmsā, and Vedānta). He also refers to the six religions at 3:19. But there is disagreement among commentators about which six religions Māṇikkavācakar is talking, some of it designed to protect his orthodoxy, hence, Citpavāṉantar who lists the six religions as Lokāyata, four branches of Buddhism, and Jainism (*Tiruvācakam*, pp. 205–206). The *Tamil Lexicon* (vol. 1, p. 179) defines *aṟucamayam* as "the six religious systems which are considered to be Vedic, viz., Śaiva, Vaiṣṇava, Śākta, Gaura, Gāṇapatiya, and Kaumāra", thus taking major Hindu deities as the determining factor, although no historical provenance for such a usage is given. One can be certain, however, that the concept of *ṣaḍdarśana* was current in the ninth century, and it is likely that a Brahmin who was educated would have been familiar with this notion. Besides, these "six religions" were philosophical schools and thus teachings uncongenial to Māṇikkavācakar's fervent devotionalism. We notice also that those who try to drink at this mirage practice *tapas*, a further rejection of more orthodox Hindu ideology and practice. Māṇikkavācakar rejects the efficacy of *tapas* at other places in the text as well. While *tapas* is useless and Śiva's grace arrives as the monsoon storm, sweeping all before it, in this passage it is noteworthy that the devotees do put forth some effort: they build a dam to catch the waters of grace.

9. J.V. Chelliah, ed. and trans. *Pattupattu: Ten Tamil Idylls*, (Madras: South India Saiva Siddhanta Works Publishing Society, 1962), p. 358. For a good brief introduction to the *Tirumurukāṟṟuppaṭai*, see Kamil Zvelebil, *Smile of Murugan*, pp. 125–130. Also, see the French translation by J. Filliozat, *Un Texte de la religion Kaumāra, le Tirumurukāṟṟuppaṭai*, (Pondichéry: Institut français d'indologie, 1973).

10. On this point see C.A. Keller, "A Literary Study of the *Tirumurukarruppadai*", *Proceedings of the First International Conference Seminar of Tamil Studies*, (Kuala Lumpur: International Association of Tamil Research, 1969), vol. 2, p. 60.

11. Examples of textual citations for each term include: *kamalam* (Skt. *kamala*)—5:93; 7:13; 10:2; 20:1, 6; 22:6; 39:1; 43:7; 48:3; *tāmarai*

(Skt. *tāmarasa*)-5:26, 45; 6:29; 8:6; 35:6; 40:9; *paṅkayam* (Skt. *paṅkaja*)-7:13, 17; 15:10.

12. For example, 5:12, 46; 6:29; 7:14; 8:16; 9:19; 13:5, 13; 16:6, 9; 17:10; 35:7; 43:8.

13. Examples of each word in order of frequency of use: *malar*-4:84; 5:5, 26, 37, 52; 6:11; 10:17; 13:9; 16:2; 20:1; 23:1; 26:5; 30:7; 38:3; 41:7; 44:1; 49:4; *pōtu*-6:25; 7:1, 10; 9:12; 13:14; 16:6; 27:10; 36:1; 43:7; *pū*-3:115; 6:5; 7:12; 13:1-20 (the "creeper flower" hymn); 45:6; 49:6.

14. Several examples of the many vocative uses of *amutu* include: 1:63; 4:142; 5:10, 55; 6:13; 20:9; 22:5; 28:8; 32:4; 38:6.

15. The Tamil Vaiṣṇava Āḻvārs were deeply influenced by the forms and conventions of the Caṅkam "interior landscape", perhaps even more so than their Śaiva counterparts. In this regard one need only refer to Nammāḻvār's *Tiruviruttam* and Tirumaṅkai's *Siṟiya Tirumaṭal* and *Periya Tirumaṭal*. The *Tiruviruttam* is modelled on Tamil Caṅkam poetry of the *akam* type. The *maṭal* is a palmyra stem which the frustrated lover fashions into a type of saw-horse and then rides through the streets while proclaiming his love. The *maṭal* custom is mentioned in *Kuṟuntokai* 17 and 32, both verses translated in Ramanujan, *Interior Landscape*, pp. 27, 34. Also see *Kuṟuntokai* 17, 173; and *Naṟṟiṇai* 146, 152, 342, 377. A brief but useful essay on Āḻvār symbolism is A. Srinivasa Raghavan, "Mystical Symbolism in the Work of the Alwars", *Proceedings of the First International Conference Seminar of Tamil Studies* (Kuala Lumpur: International Association of Tamil Research, 1969), vol. 2. One also recalls that Māṇikkavācakar's other work, the *Tirukkōvaiyār*, uses *akam* poetry as its model.

16. Taylor (1642–1729), pastor of a Puritan church on the Massachusetts frontier, left a collection of religious poetry rich in crude, extraordinary images. Prompted by the Christian Eucharist, his Preparatory Meditations abound with images of eating and drinking, used as metaphors for the infusion of grace. In addition to the expected bread and wine, God's grace is referred to among others as "sweet junkets" and "my soul's plum cake" (Second Series, Meditation 81), and a "sugar mill" and "honey hive" (Second Series, Meditation 163). The parallels with some of Māṇikkavācakar's usages in this case, and also in other matters, are sometimes quite remarkable. See *The Poems of Edward Taylor*.

17. Hart, *Poems of Ancient Tamil*, p. 25.

18. Ibid., pp. 65–80, 191–196.

19. Other passages in the *Paripāṭal* displaying a similar perspective are 1:42–48 and 3:63–76. For the text, French translation, extensive notes, and introduction, see François Gros, trans. *Le Paripāṭal: Texte tamoul* (Pondichéry: Institut français d'indologie, 1968). The above passage is also commented upon by Varadarajan, *Treatment of Nature in Sangam Literature*, pp. 409–410; and by Xavier S. Thani Nayagam, *Landscape and Poetry: A Study of Nature in Classical Tamil Poetry*, 2d ed. (London: Asia Publishing House, 1966), pp. 65–66.

20. Hart, *Poems of Ancient Tamil*, p. 195.

21. Both quotations are from William Blake, the first from plate 14 of the "Marriage of Heaven and Hell", and the second being the first four lines of his "Auguries of Innocence"; see David V. Erdman, ed., *The Poetry and Prose of William Blake* (Garden City, N.Y.: Doubleday & Company, 1965), pp. 39, 481.

22. This is a view which has been widely held in the west and is particularly associated with the name of Albert Schweitzer, whose book advancing this thesis continues to be reprinted: Albert Schweitzer, *Indian Thought and Its Development*, trans. Mrs. Charles E.B. Russell (Boston: Beacon Press, 1936).

23. Examples of such terms include *ēḻai* (7:8; 33:3), which connotes the weakness and simplicity of a woman; *taiyal* (10:15; 17:9; 51:3) which means a beautiful woman; *peṇ* (2:78; 8:8 10) and *mātu* (2:107; 5:30; 8:7, 19; 10:14; 19:3; 43:1; 51:8), the last two being common Tamil words for the female sex. Māṇikkavācakar also applies to the goddess several words which can signify a female at a particular age, e.g., *pētai*—between the ages of five and seven (7:10); *maṅkai*—between the ages of twelve and thirteen (2:26; 5:65, 67, 75; 6:41; 9:7; 11:6; 18,3 38:2; 42:2), and *maṭantai*—between the ages of fourteen and nineteen (6:37; 7:11; 29:1, 5). Thus, the goddess is presented as an eternally young woman, eminently marriageable. Although in the *Tiruvācakam* she is decidedly married, she seems more a maiden than a matron. The same terms are also used to describe the goddess by Cuntarar, on which see Dorai Rangaswamy, *Religion and Philosophy of Tēvāram*, bk. 1, pp. 218–219. I have followed the *Tamil Lexicon* in assigning age distinctions to *pētai*, *maṅkai* and *maṭantai*. For slightly differing ages, see S. Singaravelu, *Social Life of the Tamils: The Classical Period* (Kuala Lumpur: Department of Indian Studies, University of Malaya, 1966), p. 82.

24. Hence, the terms *imavāṉmakaḷ*—"Himavān's daughter" (9:13); *malaimakaḷ*—"daughter of the mountain" (12:7); *malaimātu* (23:10) and *malaiyāḷ* (6:40)—"mountain woman"; *malaiyaraiyaṉ poṟpāvai*—"golden daughter of the mountain king" (12:13); and *varaimaṅkai*—"mountain woman" (11:6; 36:1).

25. For example, see 5:30; 8:7; 9:2, 3, 6; 10:14, 15; 11:6; 16:4; 20:8; 26:2; 34:1; 41:4, 6.

26. For example, see 2:25–26, 107; 5:53; 13:7.

27. For example, see 4:146; 5:21, 64; 6:26; 12:7; 23:9; 24:2; 38:1.

28. On Śiva's 'taming' Kālī, see David R. Kinsley, *The Sword and the Flute: Kālī and Kṛṣṇa, Dark Visions of the Terrible and the Sublime in Hindu Mythology* (Berkeley: University of California Press, 1975), pp. 105–106, 146. Kinsley's claim that Māṇikkavācakar equates Kālī with *prakṛti* (p. 106) has no basis in the *Tiruvācakam* itself but rather is drawn entirely from his secondary source (Dorai Rangaswamy, *Religion and Philosophy of Tēvāram*, bk. 1, p. 491).

29. Hart, *Poems of Ancient Tamil*, pp. 93–119; and by the same author, "Women and the Sacred in Ancient Tamilnad"; "Some Related Literary Conventions in Tamil and Indo-Aryan and their Significance"; "Some Aspects of Kinship in Ancient Tamil Literature"; and "Ancient

Tamil Literature".

30. Lawrence A. Babb, *The Divine Hierarchy: Popular Hinduism in Central India* (New York: Columbia University Press, 1975), pp. 215–246; and by the same author, "Marriage and Malevolence: The Uses of Sexual Opposition in a Hindu Pantheon", *Ethnology* 9, no. 2 (April 1970): 137–148.

31. Ibid., pp. 225–226.

32. Hart, *Poems of Ancient Tamil*, pp. 110-112. This entire paragraph summarizes ideas found on these pages. Hart translates passages from two *puṟam* poems whose imagery supports this distinction between men and women: *Puṟanāṉūṟu* 86, 251.

33. On *maṇāḷar* (bridgegroom), see 4:183; 17:3. The following words for "husband" could also be taken to mean "ruler" or "lord", although in the instances cited below the context makes the marital meaning perferable: *talaivaṉ*-4:113; 5:59; 6:9, 40; 21:9; 29:3; *nāyakam/nāyakaṉ*–29:3; 33:7; 49:3; 50:2, 4; *nātaṉ*–23:5; 44:3.

34. That the women wear bangles is further confirmation that they consider themselves married or aspire to be married to Śiva; for as Dorai Rangaswamy says, "Bangles are the insignia of married or marriageable beauty. On the death of the husband the bangles are broken" (*Religion and Philosophy of Tēvāram*, bk. 1, p. 212).

35. The image here is that of a very small waist. Just as a jagged bolt of lightning makes an acute angle, so the ideal female figure is sharply tucked at the waist relative to the breast and hips.

36. The drum is called a *tuṭi*, which the *Tamil Lexicon* (vol. 4, p. 1959) defines as "a small drum shaped like an hour-glass". The image is virtually identical to that evoked when the waist is compared to lightning.

37. The *Brahmavaivarta Purāṇa* is a text which mixes devotion to the goddess with asceticism and roundly condemns women as impediments to the achievement of *mokṣa*. See Cheever Mackenzie Brown, *God as Mother: A Feminine Theology in India, An Historical and Theological Study of the Brahmavaivarta Purāṇa* (Hartford, Vermont: Claude Stark & Co., 1974), pp. 181–186.

38. Specifically, Māṇikkavācakar sees *tapas* (Tamil *tavam*) as inefficacious; for Śiva does not reveal himself to those performing austerities, although he does bestow grace on undeserving Māṇikkavācakar (e.g., 3:135–138; 5:54; 23:2, 4; 34:10; 38:10). At one point the poet says that "by means of His mercy the Father transforms all my actions into *tapas*" (15:6). But this last does not connote *tapas* in the usual sense of disciplined physical and mental self-mortification. On *tapas*, see n. 8 above.

39. This verse states that "Peruntuṟai's great Flood (i.e., Śiva) bestowed that unique *kaṟpu* which is unwavering". One can interpret *kaṟpu* as belonging to Śiva, in the sense that he promises to be unswervingly faithful to his devotee (see Vanmikanathan, *Pathway to God through Tamil Literature: I—Through the Thiruvaachakam*, p. 389). But this interpretation is unlikely for two reasons: (1) bestowing (*aḷi*)

kaṟpu seems to imply that it is the power to be faithful which is granted, not fidelity on the part of the bestower; and (2) *kaṟpu* in early Tamil literature is commonly a quality of women rather than men, which suggests that it is Māṇikkavācakar's *kaṟpu*, as the bride of Śiva, rather than Śiva's which is meant here. Thus, V. Sp. Manickam: "The well-known meaning of the word '*kaṟpu*' is chastity or loyalty to the husband" in *The Tamil Concept of Love* (Madras: South India Saiva Siddhanta Works Publishing Society, 1962), p. 95. See also N. Subrahmaniam, *Śaṅgam Polity: The Administration and Social Life of the Śaṅgam Tamils* (Bombay: Asia Publishing House, 1966), pp. 286–288, 293, 386. To be a genuine bhakta is to have *kaṟpu*. That Māṇikkavācakar sometimes fails in his "unwavering *kaṟpu*" to Śiva (see Vanmikanathan, p. 388) does not seem to me a very persuasive argument that at the time he composed hymn 41, the poet did not feel himself capable of fidelity, thanks to Śiva's gift of grace. Indeed, if it is Śiva's *kaṟpu* that is in question, then the deity also fails to be faithful; for Māṇikkavācakar sometimes complains quite vociferously about Śiva's abandonment of him (see especially hymn 6).

40. See Manickam, *Tamil Concept of Love*, pp. 103–105, with references to *Aiṅkuṟuṉūṟu* 294; *Akanāṉūṟu* 180; *Kalittokai* 107, 115; *Kuṟuntokai* 312; *Naṟṟiṇai* 143.

41. *Tirukkural* (Tamil text with English translations by G.U. Pope et. al.) (Madras: South India Saiva Siddhanta Works Publishing Society, 1970), pp. 353–355.

42. On *ūṭal* in the Cittarai festival of the Mīṇāṭci-Cuntarēcuvarar temple at Madurai, see Carl Gustav Diehl, *Instrument and Purpose: Studies on Rites and Rituals in South India* (Lund: CWK Gleerup, 1956), p. 165; and on a festival in the Śrī Vaiṣṇava tradition, see James L. Martin, "The Cycle of Festivals at Pārthasārathīswami Temple", *Asian Religions: 1971*, ed. Bardwell L. Smith (Chambersburg, Penna.: American Academy of Religion, 1971), p. 228.

43. My count shows 70 references to the Ardhanārīśvara form in the *Tiruvācakam*: 2:25, 77, 207; 3:64,65; 4:152, 184;5:17, 30, 38, 55, 65, 67, 73, 75, 85, 92, 94; 6:3, 30, 31, 41; 7:8, 10, 13, 16; 8:7, 8, 10, 11, 18, 19; 9:7; 10:15, 18; 11:6, 11; 12:7; 14:4, 8; 16:6, 9; 17:2; 19:3; 23:20; 24:5, 8; 25:10; 26:2; 28:5, 6, 8, 10; 29:1; 32:5, 10; 33:2, 3; 34:1; 36:1; 38:2; 39:1; 40:10; 42:2, 5; 43:1, 8; 45:9; 51:3, 8. On the Indian historical background of the Ardhanārīśvara form, see Jan Gonda, *Die Religionen Indiens II: Der Jüngere Hinduismus* (Stuttgart: W. Kohlhammer, 1963), pp. 206–208.

44. Some of the relevant terms with a few examples of each are *kūṟu* (part, share, half) and variants (3:64; 5:38, 67; 39:1; 40:10), *pākam* (share, part, half) and variants (5:17; 8:8, 10; 14:8; 34:1; 42:2), *pāti* (half) and variants (8:7, 19), and the extremely frequent *paṅku* (share, part, half) and variants (5:55, 73, 75, 85; 6:3, 41; 8:7; 9:7; 11:11; 32:5; 33:3; 36:1; 42:5).

45. There are two very common words which are relevant here: *attaṉ* (e.g., 1:79; 4:123; 5:3; 7:3; 9:1, 10; 11:16; 15:6; 16:7; 23:1; 26:4, 7;

42:6; 47:2, 6; 49:6; 51:1) and *appaṉ* (e.g., 8:11, 19; 9:13; 22:3; 26:1; 29:6; 35:6, 8; 41:7; 42:8).

46. For example, *ammai* (37:3; 40:10; 51:9), *tāy* (4:87, 136; 27:9), and *aṉṉai* (26:3).

47. For example, see 1:61; 4:86–87; 8:7; 10:10, 12; 13:3; 50:5.

48. See Chapter 7.

49. The image of Śiva as the "uncut Gem" is quite similar to that used several times in the *Tao Tê Ching* where the Tao is likened to an "uncarved block" (e.g., *Tao Tê Ching* chaps. 19,32, 57). Ultimately, like the Tao, Śiva is that which is basic and simple, the unity in which all multiplicity is rooted.

50. Wendy Doniger O'Flaherty, *Asceticism and Eroticism in the Mythology of Śiva* ,(London: Oxford University Press, 1973), p. 315.

51. Cf. William James, who speaks of his own mystical experience as involving a "reconciliation . . . as if the opposites of the world were melted into unity", *The Varieties of Religious Experience* (New York: New American Library, 1958), p. 298.

52. Although Śiva and the goddess are never specifically described in the *Tiruvācakam* as "sporting" (*viḷaiyāṭu*) together, at one point Māṇikkavācakar says they rejoice (*makiḻ*) in each other's company (2:80).

6

The Image of Śiva

The leading ideas of the *Tiruvācakam* converge on a common center; for all the major themes in this text vein in towards Māṇikkavācakar's immediate, intuitive experience of his union with Śiva. Such an experience is the *raison d' être* of the religious life for Māṇikkavācakar. *Mokṣa* is not simply a release *from* bondage but a release *to* a new dimension of existence whose positive characteristics are at least as important as the absence of the old problems which plagued the poet. In so far as Śiva is not only the one who severs bondage but also the being to whom Māṇikkavācakar is enslaved and with whom he desires to be united, the nature, the personality, of this deity assumes great significance in understanding both the beginning and the goal of Māṇikkavācakar's spiritual journey. With what kind of god is Māṇikkavācakar dealing? What would union with this "uncut Gem" be like?

In discussing the goddess in the last chapter we gained a glimpse of Māṇikkavācakar's image of Śiva. But just one side of this deity's character was visible there; for in association with the goddess, only the gentler features of his personality emerge. Śiva does not always, or even typically, appear to Māṇikkavācakar as one who is more compassionate than a mother (1:61; 13:3). The present examination of the deity will give a more comprehensive view of this intriguing figure. It will be seen that in Māṇikkavācakar's experience Śiva's multifaceted personality is a synthesis of several 'histories' of this god.

Sanskritic Myth and Personal Experience

In many ways the god experienced by Māṇikkavācakar is also the god known to the writers of the Sanskrit Epics and Purāṇas. When Māṇikkavācakar refers to various aspects of Śiva's character, he frequently does so by alluding to one or another of the pan-Indian myths about the god. Although the poet's use of such myths is extensive, it is also selective. Not all the myths about Śiva, related in the major purāṇas find mention in the *Tiruvācakam*. When Māṇikkavācakar cites one of the widely acknowledged incidents in Śiva's biography, he does so because it correlates closely with his personal experience of the deity. There is no idle retelling of the myths in this text. These myths are referred to because they illuminate some aspect of the god's character which Māṇikkavācakar knows first hand. In fact, the most useful way of organizing our discussion of those myths, to which the poet refers, is to consider them according to three aspects of Māṇikkavācakar's personal experience of Śiva.

As noted previously, Śiva's action vis-à-vis Māṇikkavācakar could be captured in three of the poet's favorite verbs — *aruḷ*, *āṭkoḷ*, and *aṟu* (p. 78). In considering Śiva's image in the *Tiruvācakam*, it seems more appropriate to use three nouns, which indeed subsume the activities designated by the above verbs, particularly in the case of *aruḷ* which is both a noun and a verb. The catchwords chosen to mark these three facets of Śiva's revelation to Māṇikkavācakar are *vīṭu* (release), *aruḷ* (grace), and *pittam* (madness), closely related aspects of the poet's personal experience of the deity which are much like different voices in a fugue. They imply and develop from each other.

Vīṭu (Release)

Śiva is the great bestower of release (*vīṭu, mokṣa*). He "cuts off", "destroys"the various chains of Māṇikkavācakar's ordinary existence. As the destroyer of bondage, Śiva initiates a change in Māṇikkavācakar's ontological status; for the poet's relationship to the fundamental processes of birth and death, karma, *pācam*, and social relations is decisively changed. As was discussed in chapter 4, a dramatic battle has taken place in which Śiva has captured Māṇikkavācakar from the forces of darkness that impede human existence. Not surprisingly perhaps, this victory at the level of Śiva's interaction with Māṇikkavācakar reflects various widely known actions of the god to which reference is often made by his devotee.

One of Māṇikkavācakar's favorite episodes in the myths about Śiva is the god's destruction of the Tripura, the three fortresses of the *asuras*, which were invulnerable to the attacks of the *devas* and from which the demons terrorized the cosmos.[1] Śiva is pictured as having demolished all three fortresses with a single arrow (14:2) or, sometimes, is said to have caused their destruction merely by smiling (3:158). Essentially, this is an act of release from bondage. The world is released from the tyranny of the *asuras* just as Māṇikkavācakar's bondage to karma-saṃsāra is destroyed by Śiva. For example, the parallel is clearly stated:

> Just as on that day
> His beautiful smile
> brought fiery destruction
> to His foes' ancient city,
>
> in a great fire of grace [*aruḷ*]
> He completely did away with
> the vile huts
> where all of us devotees
> (used to dwell).
>
> (3:158–161)

Furthermore, the *asuras* themselves escape punishment. They are released too — from their own bondage — and become Śiva's door guardians (14:4; 15:9).

Another myth beloved by Māṇikkavācakar is that of Śiva's drinking the Hālāhala poison.[2] The dreadful poison, which surfaced when the *devas* and *asuras* attempted to obtain *amṛta* by churning the ocean of milk, threatened to destroy the world. But Śiva came to the rescue and drank the noxious substance. This turned his throat blue, hence his Sanskrit epithet Nīlakaṇṭha, to which Māṇikkavācakar alludes several times (6:7, 32, 46; 23:7). The poet clearly draws the parallel between his own situation and that of those saved by Śiva's ingestion of the poison.

> O You
> who had mercy on lowly souls
> and ate the hot, fiery poison
> so that a base person like me
> might feed on ambrosia. (6:50)

A myth already encountered in connection with the goddess is that of Śiva's catching the falling Ganges in his hair. While not referred to as often as the Tripura and Hālāhala myths, this incident is nonetheless of interest as one of the god's specifically salvific acts. Usually, Śiva's role as bearer of the goddess Gaṅgā is simply cited along with other of his 'physical' features (e.g., 6:26, which describes Śiva's matted hair containing both Gaṅgā and the crescent moon).[3] In one verse, however the rationale for this action is stated:

> Had She [Gaṅgā] not plunged
> into His matted locks,
> there would have been great destruction
> and the whole world would have plunged
> into the nether regions.
> (12:7)

Or reference to Śiva as Gaṅgādhara occurs in contexts where he is praised as the destroyer of rebirth.

> O Subduer of the raging Gaṅgā in Your matted hair!
> O One who severs the root of my birth
> by means of Your holy grace [*aruḷ*]!
> (24:2)

Again, Śiva saves the cosmos from ruin just as he saves his devotee from the ruin of rebirth and karma. As before, the poet renders the myth personal and concrete. Śiva's drinking the poison and bearing the Ganges are cited to show that Māṇikkavācakar's individual experience of release is confirmed in Śiva's world-saving acts. There is little interest in the myths apart from their immediate, existential significance.

Less frequently met with, in the *Tiruvācakam*, are a number of other myths which have much the same point: they show Śiva as the one who saves the world or individual men from evil forces. Hence, he destroys the demonic Jalandhara with a discus (12:18) and presents this weapon to Viṣṇu (12:18; 15:10). Also meeting their demise at Śiva's hands, although their destruction is not always permanent, are the great *rākṣasa* Rāvaṇa (13:15; 14:19; 40:7), the *asura* Andhaka (12:4; 13:15), and Yama, the god of death.[4] Thus, Śiva's feet so fervently sought by the devotees are the same feet that kicked Yama and subdued Rāvaṇa.

> O the final bliss [*patam*]
> attained by those exalted ones
> who know those fragrant blossoms (of Your feet)
> which subdued cruel Yama [*kūṟṟu*]!
>
> (6:25)

> The mighty *rākṣasa* [i.e., Rāvaṇa],
> whose strength is much esteemed,
> had his shoulders crushed
> when trampled by the sacred feet.
> Those same feet are enthroned on my head.
> I'm completely free
> of that overwhelming creaturely bondage [*pacu pācam*].
> Thus I'm rejoicing and shouting here.
> Is it not so that I acquired resplendent Tillai's Lord?
>
> (40:7)

In this connection we also note Śiva's slaying the boar and elephant demons, already mentioned in the previous chapter.[5]

Aruḷ (Grace)

Turning from Śiva as the breaker of the chain of Māṇikkavācakar's bondage, we begin to see the subjective effects of his interaction with the poet. Śiva bestows *aruḷ* on Māṇikkavācakar, and while in one sense this certainly includes the already mentioned release from 'births' and 'deeds', it connotes much more. In addition, the extremely common references to Śiva's gracious action toward his bhakta are often accompanied by descriptions of how God enters into, enslaves, or possesses Māṇikkavācakar. The result of Śiva's taking possession of Māṇikkavācakar is that the poet's heart melts. In the following verse these key aspects of Māṇikkavācakar's experience are all enumerated:

> O Lord Śiva,
> who severed my births,
> You dwell right here in southern Perunturai
> where the celestial ones can't know You.
> Our Lord,
> on that day when You looked at me
> You enslaved [*āṭkoḷ*] me,
> in grace entered [*pukuntaruḷ*] me,
> and out of love [*aṉpu*] melted [*neka*] my mind [*akam*].
> (38:7)

It is interesting that this verse mentions Śiva's inaccessibility to the gods; for Māṇikkavācakar repeatedly combines description of his own enjoyment of the deity's grace with references to the gods' lack of success in understanding Śiva. The single most frequently cited myth in the *Tiruvācakam* is that of Brahmā's and Viṣṇu's failure to comprehend Śiva's immeasurable *liṅga* of fire.[6] Although Viṣṇu takes the form of a boar and tries to reach the base of the *liṅga* and Brahmā becomes a swan in an attempt to discover its summit, neither are successful, thus showing themselves to be inferior to Śiva, the supreme lord of the universe.

While this myth obviously proclaims Śiva's pre-eminence in the pantheon, it also functions for Māṇikkavācakar as a primary indicator of Śiva's inability to be known, to be comprehended, and consequently to be controlled by the thought or action of all other beings, be they the divine likes of Brahmā and Viṣṇu or humans who would seek power and understanding through the practice of austerities. As presented in the *Tiruvācakam*, the myth makes a very definite and unmistakable epistemological-theological point about the primacy of revelation in the devotees' relationship with Śiva. The relationship is God-initiated and is sustained by God's willingness to continue his gracious manifestations toward his devotees. This idea is clearly intended; for mention of the illustration of Viṣṇu and Brahmā is commonly juxtaposed with descriptions of Śiva's willingness to reveal himself to his unpretentious, apparently undeserving bhaktas. For example, the following verse:

Although great, red-eyed Māl [Viṣṇu] dug down,
  that expanding flowery foot he could not see.
But the Lord of that same foot
  graciously [*aruḷ*] came upon the earth,
  cut off our rebirth,
  and enslaved [*āṭkoḷ*] even people like us.
The Lord of the South,
  where abundant coconut groves grow,
the Lord of Peruntuṟai,
He with the beautiful eyes,
  appeared as a Brahmin [*antaṇaṉ*],
  called us,
  and graciously granted [*aruḷ*] us release [*vīṭu*].
Let us sing about
  His beautiful, merciful, adorned feet.

(8:1)

I nits purāṇic forms, this myth is usually played out against a cosmic backdrop (cf. 12:6; 15:11). Neither Viṣṇu nor Brahmā can claim to create the universe; for Śiva precedes, transcends, and contains them both.[7] Hence, Śiva is superior. He is the lord of the universe. From this cosmic framework of the myth, Māṇikkavācakar quickly shifts to the personal idiom of grace and release — and in highly concrete terms. The cosmic being who hid himself from Viṣṇu and Brahmā is the same god who assumed the form of the Brahmin guru whom Māṇikkavācakar met in Peruntuṟai. Thus, the myth of the *liṅga* with its cosmic focus is appropriated in a highly personalized context. That the one who revealed himself in such concrete form at Peruntuṟai is also the lord of the cosmos only serves to heighten the miracle of Māṇikkavācakar's conversion experience.

Again and again, Māṇikkavācakar contrasts his own undeserved good fortune with Śiva's keeping himself hidden from Brahmā and Viṣṇu. In summary, this most frequently attested myth in the *Tiruvācakam* serves several related functions: (i) it establishes Śiva's supreme sovereignty and transcendence; (ii) it attests God's absolute freedom and unpredictability in revealing himself to whom he wants; and (iii) it makes vivid the paradox of a religion of grace, i.e., a gift not revealed to the likes of Brahmā and Viṣṇu is granted to "false", "shameless", "base", "dog-like" Māṇikkavācakar.[8]

Myths mentioning the goddess also figure in Śiva's bestowal of grace on Māṇikkavācakar. We shall not repeat here what was extensively discussed in the previous chapter.

Pittam (Madness)

If Śiva releases Māṇikkavācakar from karma-saṃsāra by granting him grace, enslaving him, and entering his very being, the ultimate subjective result is that Śiva makes Māṇikkavācakar crazy. Indeed, the melting of the poet's mind and heart, occasioned by Śiva's bestowal of grace, can be viewed as one aspect of the madness which Śiva instills in Māṇikkavācakar. We shall focus on Māṇikkavācakar's devotional madness in the next chapter. Here our attention will be directed toward the initiator of the madness, and we shall see that Śiva himself is sometimes thought to be mad.

That Śiva is regarded as mad is confirmed by the application to him of the same epithet which elsewhere refers to Māṇikkavācakar, viz., *pittaṉ* (madman) (11:16; 12:9; 30:2; 37:8; see also *pitta vaṭivu* in 13:19). Without recounting the various stories upon which Śiva's reputation as madman is founded, here are two verses from the *Tiruvācakam* in which a very desperate Māṇikkavācakar threatens to mock Śiva for not revealing himself.[9] Clearly, Māṇikkavācakar's intentions of abusing Śiva are well served by the god's mythology.[10]

O Hero who is adorned
  by a garland of skulls like a cluster of stars,
  by fire,
  by snakes!
Look here, don't leave me!
If You leave me
and if men of knowledge ask me

"Whose slave are you?"
I'll give them cause to ridicule You by saying,
"I'm the servant of the glorious devotees
of Uttarakōcamaṅkai's King."

I'll give them cause to ridicule You by revealing
how my disgusting faults and service are dedicated
to You, the Lord.
Look here, don't leave me!
I'll insult You saying,
"O Madman [*piccaṉ*] who wears the fierce
elephant's skin!
"O Madman [*piccaṉ*] who wears the tiger's skin!
"O Madman [*piccaṉ*] who ate the poison!
"O Madman [*piccaṉ*] surrounded by the fire of the
town's crematorium!
"O Madman [*piccaṉ*] who has me as His slave!"
(6:48–49)

While certain of Śiva's bizarre actions became the model for the behavior of Śaivas such as the Kāpālikas, there is no evidence which suggests Māṇikkavācakar performed a *sādhana* involving an *imitatio dei*.[11] Nevertheless, we note in his descriptions of the ecstatic consciousness induced by Śiva's grace a sense of transcendence of all worldly limitations — physical, personal, and social. And in this transcendence Māṇikkavācakar participates in the divine madness of God himself; for whatever other meanings the myths about Śiva may have, they show him to be the transcendent figure *par excellence*. Everyday values are set on their heads. By the world's standards Śiva is mad. Imagine him, as Māṇikkavācakar does, dancing in the crematorium:

The One who did not appear (to Viṣṇu),
our eternal Lord,
is dancing [*nāṭakam āṭu*] right now in the burning ground
with the demons,
whirling and swaying,
mad [*uṉmattam*],
clad with a tiger's skin,

homeless.

(5:7)

As can be seen from the above verse, Śiva's appearance is anything but ordinary. His attire definitely contributes to his reputation as a madman. He dresses in various animal skins (e.g., that of the elephant and tiger),[12] wears snakes,[13] and is adorned with ashes, skulls, and bones,[14] all indicative of his transcendence of birth and death, of surpassing the limits of ordinary reality. He wears the matted hair of an ascetic (*caṭai*, Skt. *jaṭā*[15]). And in his hair are the hallucinogenic datura flowers (9:19; 17:10).[16] The invocation of him at the end of 6:30 combines a number of these motifs.[17]

Look here, don't leave me!
O real One [*caccaiyaṉ*],
who wears skulls as ornaments,
who is adorned with a cluster of flowers,
who wreathes himself with a long garland of entrails,
who smears himself with ashes,
who wears red sandal paste

(6:30)

Many of these features are associated with asceticism, with Śiva's role as Mahāyogin. Māṇikkavācakar, however, takes little specific note of Śiva's connection with yoga practice, most likely because this aspect of the god's character has very little relevance to the poet's own experience and devotional practice. He once calls him the "king of ascetics" (*tavarkku aracu*–37:4) and twice uses the word yoga (Tamil *yōkam*) in a non-technical sense to describe Śiva as the union or juncture of all reality (37:1, 4).

Māṇikkavācakar also mentions another of Śiva's features which reinforce the image of the god's madness. His wanton behavior as Vīrabhadra at Dakṣa's sacrifice is vividly described several times by the poet,[18] particularly in the fourteenth hymn where the following results are enumerated: Agni's hands were cut off; the priest's head was severed; Dakṣa was given a goat's head; Bhaga's eye was plucked out; Sarasvatī had her nose and Brahmā his head removed; Soma's face was crushed;

and Sūrya's teeth were broken and swept away (14:5-16). At a few places, in his delineation of this riotous tableau, Māṇikka-vācakar makes what must be the understatement of the *Tiruvā-cakam*: "the sacrifice was confounded' (vv.5, 7, 15; cf. v. 16). In this particular account, Viṣṇu is the only participant to escape unscathed (v. 6). Śiva's cutting off Brahmā's fifth head is also mentioned in the *Tiruvācakam* (9:18; 12:4; 13:15; 14:18; 15:11).[19] A somewhat similar episode, although only rarely referred to, is Śiva's burning of Kāma (12:4; 15:11; 29:3). The god's unruliness is celebrated in a verse praising several of his seemingly rowdy acts.

> Sing how He played ball with Brahmā's [*ayan̲*] head.
> Sing how He pulled out Sūrya's [*arukkan̲*] teeth.
> Sing how He killed the elephant and wore its skin.
> Sing how He kicked Yama [*kālan̲*] with His feet.
> Sing how He shot at the three united fortresses.
> Sing how He enslaved [*āṇṭukoḷ*] and loved us helpless [*ēl̲ai*] devotees.
> And dancing, dancing,
> let us pound the golden powder for our beloved Lord [*nātan̲*].
> (9:18)

Śiva's enslaving his devotees is thus seen to be on a par with his other crazy actions. And while the goddess is not mentioned in connection with her spouse's weird behavior, his wifely devotees obviously do not consider such actions offensive.

How is a myth such as that of Dakṣa's sacrifice related to Māṇikkavācakar's personal situation? It is cited as a type of antidote for spiritual arrogance; for such was the pride of Dakṣa and the *devas* in not inviting Śiva to the sacrifice (13:4). Twice Māṇikkavācakar simply announces that Śiva acted in such a way that rebirth might cease (14:10, 12). But, perhaps more basically, this myth exemplifies the same sort of apparent arbitrariness in Śiva's character displayed in his relationship with the poet. His capricious behavior at Dakṣa's sacrifice and his periodic revelations to and abandonment of Māṇikkavācakar are all of a piece. The epithets "madman", "deceiver" (*kaḷvan̲*

–5:6; cf. 2:55, 65),[20] "simpleton" (*pētai*–27:9), "thief" (*cōraṉ* –3:141), "trickster" (*ettaṉ*–37:8; 42:4), "conjurer" (*māyaṉ*–23:7) "magician" (*viccaiyaṉ*–6:31), and "dissembler" (*vikirtaṉ*–4:96, 105; 29:7) are based as much on Māṇikkavācakar's personal experience as they are upon Śiva's mythical actions.[21] His is not always a gentle love, even though he can be kinder than a mother. Rather, Śiva's grace is often aggressive, possessing and intoxicating, but also by fits leaving his devotee in moods of rejection and utter desolation, testing Māṇikkavācakar's faithfulness to him. Indeed, in a religious world of such divine unpredictability there is little room for pride of spiritual achievement.

The figure of Śiva presents a powerful concrete image of transcendence of everyday reality. Birth and death, family and caste, decorum and attachment to possessions are all strikingly disregarded by Śiva. They exercise no effect upon him. Thus, the eyes of the world perceive Śiva as being mad. It is hardly surprising, as we shall see in the next chapter, that some of his devotees should also appear to be mad.

Basically, Śiva both symbolizes in himself and offers his devotees participation in a new kind of consciousness, a type of consciousness opposed to ordinary modes of experience. In this mystical state of awareness, not just social hierarchy and egotism are abandoned, but necessity, purpose, and volition based on the choice between a variety of options have also been eliminated.[22] Such utter spontaneity is incomprehensible to most of us, and perhaps madness is quite a profound image of what it must be like.

At one point, Māṇikkavācakar addresses Śiva in the following way:

> O King of loving devotees!
> O Father who owns me as Your slave!
> You entered me body and soul,
> abiding in me
> so that all my bones become soft and melt.
> O Light of truth who dispels the darkness of falsehood!
> O abiding, clear, calm Sea of ambrosia!
> O Śiva who dwells in holy Peruntuṟai!
> O unique Consciousness [*ōr uṇarvē*],

> which is realized [*uṇarvatu*] as standing firm,
> transcending words and (ordinary) consciousness [*uṇarvu*]
> O, let me know [*uṇarttē*] a way to tell of You!
> (22:3)

The last two lines of this stanza are a linguistic *tour de force*. Of the twelve words in these two lines, four are derivatives of the root *uṇar*—to be conscious of, to know, to understand. Linguistic virtuosity notwithstanding, these lines make an important substantive point. Although Śiva is understood rather abstractly as a mode of consciousness opposed to ordinary awareness, by referring to the immediately preceding line we see that this unique consciousness is objectified, concretized, in the one who dwells in holy Peruntuṟai. Here we touch upon two new dimensions of Māṇikkavācakar's image of Śiva: (i) abstract philosophical concepts of the deity such as that mentioned in the above quoted passage ("unique consciousness"), and (ii) the local myths relating to the "public" manifestation of Śiva in Māṇikkavācakar's life, e.g., Śiva's appearance as a guru at Peruntuṟai. We shall next attend to these two additional components of Māṇikkavācakar's image of Śiva.

Philosophical Concepts

The *Tiruvācakam* is a work of devotional poetry, not systematic philosophy. For the most, it does not argue or analyze; rather it praises, petitions, and bears witness. Nonetheless, rather abstract philosophical terminology is not uncommonly applied to Śiva in our text. But, with regard to a philosophical understanding of Śiva's nature, Māṇikkavācakar's method might be called philosophy by epithet rather than philosophy by logical argument. Indeed, it is in those very passages that most bear the stamp of ecstatic utterance that philosophical ways of addressing Śiva are most numerous. Māṇikkavācakar's 'philosophy' of God is frequently in the vocative.

In the *Tiruvācakam*, there are a number of commonly used quasi-philosophical names of the deity which cluster around the ideas of lordship and transcendence. The one-word titles of Śiva, which appear most often, are words suggesting sovereignty, e.g., *kōṉ* — "king" (1:9; 2:40; 32:10); *aracu* — "king" (4:90; 7:17; 37:1); *īcaṉ* (Skt. *īśa*) — "lord" (1:11; 15:7; 30:7); *uṭaiyāṉ* — "master" (5:37; 21:10; 45:1); *iṟaivaṉ* — "supreme one" (1:5; 22:5; 36:4); *pirāṉ* — "lord" (4:177; 23:5; 51:3); and *perumāṉ* — literally, "great person" (18:1; 24:3; 44:2).[23] To these terms we can add titles and phrases which designate Śiva as the creator, the source, of the universe. He is the beginning (*āti*, e.g., 7:14; 26:6; 51:8), the source (*tōṟṟam*, e.g., 5:70; 7:20), the one who creates (*paṭai*, e.g., 3:13; 4:100; 5:16; 27:10), and the first one (*mutal/mutalvaṉ*, e.g., 4:94; 5:30; 27:10; 42:1). And as previously noted, Māṇikkavācakar also frequently calls Śiva "father" (*attaṉ*, e.g., 5:3; 7:3; 23:1; *appaṉ*, e.g., 26:1; 29:6; 42:8).

Śiva transcends (*kaḻi*, *iṟa*, *kaṭa*) all conceivable reality — speech and mind (1:45), all things (4:134), the "fourth" (*turiyam*, Skt. *turya*) state of consciousness (4:195), all endless states (22:1), words and ordinary consciousness (4:124; 22:3). In short, Śiva is supremely unique (*oruvaṉ* and variants, e.g., 3:43; 7:7; 36:1). He is without compare (*oppil*[*ā*], e.g., 5:61, 68; 6:29; 37:7). He, thus, is the rare one difficult to see, to understand, to know (*aru/ariya*—"rare", "difficult" and variants, e.g., 3:47; 5:17; 50:7).

At the same time, Śiva is also omnipresent, all-pervading (3:44, 50; 5:46; 8:13; 49:8). Specifically, he is said to abide in the five elements — earth, water, fire, wind, and ether (e.g., 6:20, 31; 22:6; 27:7). At a few places, the list of elements he pervades is expanded to eight, adding the sun, the moon, and life to the more usual five (5:63; 15:5; 42:2). A strongly philosophical verse which combines notions of transcendence and immanence is the following:

> Him who is
> the five elements,
> the senses
> and their objects,
> every distinct thing
> and yet Himself the great one without distinction
> [*pētamilā*, Skt. *abheda*],

the Emerald shining resplendently
who destroyed my afflictions and ruled [*āḷ*] me —
I saw Him in gleaming Tillai
which the Vedas worship and extol.

(31:10)

Again, we see how Māṇikkavācakar juxtaposes philosophical concepts with mention of local sacred places (in this case Tillai, i.e., Cidambaram) which were of great personal significance in his own spiritual development.

Śiva is the eternal one (*nittaṉ*, Skt. *nitya*, e.g., 4:175; 23:3). He is life (4:181; 20:9), time (5:43; 30:5), truth (6:7; 9:12; 18:8; 37:2), the Veda,[24] the Āgama (1:4; cf. 2:9-10, 18),[25] and the Oṃkāra (1:33). These relatively 'intellectual' apprehensions of the deity, however, are less frequently encountered than Māṇikkavācakar's more sensual experiences of Śiva as light (*oḷi*; *cuṭar*; *cōti*, Skt. *jyotis*),[26] bliss (*āṉantaṉ*, e.g., 5:98; 7:3), and ambrosia (*amutu*, e.g., 1:63; 20:8; 32:4), and the several kind of sweetness discussed in chapter 5 (pp. 109–11). At one point, Māṇikkavācakar simply addresses Śiva as the "enjoyment (*pōkam*, Skt. *bhoga*) which transcends praise" (37:4).

The synthesis of the abstract and the tangible in Māṇikkavācakar's image of Śiva in some ways foreshadows the final philosophical aspect of Śiva's nature which we shall consider. Māṇikkavācakar is fond of the language of paradox, which, when expressed in philosophical terms, quickly reminds us of images of the deity based on Śiva's mythology and the poet's personal experience. The procedure here, already known in the Upaniṣadic statements about Brahman and Ātman, is to view God as both something and its opposite, or as opposites and yet neither. Hence, Śiva has form and is formless (4:193; 11:2; 22:9). He is male, female, and neither male nor female (e.g., 5:29; 7:18). He is first, last, and whole (6:43). He is beginning, middle, and end (4:212); one and many (1:5; 5:25); light and darkness (6;17; 9:20); heat and cold (1:36); delight and sorrow (1:70; 9:20); good and evil (33:5; cf. 33:7); existence and non-existence (5:15; 38:8); bondage and release (3:52; 9:20). He is both near and far (1:44). He pervades the universe yet is smaller than an atom (3:44–45). Śiva has in his hair both the moon with its hare spots and a snake, thus reconciling inveterate animal enemies, parallel to the lamb and lion of the biblical tradition (6:35). Having already discussed the implications of Śiva's tendency to unify opposites in connection with his Ardhanārīśvara form,[27] we can proceed to what the local myths appearing in the *Tiruvācakam* reveal about his character.

Local Tradition

There are several kinds of local tradition which find mention in the *Tiruvācakam*. First, Śiva is often identified with "the South" or the Pāṇṭiyan kingdom. He is called the southerner (*teṉṉaṉ*, e.g., 8:2, 4–7, 11; 9:9; 43:9), the Pāṇṭiyaṉ (36:6, 9), and the one who dwells in the Pāṇṭiyan country (8:10, 19; 49:1). The entire thirty-sixth hymn is addressed to Śiva as lord of the Pāṇṭiyan region. In 8:10 Śiva is described as the "Inhabitant of the cool Pāṇṭiyan country who patronizes (*aḷi*) refreshing Tamil." This could be a reference to various of the popular traditions associating Śiva with Tamil, e.g., as the head of the first Caṅkam, as the teacher of Tamil to Agastya, or as the one whose two-headed drum emits Sanskrit from one end and Tamil from the other.[28] In any case, it shows a typical Tamil love of the language that is also widely attested in Tamil literature.

More concrete than the association of Śiva with the South or with the Pāṇṭiyan kingdom are the descriptions which picture him as peculiarly related to specific temples and sacred places throughout the Tamil country.[29] In this, Māṇikkavācakar continues a practice well known in the lyrics of the Nāyaṉmārs, the Tamil Śaiva bhaktas antecedent to him.[30] To some extent, this concretization of the sacred seems to be a distinctively South Indian phenomenon related to the Caṅkam view of the immanence of sacred power and Tamil affection for the landscape. It may be that certain places originally derived their sacredness from a tree or stone. Be that as it may, by Caṅkam times shrines associated with particular deities were flourishing in South India. This is particularly true of the god Murukaṉ, who is said to favor hilltops for his abode. The *Tirumurukāṟṟuppaṭai* reveals in its very structure of presentation the shrine-oriented worship of the early Tamils. This text is divided into six parts, each of which bears a subtitle referring to one of Murukaṉ's hill shrines, at least three of which, however, can no longer be traced historically.[31] There are more instances where shrines are mentioned in pre-bhakti Tamil literature,[32] and when we reach the period of bhakti itself, the strong identification of religious experience and practice with particular places, where a god is thought to dwell, becomes very pronounced indeed. Reference is made to over 500 shrines and temples in the Śaiva devotional literature alone.[33]

But unlike the three great Nāyaṉmār poets of the *Tēvāram*, Māṇikkavācakar is principally concerned with only three or four sacred places which were of great personal significance to him. He does, however, mention quite a number of other temples, although for the most part these references are concentrated in a single hymn. Hymn 2 of the *Tiruvācakam* is a summary of Śiva's activities in Tamilnad. No less than thirty-one different locations are cited, almost in serial fashion, in connection with the god's feats. We discover here a subtle fusion of pan-Indian myth and local tradition, as in the mingling of a local story involving the Pāṇṭiyan king with the myth of Śiva's immeasurable *liṅga* of fire (2:33-36). The remarkable ability of the Tamil bhakti movements to give concrete spatial focus to their teachings — no insignificant factor in their success — is amply evident in this hymn.

The places receiving more frequent attention in the *Tiruvācakam* are Peruntuṟai, Uttarakōcamaṅkai, Tirukkaḻukkuṉṟam, and Tillai (Cidambaram). Each figures in Māṇikkavācakar's personal history. Of the four, Tirukkaḻukkuṉṟam is least important and is discussed here because it is the subject of one entire hymn. Hymn 30 has the title "Tirukkaḻukkuṉṟappatikam" (Song of Tirukkaḻukkuṉṟam). It is a short hymn.[34] The beginning of each stanza (except for the final one) mentions Śiva at Peruntuṟai, while the last line of each of the seven stanzas is a refrain, "You revealed Yourself in Kaḻukkuṉṟam." Although there is a well-known Śaiva temple at this place with its own local traditions about Śiva's activities there,[35] Māṇikkavācakar mainly has in mind a personal revelation of the god which he enjoyed in Tirukkaḻukkuṉṟam at some point after his initial experience at Peruntuṟai and before his arrival in

Cidambaram.

Uttarakōcamaṅkai was the site of a Śiva temple where Māṇikkavācakar went for a short stay not long after his conversion experience.[36] According to tradition, a sense of disillusionment overcame the poet while at Uttarakōcamaṅkai, and it is there that he recited the "Nīttalvinnappam", the sixth hymn of the *Tiruvācakam*. In this hymn, Māṇikkavācakar pleads with Śiva not to desert him and addresses each of its first twenty stanzas to the "King of Uttarakōcamaṅkai" (6:1–20). There are also scattered references to Uttarakōcamaṅkai elsewhere in the text (e.g., 2:48, 220; 17;6; 19:3; 20:7).

By far the most frequently attested places in the *Tiruvācakam* are Peruntuṟai and Cidambaram, the place of conversion and the place of final consummation. If we follow the legends about Māṇikkavācakar's life, the *Tiruvācakam* is the product of the saint's physical *cum* spiritual journey from Peruntuṟai to Tillai. Peruntuṟai ("great port"), a harbor city of ancient Tamilnad probably on the Coromandel Coast,[37] was the scene of Māṇikkavācakar's radical transformation at the feet of a guru whom he took to be Śiva himself. Peruntuṟai is mentioned repeatedly in these hymns, as we have already seen in a number of the passages translated.[38]

Although Māṇikkavācakar does not use the name Cidambaram, he sings of Tillai (e.g., 1:90; 5:55; 31:1–10), Puliyūr (2:145), the Poṉṉampalam (21:1–10), and the Ampalam (5:51; 10:2, 17; 38:6), all ways of referring to Cidambaram and its great temple. The twenty-first and twenty-second hymns of the *Tiruvācakam* both bear titles referring to *the* temple (*kōyil*), i.e., the Naṭarāja temple at Cidambaram. Twenty-five of the *Tiruvācakam's* fifty-one hymns are said to have been composed during the period Māṇikkavācakar lived in Cidambaram. The poet's connection with Cidambaram is still quite evident today; for the entire text of the *Tiruvācakam* has been engraved on stone slabs mounted on the walls of the portico surrounding the Śivagaṅgā, the tank of the Naṭarāja temple.[39]

A text which records Śiva's activities in Madurai and its vicinity is the previously mentioned *Tiruviḷaiyāṭal Purāṇam* (The Story of the Sacred Sports [of Śiva]).[40] This text is the *sthalapurāṇa* of the Mīṉāṭci–Cuntarēcuvarar temple in Madurai and is of interest to us here for two reasons: (i) of the sixty-four 'sports' related in the *Tiruviḷaiyāṭal Purāṇam*, four are about Māṇikkavācakar, specifically about his relations with the Pāṇṭiyan king whose capital was at Madurai (chaps.58–61)[41]; (ii) two of these four 'sports' are mentioned in the *Tiruvācakam* itself.[42] Moreover, Māṇikkavācakar makes reference at one place or another in the *Tiruvācakam* to no less than sixteen of the remaining sixty 'sports' recorded in the purāṇa. Most of these non-autobiographical 'sports' mentioned in our text are listed in summary fashion in the second hymn when Śiva's manifestations at different places are praised.[43] Of those referred to apart from hymn 2, we note examples of three here. *Tiruviḷaiyāṭal* 2 relates how Śiva delivers Indra's albino elephant from a curse and is alluded to at *Tiruvācakam* 4:163 and 11:12. The story of Śiva's becoming a fisherman in order to deliver his spouse from a curse and to recover the Āgamas (*Tiruviḷaiyāṭal* 57) is mentioned at 2:17-20; 8:2; 16:8; 43:3; and 49:1. And twice (42:3; 43:10) Māṇikkavācakar refers to the incident when Śiva appeared in Madurai as a bangle merchant and dazzled the local women-folk (*Tiruviḷaiyāṭal* 32).[44]

Śiva's sportive character is especially evident in the two stories related to Māṇikkavācakar's 'life'. According to chapter 59 of the purāṇa, the Pāṇṭiyan king had Māṇikkavācakar jailed for malfeasance after he returned empty-handed from Perunturai with neither horses nor treasure. As we have seen in chapter 3 (p. 52), Śiva came to the rescue, however, by transforming all the jackals in the area into horses and driving them to Madurai. In one way or another, this story is referred to no less than twenty-five times in the *Tiruvācakam.*[45] It is never fully narrated but rather is cited in epithets and brief descriptions, as is the case with virtually all the myths, both local and pan-Indian, mentioned in Māṇikkavācakar's poems. As noted in chapter 3 (p. 49), Śiva's 'sport' of changing jackals into horses was also known to Appar, although Appar did not connect this incident with Māṇikkavācakar. The story of the jackals' transformation into horses probably antedates Māṇikkavācakar's time by several centuries, and only in a later period, perhaps because it is mentioned so frequently in the *Tiruvācakam*, did it become incorporated into the poet's legendary biography.

The third of the four Māṇikkavācakar episodes in the *Tiruviḷaiyāṭal Purāṇam* is never referred to in the *Tiruvāckam*.

This 'sport' was Śiva's changing the horses back into jackals while they were in the king's stables. The fourth incident, however, which is connected with the third, is mentioned four times in the poet's devotional hymns (2:46–47; 8:8; 13:16; 30:2). This 'sport' concerns how Śiva came to earth and carried dirt in helping to stem the flooding Vaikai river at Madurai. According to the purāṇa, these are the events leading up to this episode. After the horses reverted to being jackals, the Pāṇṭiyan king again had Māṇikkavācakar arrested and this time tortured. Śiva then caused the river Vaikai to flood during the dry season. The king decreed that every citizen participate in helping to reinforce the city's dikes.

In Madurai there lived an old woman named Vanti who sold steamed rice cakes (*piṭṭu*) for a living.[46] Not able to do the heavy work of reinforcing a section of the dike herself, she appealed to Śiva for assistance. The god then appeared at her house disguised as a day laborer willing to work for a wage. She hired him, agreeing to pay him with rice cakes. The laborer/Śiva, however, behaved most unusually (or should we say typically?). He danced and sang, interfered with the work of others, threw his basket for carrying dirt into the river, jumped into the water after it, and swam with the current in an attempt to recover the basket. When the king came to inspect the work and found Vanti's section unfinished, he struck her laborer's back with a stick. The whole universe felt the blow, and the laborer/Śiva vanished. The upshot of the beating was that the king realized his mistake and had Māṇikkavācakar released from his service, free to go to Cidambaram in keeping with Śiva's instructions to the devotee.

The expression of this local myth in the *Tiruvācakam* connects with aspects of Śiva's image already considered. First, it shows Śiva as a god of grace. In two of the four places where Māṇikkavācakar mentions the episode he also uses the term *aruḷ* — "out of grace (*aruḷ*) He carried dirt for His devotee" (2:46-47), and "in Madurai as a carrier of dirt He graciously (*aruḷ*) ate the rice cakes" (13:16). Furthermore, Śiva is seen as a god who will go so far as to suffer for his devotees; the beating is mentioned in 8:8 and 13:16. Finally, Māṇikkavācakar views the whole incident as an aspect of Śiva's inveterate craziness; "O Perunturai's great Madman (*pittaṉ*) who carried dirt for rice cakes" (30:2).

These peculiarly Tamil traditions do not alter the experientially, mythically, and philosophically based image previously discussed; they merely serve to broaden and deepen it. The *Tiruvācakam* presents a richly textured image of the deity, a collage of pan-Indian myth and symbol, local tradition, and philosophical concept, all superimposed on the field of Māṇikkavācakar's own distinctive experience.

Līlā

To conclude this chapter, I shall venture a generalization. The dominant feature of Māṇikkavācakar's Śiva, the feature which underlies, unites, and animates the various limbs of that image singled out here, is *līlā* — sport, play. The caprice, the abandon, the crazy unpredictability, the uniqueness of Śiva, all converge around the image of playfulness. Whatever he does, he does in sport. Sometimes his sports may seem cruel or at best 'meaningless'. But perhaps that is the meaning. God is free, free from having to account for, rationalize, what he does. He is free of all the necessities of our ordinary life — free of 'must' and 'ought', free of the obligations of family and caste, of the constraining attachments and desires of the ego, free of the structure, the seemingly 'inexorable' web of karma, birth, and death.

Viṭu, *aruḷ*, and *pittam* are all aspects of Siva's *līlā*. To be released, to be free of karma-saṃsāra, is to join Śiva in a realm transcending purposive action, effort, and the nexus of cause and effect. Likewise, *aruḷ* has no connection with the world of work and just reward. Grace is undeserved, unpredictable, free. And the madness of Śiva and his love-filled devotee graphically represents the discontinuity between their state of consciousness and non-playful, common sense sanity.

The concept of *līlā* is usually associated with Kṛṣṇa.[47] But it is also a typically Tamil Śaiva notion, as we have already seen in the *Tiruviḷaiyāṭal Purāṇam*. The concept of God's *līlā* (Tamil *viḷaiyāṭal*) is well known to Māṇikkavācakar too. Several quotations from the *Tiruvācakam* should suffice to indicate the scope of this image. The first mentions a number of motifs already referred to.

He graciously [*aruḷ*] severed
the bondage [*pācam*] of a creature [*pacu*] like me
who has neither devotion nor good reputation.
He changed me so that people said,
"This fellow's a madman [*pittaṉ*]."
. . . .
In gleaming Tillai I saw
the sports [*viḷaiyāṭal*] of the wise One [*vittakaṉār*].
(13:17)

It is not insignificant that Māṇikkavācakar designates Cidambaram, the site *par excellence* of Śiva's dance, as a scene of his sports. The Tamil word *viḷaiyāṭu* ("to sport", "to play") is a compound, one of whose components is the verb *āṭu* ("to move in a rhythmical manner", "to dance"). A very popular name for Śiva in the *Tiruvācakam* is "the Dancer"[48] often in connection with his Naṭarāja form at Cidambaram.[49]

Sometimes images of *līlā* and dancing explicitly occur together.

Let us praise
the Dancer [*kūttaṉ*],
who in good Tillai's hall
dances [*āṭu*] with fire,

who sports [*viḷaiyāṭu*],
creating,
protecting,
destroying
this heaven and earth
and all else. (7:12)

Thus seen, the cosmic dance of creation and destruction is effortless play. It is in this play that Māṇikkavācakar so intensely desires to participate.

To me who passionately pleads again and again,
"Have pity on me, O Dancer [*kūttaṉ*] in
(Tillai's) hall."
You taught a precious lesson and became my lord [*āḷ*].

Will I now become a bull without a master?

O that place close by where
You and Your thronging devotees
live and play [*viḷaiyāṭu*] so splendidly together.
O our Life,
act in grace [*aruḷ*],
bid me come join You!

(21:7)

All Śiva's acts are acts of *līlā*. In a verse which even has a playful tone, his granting grace and enslaving his devotees are said to be done in sport.

We entered the crowded, wide tank.
We scooped up water and splashed while bathing.
And we sang about Your foot.
See, O Lord, how we generations of devotees have flourished.
O One who is red like a blazing fire!
O One besmeared with white ashes!
O blessed One!
O Bridegroom of the slender-waisted Lady [*maṭantai*]
whose wide eyes are black with collyrium!
O Lord,
because of Your sport [*viḷaiyāṭṭu*] of enslaving and granting grace [*āṭkoṇṭaruḷ*]
we've lived in all the ways
in which those who've been released live.
Watch over us so that we don't grow weary.

(7:11)

Śiva is said to "delight in" (*uka*) wreaking havoc at Dakṣa's sacrifice (8:14). And Māṇikkavācakar portrays the god's relations with himself as simply being incomprehensibly ridiculous.

O my uncut Gem!
I'm not fit to join Your devotees.
Is it proper —
how You enslaved [*āṭkoḷ*] me?
how You raise up base people so high

and put down the heavenly ones?
O unapproachable Ambrosia!
My God,
the comedy [*nāṭakam*] You acted with me
is something to laugh at.[50]

(5:10)

But this is a farce in which Māṇikkavācakar gladly takes part.

O You whom even the inhabitants of heaven cannot know!
O You whom even the end of the Veda [i.e., the Upaniṣads] cannot seek out!
O You whom even the people of other lands cannot explain
O You who sweetly enslaved [*āṇṭukoḷ*] me!
O You who caused my body to dance [*nāṭakam āṭuvittu*]!!
O You who made me melt and relish You!
O You who made me dance the comedy of wisdom [*ñāṉa nāṭakam āṭuvittu*]
so that I could be free of earthly knowledge!

(5:95)

Śiva acts not out of purpose, not out of a sense of justice or righteousness (which is a central impulse of the Judeo-Christian-Islamic monotheisms). Certainly, this is a way of conceptualizing ultimate reality different from that which has been dominant during much of western history. This is not to deny or discount some important similarities in basic structure between Indian and Western monotheisms. But, the devotion of a Māṇikkavācakar is as different from that of a Loyola or a Wesley as is a dancing, sporting god from one who is crucified.

Śiva is an end in himself; he serves no outside ideals. In popular idiom I suppose we might say "he does what he damn well pleases, just for the hell of it." That kind of total spontaneity can be an enormously powerful and attractive image of what God is like — and, by extension, of what it must be like to be possessed by, saved by, transformed by, such a god.

Notes

1. Māṇikkavācakar does not use the term *asura*, which is the common Sanskrit designation for the inhabitants of the Tripura. Twice, however, he calls them *rākṣasas* (Tamil *irākkatar* in 15:9, *arakkar* in 28:4). Usually, Māṇikkavācakar simply refers to the three fortresses (e.g., 12:16; 13:6; 14:1, 2, 3; 43:6) without specifically mentioning the inhabitants. The Tripura myth is mentioned a total of twenty-two times. In addition to the above references, see 3:158; 4:221; 5:13; 6:10, 29; 9:5, 16, 18; 12:15; 13:10; 14:4; 23:3; 26:10; 29:7.

2. There are twenty-one references in the *Tiruvācakam*: 4:173; 5:69; 6:7, 18, 28, 32, 46, 49, 50; 9:17; 11:20; 12:8, 19; 13:10, 12; 16:4, 5; 23:7; 35:9; 36:5; 38:3.

3. Other references include 4:146; 5:21, 64; 6:26, 37; 12:7; 23:9; 24:2; 38:1.

4. There are nine references to Śiva's kicking Yama when the god of death tried to take the life of Śiva's devotee Mārkaṇḍeya: 5:45; 6:25; 9:18; 12:4; 13:15; 15:11; 23:9; 29:7; 36:10.

5. See p. 102 and the translation of 40:8 on the demonic boar. On the elephant demon, see p. 102 and p. 117. There are seven references in the text to Śiva's killing the *gajāsura* or wearing its skin: 6:19, 24, 31, 49; 9:18; 13:19; 28:9.

6. There are no less than forty-four references to this myth in the *Tiruvācakam*: 2:35, 115; 3:38, 126, 182; 4:1-9; 5:7; 7:5, 20; 8:1, 18; 10:20; 11:1, 3, 5, 7, 14, 19; 12:6; 13:17; 15:2, 12; 16:15; 17:6; 18:8; 23:1, 10; 24:3; 27:1, 3, 5; 28:2, 4, 9; 29:1, 4; 33:6; 35:2, 5; 36:5; 39:1; 41:9; 47:5; 48:1.

7. See Heinrich Zimmer, *Myths and Symbols in Indian Art and Civilization*, ed. Joseph Campbell (New York: Harper Torchbooks, 1962), pp. 128-130; and Dorai Rangaswamy, ***Religion and Philosophy of*** *Tēvāram*, bk. 1, pp. 196-199.

8. In addition to calling himself a dog (see pp. 83), some of the other terms in Māṇikkavācakar's vocabulary of self-disparagement are: "false"—*poy*, e.g., 5:73, 90; 6:7; 41:4; "shameless"—*nāṇamillā*, e.g., 5:60; and "base"—*kaṭai*, e.g., 5:23, 91, 97; 6:1, 50; 27:1.

9. On Śiva's madness, in particular, and madness generally in the Hindu tradition, see the following article: David Kinsley, "'Through the Looking Glass': Divine Madness in the Hindu Religious Tradition", *History of Religions* 13, no. 4 (May 1974): 270-305 (274-278 on Śiva). This is quite an interesting essay, which argues for a number of conclusions similar to points made in this section. Kinsley's scope, however, is much broader than that here, since his range of inquiry extends well beyond a single bhakta or even a single deity or sect to include the phenomenon of madness in the entire Hindu tradition.

10. These verses are rather like *nindāstuti* (blame-praise, invective praise) known in other Hindu religious poetry. On an example of this in Vīraśaivism, where one of Basavaṇṇa's *vacanas* refers to Śiva as a

whore, see Ramanujan, *Speaking of Śiva*, p. 81 and p. 192 (n. 23). Also see 6:46 where Māṇikkavācakar in a series of *double entendres* calls Śiva a worthless person, a fool, and an old beggar. On *nindāstuti* in Śaiva mythology, see O'Flaherty, *Asceticism and Eroticism in the Mythology of Śiva*, p. 236.

11. On the aspects of Kāpālika practice which imitate various of Śiva's mythical actions, see David N. Lorenzen, *The Kāpālikas and Kālāmukhas: Two Lost Śaivite Sects* (Berkeley: University of California Press, 1972), pp. 73-95.

12. On Śiva's flaying the elephant and wearing its skin, see n. 5 above. References to his wearing the tiger's skin include 3:22; 6:1; 10:18; 12:12; 17:4.

13. For example, 6:35; 12:1; 13:17; 17:4; 24:2; 26:5; 29:9. Also when Śiva is called Puyaṅkaṉ (Skt. Bhujaṅga), this too refers to his being adorned with snakes, e.g., 4:223; 5:62; 6:37; 18:7; 45:1–10.

14. There are many references to Śiva's wearing *vibhūti* (Tamil *tiṟu nīṟu*), e.g., 3:33, 108; 5:33; 6:11, 30; 7:11; 8:9, 13; 10:4, 18; 12:1; 17:1, 4; 25:5; 29:1; 35:4; 43:9; 49:4. Far fewer are the times Śiva is said to wear skulls, bones, and entrails (6:30, 48; 12:11, 12).

15. References to Śiva's matted hair (*jaṭa*) are quite common. Examples include 5:64; 6:1, 36; 8:11; 12:7; 16:6; 23:7; 34:2, 6; 35:1; 39:2.

16. See Frits Staal, *Exploring Mysticism: A Methodological Essay* (Berkeley: University of California Press, 1975), p. 161. The Tamil term for this plant is *mattam*, the Sanskrit is *dhuradhura* (Staal, p. 161). The verse 17:10 will be translated and discussed in the next chapter.

17. For a description in classical Sanskrit literature of Śiva's dreadful appearance and Pārvatī's positive interpretation of it, see Kālidāsa's *Kumārasambhava*, canto 5. The relevant section has been translated in a recent article by Daniel H.H. Ingalls: "Kālidāsa and the Attitudes of the Golden Age", *Journal of the American Oriental Society* 96, no. 1 (January-March 1976): 25-26.

18. For example, in addition to 14:5-16, see 5:4; 8:15; 9:18; 12:5; 15:11.

19. It is unclear, especially at 13:15 and 15:11, whether Māṇikkavācakar views the severance of Brahmā's head as simply part of the Dakṣa story or as a separate myth independent of the account of Śiva's destruction of Dakṣa's sacrifice. On the various versions of Śiva's beheading Brahmā, see O'Flaherty, *Asceticism and Eroticism in the Mythology of Śiva*, pp. 123-127.

20. In Caṅkam times there was apparently a tribe or caste of thieves called Kaḷvar (forerunners of the modern-day Kaḷḷar?) who are mentioned in *Akanāṉūṟu* 63. Hart refers to this passage in *Poems of Ancient Tamil*, p. 140.

21. Māṇikkavācakar frequently mentions Śiva's role as trickster without specifically addressing him as such. Thus, his actions are called a trick (*paṭiṟu*—34:3, 6; see 34:3 translated in chapter 7, and 10:6 translated on p. 82), a magic show (*intirañālam*, Skt. *indrājala*—2:43, 94; *ñālam*—16:8; 50:7), magic (*viccai*, Skt. *vidyā*—5:28, 29, 94), a scheme

(*tantiram*, Skt. *tantra*—3:132), and a comedy (*nāṭakam*, Skt. *nāṭaka*—5:7, 10, on which see the final section of this chapter). And his various forms of appearance are sometimes referred to as disguises (*vēṭam*—2:15, 49, 93; 17:4, 9).

22. In this regard there are a number of parallels between Māṇikkavācakar's experience and the "unmediated vision" of the somewhat later (tenth through twelfth centuries) Vīraśaiva saints of the Karṇāṭaka, on which, see Ramanujan, *Speaking of Śiva*, especially pp. 29-37.

23. Since each of these terms is so frequently mentioned throughout the *Tiruvācakam*, I have simply listed three representative examples in every case. Each set of examples includes at least one vocative use of the word. The tendency to think of God and treat him as a king could have a peculiary Tamil dimension, although most of the above terms have Sanskrit counterparts. George Hart has claimed that the Tamil bhakti movements tended to apply to the gods the attitudes and reverence originally accorded to kings in ancient Tamilnad, who along with women were considered primary repositories of sacred power: "Cosmic Imagery in Kamban" (Paper delivered at the Twenty-seventh Annual Meeting of the Association for Asian Studies, San Francisco, March 25, 1975). Of all the hymns in our text the nineteenth, Tiruttacāṅkam, "The Holy Ten Features", most systematically praises Śiva as a king, much in the manner of the Caṅkam poems of the *puṟam* type (see Hart, *Poems of Ancient Tamil*, pp. 13-20).

24. Śiva's connection with the Vedas is referred to fairly often (e.g., 6:43; 17:1; 43:1). At various places he is specifically called the Veda (e.g., 7:4, 14; 9:20; 22:5; 38:8). Whenever Śiva is designated a Brahmin with either the word *vētiyaṉ* or *maṟaiyōṉ/maṟaiyāṉ*, the association with Vedic lore is also implied (see p. 92). But by contrast, he is also unknowable by the Vedas (e.g., 5:85, 95; 10:1; 12:17; 41:3; 48:1).

25. In the *Tiruvācakam*, Śiva is not only the Āgama, he also utters the Āgamas. But, he is pictured as uttering the Āgamas on Mt. Mahendra (2:9-10, 18-20) rather than on Kailāsa, as is more typical in the Sanskrit literature mentioning this incident—a good example of the parochialization of a pan-Indian myth.

26. There are many citations for each of these words. Examples of each include: *oḷi*—26:7; 28:7; 37:5; *cuṭar*—29:1; 34:3; 49:8; *cōti*—1:72; 29:1; 50:7.

27. See pp. 123-128, including the translation of 9:20 on p. 128.

28. I am indebeted to Professor M. Shanmugam Pillai for this information.

29. On the significance in the Hindu tradition of sacred presence manifested at specific places, see the insightful essay by Kees W. Bolle, "Speaking of a Place", *Myths and Symbols: Studies in Honor of Mircea Eliade*, ed. Joseph M. Kitagwa and Charles H. Long (Chicago: University of Chicago Press, 1969), pp. 127-139.

30. See George Spencer, "Sacred Geography of the Tamil Shaivite Hymns", *Numen* 17 (December 1970): 232-254. Zvelebil also points out the importance of the "cult of sacred places" to both Śaiva and Vaiṣṇava

bhakti in Tamilnad: *Smile of Murugan*, pp. 198-199. On the Nāyaṉmārs mentioned in the *Tiruvācakam*, see chapter 7. Some commentators (e.g., Pope) have found a reference to Kāraikkāḷammaiyār at 7:15, but the text is probably better read as simply depicting the intense devotional ecstasy of an undesignated female devotee rather than that of the mother of Kāraikkāl in particular.

31. Fred W. Clothey argues that the tradition of *six* Murukaṉ cult centres is a late accretion: "Pilgrimage Centers in the Tamil Cultus of Murukan", *Journal of the American Academy of Religion* 40, no. 1 (March 1972): 84-88. A probable conclusion is that early Murukaṉ worship was oriented toward particular sacred places but that it did not necessarily center on *six* specific sites, a number indicative of symbolism associated with Skanda.

32. For example, *Paṭṭiṉappālai* 52, 249-250; *Maturaikkāñci* 467, 615; and the *Cilappatikāram*, especially cantos 9, 12, 14, 28.

33. M. Rajamanickam, *The Development of Saivism in South India* (AD *300–1300*) (Dharmapuram: Gnanasambandam Press, 1964), whose lists, however, sometimes include the same site mentioned under different names. In the *Tēvāram* hymns alone Spencer has counted 260 identifiable places: "Sacred Geography of the Tamil Shaivite Hymns", p. 236.

34. There are only seven stanzas. Most *patikams* have ten stanzas. Perhaps three verses of this hymn have been lost.

35. Tirukkaḻukkuṉṟam means "sacred hill of the vultures". The name relates to a local legend, for which see Das, *Temples of Tamilnad*, p. 228.

36. We rely here on the *Tiruvātavūrar Purāṇam* by Kaṭavuḷmāmuṉivar: Puṉṉaivaṉaṉāta Mutaliyār, ed. and commentator, *Tiruvātavūraṭikaḷ Purāṇam*, pp. 188, 203-204. Two verses of the hagiography mention Uttarakōcamaṅkai, 341 (4:93) and 369 (5:26). According to this text, Māṇikkavācakar was told by Śiva himself to go to Uttarakōcamaṅkai (v. 341).

37. Ancient Peruntuṟai is commonly identified with the modern-day Āvuṭaiyārkōyil in Tanjore District, although Āvuṭaiyārkōyil is about twelve miles inland. The Śaiva temple there contains an image of Māṇikkavācakar which is the object of regular *pūjā* rituals. See above p. 13 (n. 23).

38. Several of the many references are 20:1-6, 8-10; 22: 1-7, 9-10; 23:1-10; 30:1-6; 34:1-10; 39:2; 50:7.

39. There are a number of modern, popular works on Cidambram and the Naṭarāja temple, e.g., B. Natarajan, *The City of the Cosmic Dance* (New Delhi: Orient Longman, 1975); J.M. Somasundaram Pillai, *Śiva-Nataraja—the Cosmic Dance in Chid-Ambaram* (Annamalainagar: J.M. Somasundaram Pillai, 1970); and J.M. Somasundaram Pillai, *The University's Environ..: Cultural and Historical*, 4th ed. (Annamalainagar: Annamalai University, 1963). Two thoroughly researched monographs on particular aspects of the temple and its history are James C. Harle,

Temple Gateways in South India: The Architecture and Iconography of the Cidambaram Gopuras (Oxford: Bruno Cassirer, 1963); and Hermann Kulke, *Cidambaramāhātmya: Eine Untersuchung der religionsgeschichtlichen und historischen Hintergründe für die Entstehung der Tradition einer südindischen Tempelstadt* (Wiesbaden: Otto Harrassowitz, 1970). A comprehensive "temple study" volume on this important South Indian religious center is a great desideratum. On Śiva as the lord of dance, see the last section of this chapter.

40. See p. 62 above. A summary of the text is found in R. Dessigane et. al., *La legende des jeux de çiva a Madurai*, vol. 1.

41. Ibid., pp. 91-102. These four chapters relate much the same events as are found in the first four chapters of the *Tiruvātavūrar Purāṇam;* see Puṉṉaivaṉanāta Mutaliyār, *Tiruvātavūraṭikaḷ Purāṇam*, pp. 7-189.

42. Chapter 58 of the *Tiruviḷaiyāṭal Purāṇam* recounts, among other incidents, Māṇikkavācakar's conversion at Peruntuṟai, which is often alluded to in the *Tiruvācakam.* Since, however, many of the Purāṇic details and other incidents leading up to this event are not found in the *Tiruvācakam*, I have not counted it as one of the two 'sports' mentioned.

43. For example, 2:58-59 on how Śiva set up a shed (*pantal*) for dispensing water to the Pāṇṭiyan king's army (*Tiruviḷaiyāṭal* 35) and other ways in which he assisted the Pāṇṭiyan kings of Madurai (2:29-30—*Tiruviḷaiyāṭal* 13; 2:64-65—*Tiruviḷaiyāṭal* 37).

44. The wider context of this story is a parochialization of the purāṇic myth relating Śiva's seduction of the sages' wives in the pine forest, on which see O'Flaherty, *Asceticism and Eroticism in tne Mythology of Śiva*, pp. 172-209.

45. See 2:27-28, 36, 38-39, 44-45, 116; 8:20; 13:20; 16:8; 17:7; 18:6, 7, 8; 36:1, 2, 3, 4, 6, 7, 9; 38:1; 43:4; 47:9; 48:2, 3; 50:7.

46. In the *Tiruvātavūrar Purāṇam* (270) she is called Cemmaṉa Celvi.

47. On *līlā* in North Indian Kṛṣṇaite myth and thought, see David Kinsley, "'Without Kṛṣṇa There Is No Song'", *History of Religions* 12, no. 2 (November 1972): 149-180. In addition, Kinsley notes several references to *līlā* in the Rudrasaṃhitā (1:14:9; 2:1:4; 2:3:34; 2:20:6) of the *Śiva Purāṇa*; see pp. 150-153. On Kṛṣṇa's playfulness, also see Kinsley, *The Sword and the Flute*, pp. 9-78.

48. The most common term for Śiva as a dancer is *kūttaṉ* and its variants (e.g., 1:90; 5:43; 7:12; 9:2, 15; 15:8; 21:7, 8; 25:3; 39:3; 43:3; 51:2). Also encountered are *niruttaṉ* (e.g., 4:202; 5:61; 29:2) and *naṭamāti* (50:6). There are numerous instances when the verb *āṭu* is applied to Śiva (e.g., 13;7; 21:5, 6, 9, 35:3).

49. Many examples could be noted here, for almost all mention of Tillai in the *Tiruvācakam* is at least implicitly a reference to Śiva as Naṭarāja. Just a few of the many passages are 1:90; 2:140-141; 5:61; 11:20; 13:1, 7, 14; 21:1, 5, 6, 7, 8, 9; 35:3, 7; 42:4; 50:6. On the symbolism and interpretation of the Naṭarāja form, see Ananda K. Coomaraswamy,

The Dance of Shiva (New York: Noonday Press, 1957), pp. 66-78; Zimmer, *Myths and Symbols in Indian Art*, pp. 151-175; Dorai Rangaswamy, *Religion and Philosophy of Tēvāram*, bk. 1, pp. 440-499; and Natarajan, *City of the Cosmic Dance*, pp. 85-88.

50. In *Tiruvācakam* 2:138 Śiva himself is called *parama nāṭakaṉ*—the supreme actor, player, dancer.

7

Bhakti: The Means of Transformation

In the course of the last three chapters, several aspects of Māṇikkavācakar's devotion have inevitably come to light. It remains here to draw the human implications of his release from bondage and his service to Śiva in a more orderly fashion. How does a "slave" (*aṭiyāṉ*) act? What will he do? What will he not do? With whom will he associate? Is there an ethics of devotion? In sum, what is a life transformed by Śiva's intervention like? In addition to these questions which lend themselves to answers arrived at phenomenologically, historical considerations regarding the South Indian context of Māṇikkavācakar's bhakti will also be taken into account.

The discussion in this chapter will be focused on four facets of devotion in the *Tiruvācakam*. As the word bhakti implies, love and service will be the topic of the first section. From there we shall move to consideration of devotional madness, an important aspect of the transformation induced in Māṇikkavācakar's consciousness by Śiva's impartation of grace. Here the madness of the poet, rather than of the god, will command our attention. Next, some possible connections between Śiva's possession of Māṇikkavācakar and religious practices evidenced in Caṅkam literature, practices antedating the Brahmanization of religion in South India, will be suggested. Finally, the social context of bhakti will merit examination; and in this regard we shall be concerned not simply with Māṇikkavācakar's general attitude toward other devotees but also with the centrality of the guru-śiṣya relationship to the communication of devotion.

Love and Service

More than anything else, Māṇikkavācakar wants to melt in love for Śiva.[1] The images of sweetness, particularly those having to do with mellowness of ripe fruit, illuminate what Māṇikkavācakar means by melting. Melting implies maturity, ripeness, perfection. It suggests openness and freedom as opposed to the petrified self that is hammered by karma into a dense, impervious stone of a being, an atom (*aṇu*) incapable of getting beyond itself. Melting implies transformation from one state of existence to another. Green fruit ripens and becomes soft; ice becomes water. Moreover, that which has melted can flow into, become mixed with, something else. One who melts is no longer encapsulated in his own shell of desire. For Māṇikkavācakar, to melt is to become united with Śiva. The ability to melt is, of course, God-initiated.

What jugglery [*viccai*] this is!
  If one should ask—
Is there anything comparable to this?
He made me a slave of His most loving [*kātal*] devotees.
He cured my fear and enslaved [*āṭkol*] me.
He entered me
  so that ambrosia gushes up
  and my mind [*akam*] melts [*neku*].
He ruled [*āḷ*] me
  so that love [*aṉpu*] swells up (in me).

(5:29)

As often as Māṇikkavācakar lauds Śiva for enabling him to melt, he complains to the god that his mind does not soften (e.g., 5:33, 36, 100; 23:2; 26:1).

O Master!
I've seen how
  those who possess great love [*kātal*]
    which melts [*uruku*] their minds [*uḷḷam*]

think about You
and become united with Your feet.
Yet here I am
lower than a village dog.
My heart [*neñcu*] doesn't grow tender [*uruku*].
I have a mind [*maṉam*] like stone.
I won't melt [*kaci*].
I'm here safe-guarding
this worm-infested sheath (of a body)
which stinks of flesh.
Oh, when will You put an end to this?
(5:56)

Not just the mind or heart but also the body and one's bones are said to melt as a result of Śiva's grace and the devotee's reciprocating love to the god.[2]

This spiritual liquefaction is most apparent in the emotional change it produces in Māṇikkavācakar. It is not a quiet or subdued process. 'Melting' entails the onset of ecstatic behavior frequently approaching the hysterical.

Ah, when shall I get to gaze upon
the unique One to whom no other compares,
Him who is fire, water, wind, earth, and ether,
Him whom others cannot understand?
With voice stammering,
a cataract of tears gushing forth,
hands joined in worship,
when am I going to adorn Him with fragrant flowers?
When shall I be united with my uncut Gem?

With mind melting, melting [*nekku nekku uḷ*],
growing more and more tender [*uruki uruku*]—
standing, sitting, lying, rising,
laughing, weeping, serving, praising—
when shall I dancing do all these things?
With hair bristling, bristling,
when am I going to gaze upon His holy form,
which gleams like the sunset,
and enter (union) with Him?

When shall I be united with my uncut Gem?
(27:7-8)

Implicit in the above passage is the idea that unless one displays such overt signs of ecstasy, he is not a true devotee, has not really experienced the full measure of Śiva's grace and gained release. The notion that such emotional outpourings are indicators of one's spiritual condition is even more pronounced in the fourth decad of the "Tiruccatakam", where Māṇikkavācakar clamorously laments the absence of such signs in his own life.

O helpless corpse of a heart [*neñcu*]
  you don't dance,
  you have no love [*aṉpu*] for the Dancer's feet,
    with bones melting [*uruku*],
  you don't sing,
  you don't throb and shake [*patai*],
  you don't bow down,
  you don't wear His feet as flowers (on your head),
  you don't garland those feet,
  you don't seek Him in every street,
  you don't wail.
I don't know what to do!
(5:31)

In Māṇikkavācakar's emphasis on visible emotion, one is reminded somewhat of the evangelical Protestant's need for frequent stirrings of his feelings in order to remain convinced that he is truly saved.[3] It is doubtless such ecstatic behavior that led to Māṇikkavāckar's being called mad, an issue which will be taken up next.

William James has seen a positive indicator of spiritual transformation in such enthusiasm and has drawn a parallel between this religious ardor and experience common to people other than saints.

Magnanimities once impossible are now easy; paltry conventionalities and mean incentives once tyrannical hold no sway. The stone wall inside of him has fallen, the hardness in his heart has broken down. The rest of us can, I think,

> imagine this by recalling our state of feeling in those temporary 'melting moods' into which either the trials of real life, or the theatre, or a novel sometimes throw us. Especially if we weep! For it is then as if our tears broke through an inveterate inner dam, and let all sorts of ancient peccancies and moral stagnancies drain away, leaving us now washed and soft of heart and open to every nobler leading. With most of us the customary hardness quickly returns, but not so with saintly persons. Many saints, even as energetic ones as Teresa and Loyola, have possessed what the church traditionally reserves as a special grace, the so-called gift of tears. In these persons the melting mood seems to have held almost unimportant control. And as it is with tears and melting moods, so it is with other exalted affections. Their reign may come by gradual growth or by a crisis; but in either case it may have 'come to stay'.[4]

As James indicates, the spiritual fervor of weeping and melting is characterized by magnanimity; so too with Māṇikkavācakar who often mentions love in his descriptions of devotional ecstasy. The word most commonly used for 'love' in the *Tiruvācakam* is *a<u>n</u>pu*.[5] Thus, the poet does not simply melt; he melts or desires to melt with love (*a<u>n</u>pu*) (e.g., 1:57; 3:150; 4:80-81; 5:14, 29, 36, 60; 22:2). Such love is unperishing (3:150; 4:64, 86; 5:11; 31:9)[6] and is ideally directed toward Śiva's feet (5:36, 71, 74, 87, 94). Sometimes the devotees are called 'lovers' (*a<u>n</u>par*—e.g., 1:71; 5:46, 69; 22:3).

As is true of melting, the capacity to love is a gift given by Śiva who graciously bestows on Māṇikkavācakar inconceivable love (*eṇṇamilā a<u>n</u>pu aruḷ*–51:4), here understood not simply as Śiva's love toward Māṇikkavācakar but also the ability to love which he instills in the poet. In order that the devotees' love may increase, Śiva takes up residence in their minds (*uḷḷam*) (2:7-8). He produces love in his devotees (47:11). Although some of his devotees have become ripe with love, Śiva's love is praised as being still more excellent (5:69). He is the lover (*a<u>n</u>pa<u>n</u>*–18:6), the lover of his lovers (*a<u>n</u>parukku a<u>n</u>pa<u>n</u>*–1:71). Indeed, Śiva is addressed as love itself (4:198; 22:1; 37:5). Christians have thus not had a monopoly on defining God as love. In fact, a quite memorable verse identifying Śiva with love is found in the writings of Tirumūlar, one of the early Nāyaṉmārs who probably lived several centuries prior to Māṇikkavācakar. Although the following verse is more philosophical in tone than most of Māṇikkavācakar's hymns, its point of view is voiced in the *Tiruvācakam*, as the above examples show.

> Those who say,
> Love [*aṉpu*] and Śiva are two different things
> have no knowledge.
> None of them know
> love [*aṉpu*] and Śiva are the same.
> If they all knew
> love [*aṉpu*] and Śiva are the same,
> they would rest calmly in the
> love [*aṉpu*] which is Śiva.
>
> (*Tirumantiram* 257)[7]

The erotic aspects of Māṇikkavācakar's bhakti have already been discussed in connection with his attitude toward women and toward Śiva's spouse. It need only be repeated here that the love of a faithful wife toward her husband is the kind of devotion to which Māṇikkavācakar aspires. In this vein, Śiva is twice called a lover (*kātalaṉ*–2:113; 3:103), vis-à-vis both Pārvatī and his devotees, just as those same devotees are sometimes designated by the same term (*kātalar*–3:105; 19:2).[8] In one of the more explicit erotic images in the text, Śiva is said to be "the One who rules (*āḷ*) the mind and makes love (*aṉpu ceyvar*)" to his devotee (17:5).[9] The eroticism of the *Tiruvācakam*, however, is by and large non-obtrusive. As has been seen before, it is addressed primarily through the settings of hymns which show the devotees as village women. In this, it is quite different from later North Indian Kṛṣṇaite bhakti with its detailed descriptions of the love-play of Rādhā and Kṛṣṇa, its mythical paradigms, and religio-aesthetic theory of *bhāva* and *rasa*.[10]

Aṉpu and *kātal* are not the only terms Māṇikkavācakar uses for devotional love. Also encountered, but less frequently than *aṉpu*, are several terms of Sanskrit origin, e.g., *patti* (Skt. *bhakti*), *nēcam*/*nēyam* (Skt. *sneha*), and even one instance where *pācam* means 'love'.[11] There is a sea of bhakti (*pattik kaṭal*–

11:12). Siva teaches Māṇikkavācakar the path of bhakti (*patti neṟi*–51:1) and allows himself to be caught in the net of devotion (*patti vilai*–3:42). The devotees are infrequently referred to as bhaktas (*pattar*–19:3; 37:8; 56:2). And on one occasion even Śiva himself is hailed as a bhakta (*pattā pōṟṟi*–4:176).

But besides 'melting' with love, what is it that the devotees do? Primarily they perform service (*toḻumpu*) to Śiva. The devotees are sometimes called *toḻumpar* (slaves) (e.g., 6:38, 44; 10:7; 15:13; cf. 5:98).[12] When Śiva enslaves Māṇikkavācakar he accepts him into his service (*toḻumpu ukantu kaṭaipaṭṭēṉai āṇṭukoḷ*–27:1; cf. 1:43; 8:14). In the seventh hymn where the female devotees are seeking husbands who are also Śivabhaktas, *toḻumpu* connotes the submission and eagerness to wait upon the husband which characterize a good wife (7:9 translated below). Principally, service is directed towards Śiva's feet.[13]

> Look here, don't leave me
>   who am like butter dripping into the great fire
>   of those women whose eyes are sharp spears.
> Join me to Your heavenly slaves [*toḻumpar*]
>   who serve [*toḻu*] Your fragrant flowery feet.
> Praise to You, O Lord!
> Don't leave me who does what is wrong.
> O Master, I shall sing about You.
>
> (6:44(

There are literally hundreds of references to Śiva's feet in the *Tiruvācakam*.[14] The god's feet, of course, symbolize his sovereignity. By venerating Śiva's feet or wearing those feet on his head or placing his head at the deity's feet, Māṇikkavācakar is making a statement about superiority and inferiority.[15] He is the slave and Śiva is the master; thus, even the lowest and least exalted part of Śiva's anatomy is far higher than Māṇikkavācakar. One goes to the feet for refuge (*caraṇam*–4:105; 10:9; 30:6), touching them, serving them, adorning them, as a sign of deepest obeisance and respect In fact, the most commonly used word for devotee in the *Tiruvācakam* is a cognate of the most frequently encountered word for Śiva's feet. *Aṭiyāṉ* signifies a slave, literally one who is at the feet (*aṭi*) of his master (see n. 61 below). Śiva's feet are thus seen to be the appropriate object of Māṇikkavācakar's *aṉpu* (5:74, 87, 94, 99) as well as of his service.

How specifically does one serve or express love for Śiva's feet? The most typical way of venerating the feet of the deity is to place flowers on them (5:5, 6, 18, 31; 27:3; 41:2, 7; 42:6; 43:7). The offering of flowers is one of the most widespread ritual acts in the Hindu tradition and is intimately associated with many types of *pūjā*.[16] The mention of flowers in connection with the worship of Śiva is also attested at places where no specific reference is made to his feet (e.g., 5:13, 14; 26:5; 27:7; 29:8). The setting of hymn 13, "Tirruppūvalli" (The Sacred Creeper Flowers) has the devotees picking flowers in order to present them to Śiva (13:1-20).

In addition to the basic melting rapture already discussed, what Māṇikkavācakar seems mainly to have in mind when he speaks of love and service is ritual homage to the deity. Thus, one should venerate the god in ritual worship, treating him as one would a king. Not only the thirteenth hymn assumes a ritual background. Even more directly related to *pūjā* in the temple or the home is "Tiruppaḷḷiyeḻucci", which is sung to the deity in order to awaken him in the morning (20:1-10). Thes golden powder under preparation in "Tirupporçunnam" i meant for presentation to Śiva for his bath (9:1-20). Singing the praises of the deity, which is what much of the *Tiruvācakam* does, is a standard feature of much Hindu worship and is specifically recommended in our text (e.g., 5:1, 100; 25:7; 42:8).

Here are a few verses which picture some of the ritual and service activities Māṇikkavācakar envisions as appropriate expressions of love to God:

> My mind [*akam*] doesn't grow tender [*kuḻai*] for
> Your sacred feet as it should.
> I don't melt [*uruku*] in love [*aṉpu*] for You.
> I don't adorn You with flower garlands and extol You.
> I don't declare Your praises.
> O King of the gods,
> I don't sweep Your holy temple.
> I don't cleanse the (temple) floor with cow-dung water [*meḻuku*].
> I don't dance.

In such a way I hasten toward death
and aim to reach You by my cleverness [*catur*[!
(5:14)

Hang up the beautiful strings of pearls and flower garlands.
Make ready the pots of sprouting seeds, the incense, and the good lamps.
O Śakti, Somi, the Goddess of the earth, and Sarasvatī,
chant "many years".
O Siddhi, Gaurī, Pārvatī, and Gaṅgā,
come and wave your yak-tail fans.
Let us sing about the Father, the Lord of Aiyāṟu,
and let us dancing pound the golden powder.
(9:1)

Wear the beautiful ashes.
Cleanse the flower with cow dung [*meḻuku*].
Scatter pure gold.
Spread out the treasure.
Plant Indra's *kaṟpaka* [Skt. *kalpaka*] tree.
Put beautiful lights everywhere.
Hoist the flag.
For the King of the celestials,
for Brahmā's Lord,
for the Lord of him with the discus [i.e., Viṣṇu],
for the Father of good Vēlaṉ [i.e., Murukaṉ],
for Umā's Husband who rules [*āḷ*] our kind,
let us pound the golden powder fit for Him.
(9:3)

The players of the sweet-surrounding *vīṇā* and the *yāḻ* players are heıe.
Those who intone the Ṛg Veda and the *stotras* are here.
These who carry thickly entwined flowers in their hands are here.
Those who worship [*toḻukaiyar*], those who cry, and those who tremble are here.
Those who join their hands above their heads in adoration [*añcaḷi*] are here.

O Lord Śiva who dwells in holy Perunturai!
O our Lord,
who enslaves [*āṇṭukoḷ*] even me
and gives sweet grace [*aruḷ*],
arise from Your bed!

(20:4)

The intent of the above hymns seems obvious. Śiva is to be treated as a royal personage in the manner well-known to Hindu temple ritual. But, lest one should imagine that only such proper ritual activity is deemed acceptable, consider Māṇikka-vācakar's mention of two of his Nāyaṉmār predecessors. In the fifteenth hymn, the poet favorably refers to Caṇṭēcuvara-nāyaṉār, a Brahmin devotee, but hardly an orthodox one.

When the faultless *brahmacarī*
cut off both feet of his father,
also a Brahmin by caste [*cātiyum vētiyaṉ*],
after he had spoiled (his son's) offering [*karumam*] to Śiva,
the crime became merit
by the Lord's holy grace [*aruḷ*],
so that even the *devas* serve [*toḻu*] (the boy).

(15:7)

The story of Caṇṭēcuvarar, assumed as a background for this verse, is most readily accessible in the twentieth chapter of Cēkkiḻār's *Periyapurāṇam*, a well-known Tamil hagiography of the twelfth century which relates the lives of the sixty-three Nāyaṉmārs.[17] In summary outline, the legend of Caṇṭēcuvarar tells how a young Brahmin boy who tended the village cows worshipped Śiva in the form of an earthen *liṅga* which he had built. He bathed the *liṅga* with milk from the cows he was herding. When news of his behavior reached the village, his father decided to observe the boy's activities from a nearby tree where he had hidden. Incensed by what he saw, the father interrupted his son's worship, upending the pot containing the milk for the *pūjā*. At that the boy cut off his father's feet with an ax and continued his worship. Thereupon Śiva revealed himself to the boy, announcing, "On my account you cut to pieces the father who brought you into being. Henceforth I shall be your father" (*Periyapurāṇam* 20:54).[18] In addition, Śiva took the boy to Śivaloka and made him his servant and recipient of offerings made to the god.

There are two noteworthy themes here. First, as with Māṇikkavācakar, Śiva replaces the boy's biological father. Second, even though the boy's offering was crude and unorthodox by Brahmanical standards, it was pleasing to Śiva since the god is pictured as caring only about the devotedness of his worshippers rather than the propriety of their rituals.

Similar to Caṇṭēcuvarar's story is that of Kaṇṇappanāyaṉār, who also finds mention in the *Tiruvācakam*. Again, the peculiarity and perseverance of bhakti in the face of ritual orthodoxy are emphasized. And this is the very kind of intense, although socially and ritually aberrant, love to Siva which Māṇikkavācakar wants to emulate. At one point he simply says, "After seeing that there was no unique love (*aṉpu*) in me like Kaṇṇappaṉ's, He still graciously enslaved (*āṭkoḷ*) incomparable me" (10:4). The other reference to Kaṇṇappaṉ presupposes knowledge of the legend about this saint; so before translating that passage it is necessary to summarize the story of Kaṇṇappaṉ.

Kaṇṇappaṉ was a Vēṭaṉ, a hunter, hardly a very noble or high-status occupation according to Brahmanical criteria.[19] He is depicted as being crude and rough in his manners and, as we shall see, in his worship too. One day while on a hunting expedition, he discovered a Śivaliṅga in the forest whose upper part had been fashioned into a face of the god. When he saw the *liṅga*, Kaṇṇappaṉ immediately became enraptured with devotion to Śiva. His manner of worship was to present the *liṅga* with the flesh of animals he had killed while hunting. He bathed the *liṅga* with water from his own mouth and offered it wild flowers from his hair. Also, he used his leather sandals to clear away the withered flowers from the *liṅga*.

Unbeknown to Kaṇṇappaṉ, an orthodox Brahmin worshipped at the same spot during the day while Kaṇṇappaṉ was hunting for meat to present to Śiva in the evening. Upon finding the remains of Kaṇṇappaṉ's offerings, the Brahmin was utterly scandalized by what he considered to be a polluting desecration of the image. However, Śiva appeared to the

Brahmin in a dream, informing him that the worship being offered was pleasing to him and that the spirit in which the *pūjā* was performed was far more important than its lack of orthodoxy. The god told the Brahmin to hide himself early the next morning near the image and Śiva would demonstrate to him the intensity of Kaṇṇappaṉ's devotion. The Brahmin did as directed. In the morning when Kaṇṇappaṉ approached the *liṅga*, he noticed that one of its eyes was bleeding. When all else failed, Kaṇṇappaṉ ("he [who gave] an eye") cut out his own eye and placed it on the image's injured part. The wound immediately healed, but then the *liṅga's* other eye began to bleed. Just as Kaṇṇappaṉ was about to remove his one remaining eye, Śiva appeared, prevented him from doing so, and thereupon granted Kaṇṇappaṉ a place at his right side.

Referring to Kaṇṇapaṉ, Māṇikkavācakar says:

So (all) may know
  the greatness of that hunter [*vēṭaṉār*]
  who worshipped (Śiva) with intense love —
    the good sandaled foot,
    the mouth which was his water pot
    the meat as food,
      appearing as *pūjās* [*pūcaṉai*] properly performed
let us (sing)
  how he was truly satisfied
  and received garce [*aruḷ*] there,
and let us play Tōṇōkkam. (15:3)

The story of Kaṇṇappaṉ needs little interpretation. It exalts devotion, no matter how unusual the form it may take above considerations of caste and ritual orthodoxy. Love of God is what is deemed important, not social or ritual status. Brahmins are not superior to low-caste devotees simply because they are Brahmins and can perform *pūjā* according to the Vedic and Āgamic prescriptions. This story, and particularly the part Māṇikkavācakar focuses on, shows Śiva as uninterested in orderly proceedings, especially proper ritual activities. In keeping with his own unique and unpredictable nature, Śiva welcomes devotion expressed in unusual, indeed bizarre, ways, as the legends about Kaṇṇappaṉ and Caṇṭēcuvarar amply show.

Śiva is an enormously tolerant god with regard to the types of ritual which are pleasing to him. A very wide range of ritual activity is considered acceptable to this deity. He can be honored in standard Āgamic fashion, as performed, for example, by orthodox Smārta Brahmins. Or he may be suitably worshipped in the 'dark' ways of a Kaṇṇappaṉ with his meat offerings and water carried in his mouth mixed, as it must be, with polluting saliva. Both orthodox and 'deviant' ritual practice are allowed. Again, Śiva appears as an integrator of opposites, in this case of widely divergent ritual activities.

What Śiva desires most is complete self-surrender, total dedicated love to himself. He wants 'slaves'. Ritual is one very appropriate form for expressing such devotion, but ritual itself is of no particular consequence. Rather the feelings of love and service informing that ritual are all-important. Love and service in the *Tiruvācakam* are almost entirely directed toward Śiva. There is little sense of social obligation and no concern for justice or righteousness in the Western sense of these terms. Only vis-à-vis other devotees does one have social duties, as will be noted later in this chapter, and then service rendered to them is appropriate mainly because devotees are viewed as virtual extensions of Śiva himself. If one perceives ordinary reality largely as a place from which to escape, as Māṇikkavācakar does, then religious effort will most likely be directed towards transforming one's consciousness (indeed, destroying one's ordinary ego consciousness through devotion to Śiva) rather than towards transforming the 'ordinary' space-time world in accordance with some set of ideal social values.

As will be shortly pointed out, total orientation toward Śiva is a form of possession by the god. Expressed in terms that have become familiar in this section, such loving self-surrender appears as follows:[20]

> If ever they speak,
> they say, "O Lord! O our Father! O Lord of our father!"
> If ever they besmear themselves with anything,
> they rub themselves completely with sacred ashes.

O You who rule [*āl*] such people
who have transcended birth and death
through unchanging love [*nēcam*],
who say, "Praise to our Lord!"
Alas, the way in which You enslaved [*āṭkol*] me,
me a deceiver [*kaḷvaṉēṉ*] caught in a flood of base desire!
O flawless Hill of gems! O my Father!
(5:24)

Madness

Māṇikkavācakar's intense devotion leads to a behavior which is sometimes said to be "mad", the Tamil words being *piccu*, *pittu*, and *uṉmattam*.[21] These terms seem to have roughly the same connotation for Māṇikkavācakar that 'mad' commonly has for us, namely, striking deviation from normal, widely accepted personal and social behavior. While standards of normality may differ greatly between ninth-century Tamilnad and twentieth-century America, the type of phenomena indicative of "madness" in the *Tiruvācakam* would merit that label in the contemporary Western society too.

Perhaps the most vivid description of ecstatic devotional madness in the *Tiruvācakam* is found in the third hymn. After Śiva had revealed himself to Māṇikkavācakar in the form of a guru at Peruntuṟai, the poet describes his own behavior as follows:

While unperishing love [*aṉpu*] melted [*uruku*] my bones,
I cried.
I shouted again and again,
louder than the waves of the billowing sea,
I became confused,
I fell,
I rolled,
I wailed.
Bewildered like a madman [*pittar*],
intoxicated like a crazy drunk [*mattar*],
so that people were puzzled

and those who heard wondered.
wild as a rutting elephant which cannot be mounted,
I could not contain myself.
(3:150-156)

Māṇikkavācakar then goes on to tell how in this state of ecstasy his body became suffused with ambrosia. Śiva is said to pump honey into the poet's body, to inject ambrosia into the very hollow of his bones (3:170-175). All this has the result of creating for Māṇikkavācakar a new heart (*uḷḷam*) and body (*akkai*) whose very nature is to melt and ooze with love (3:176–177). Thus, the devotee's madness is a manifestation of his new form, of a life utterly transformed by Śiva's grace.

The kind of hysterical behavior associated with devotional madness is also quite evident in a verse of the seventh hymn. Here the ecstasy of one of the young women devotees is described in some detail.

Once calling out "Our Lord" again and again,
now her mouth does not cease (to sing) the glory
of our Lord.
With intense joy of mind,
with eyes pouring forth an unceasing flood of tears,
she who lies on the earth as if worshipping it
does not bow down to the celestial beings.
In this way one becomes mad [*pittu*] for the great King.
Who are such ones (who become mad like this)?
O you women
whose breasts are adorned with bodice and jewels,
let us sing with full voice about the feet
of the skillful One [*vittakaṉ*] who enslaves [*āṭkoḷ*]
people in this manner,
and let us plunge and dance
in the beautiful, flower-filled water. (7:15)

The ecstasy pictured in this passage is so intense that the devotee appears as though unconscious, lying on the ground. Notice too that in this state other gods ("the celestials") apart from Śiva are not accorded any reverence, a common theme in the *Tiruvācakam*. Pope has ingeniously seen an allusion to

Kāraikkālammaiyār in this verse.[22]

Often in the *Tiruvācakam*, Māṇikkavācakar simply states that Śiva has filled him with madness, intoxicated him (e.g., 3:107; 5:96; 8:2, 5; 24:3; 34:3; 47:6). In the following verse, both *pittu* and *mattam* are used to describe how Śiva's grace invades the devotee's mind:

> The Father, the Lord of Perunturai,
> filled me with madness [*pittu*],
> cut off my rebirth,
> came and made my mind indescribably intoxicated [*mattam*],
> enslaved [*āṭkoḷ*] me.
> He, my Medicine,
> looked on me with great grace [*aruḷ*]
> and came as undying bliss.
>
> (47:6)

Indeed, the nature of bliss itself is elsewhere characterized by confusion, bewilderment, stupor (*māl*) (47:2). This state of confusion (*māl*) contrasts with and supersedes worldly wisdom (*catur*) (36:2). Thus, it is not surprising that one result of Śiva's grace is that by it he shows Māṇikkavācakar how to become bewildered (*māl*) (50:3).

In this bewildered state of devotional ecstasy, the poet fails to notice the passage of time, and more significantly he forgets who he is. In short, he abandons all sense of ego and transcends time.

> I don't know that I am me.
> I don't know day from night.
> He who lies beyond thought and speech
> made me into a frenzied madman [*matta uṉmattaṉ*].
> The Master of the great angry bull,
> the Brahmin [*paṉavaṉ*]
> who dwells in enduring holy Perunturai —
> I don't know the mischief [*paṭiṟu*] He played on me!
> O supreme Light! (34:3)

As with Śiva's own craziness, devotional madness is another

facet of the two quite separate states of consciousness widely attested in our text. On the one hand, there is the sphere of ordinary awareness, reason, worldly wisdom, and self-seeking. Opposed to such 'normal' states of mind, however, is the madness of ecstatic devotion to Śiva. And this non-ordinary consciousness is accompanied by a whole series of physical manifestations — weeping, laughing, rolling about on the ground, trembling, babbling incoherently (*pitaṟṟi*—21:10), hair standing on end, etc.[23] The opposition between the two types of consciousness is further evidenced by the derision which Māṇikkavācakar's hysterical actions provoke. Thus, after enumerating all the signs of ecstasy—melting, crying, trembling, weeping, singing, agitation—Māṇikkavācakar says:

> Though the world mocked me
>   calling me "demon" [*pēy*],
> I abandoned shame.
> The local people's despising talk
> my mind bent
> into ornaments of praise. (4:67-70)

At a number of other places in the text, Māṇikkavācakar's strange behavior draws accusations of madness from those who observe his actions (5:3; 26:4; 31:7; 32:3). The verse 5:3 especially merits attention, for it gives further evidence of the kind of behavior which occasions such censure.

> Thinking only about the feet
>   of the supreme One,
>   the Father,
>   the Master,
> my mind melting [*uruku*] with madness [*mata maṉam*],
> and wandering from place to place
>   saying whatever is consistent with that state of mind,
>   so that people say,
>   "This fellow is confused [*māl*]",
>   everyone speaking his own mind—
> when shall I thus die? (5:3)

Thus, Māṇikkavācakar expects that the behavior of one who is god-intoxicated will meet with scornful comments of non-devotees. In the above verse he regrets that his own actions are not the object of disdain[24]; for they are presumably still too 'normal'. He desires to "die" to ordinary existence in favor of the far more attractive madness of devotion.

Devotional madness is the madness of love. As several translated passages show, madness occurs in conjunction with melting love (3:150-156; 5:3). The characteristics of madness overlap the features associated with melting (see 27:7–8 translated on pp. 169-170). To be mad is to be madly in love with Śiva. A particularly interesting verse in this regard is found in hymn 17, where a girl/devotee confesses her complete infatuation with Śiva to her mother.

> "*Konṟai* flowers and the moon,
> "*vilva* and datura [*mattam*],
> "thickly crown His head, O mother!"
> she says.
> "The datura [*mattam*] on His thickly crowned head
> "is why I'm so mad [*uṉmattam*] today, O mother!"
> she says.
> (17:10)

Here the word *mattam* refers to the datura or purple stramony, a plant capable of producing powerful hallucinogenic effects, which Śiva wears in his hair (see 9:19). Although the verse hints at a madness induced by drugs, there is no other evidence in the text which suggests that Māṇikkavācakar himself used drugs to produce an ecstatic state of consciousness. The key to interpreting this verse is probably the poet's desire to make a pun, not a veiled admission or recommendation of the religious use of drugs, although doubtless such practices have been known to some Śaivas.

The madness of Śiva's devotees reflects the madness of the god himself. This is not mystical ecstasy arrived at through disciplined meditation. Māṇikkavācakar does not achieve a state of freedom and unconditionedness through a process of withdrawal into his inmost self. Rather, he becomes enslaved, possessed, by a being whom he perceives to be different from himself. His goal is not to discover, to absorb, all things in his own self but to allow his self to be discovered, to be penetrated, by Śiva in the most intimate possible personal union. To be penetrated, entered, possessed, is to become like one's possessor. And, as was seen in the previous chapter, this god is mad. That some of his devotees also seem to be mad is in fact quite logical.

Leaving further discussion of the 'possessed' nature of Māṇikkavācakar's bhakti until the next section, this examination of madness in the *Tiruvācakam* will conclude with some interpretive comments about this phenomenon. The madness of devotional ecstasy stands opposed not only to reason and worldly wisdom but also to all egocentric attachment and precoccupation with normal social relationships. Devotional madness, in short, is a state of absolute freedom where one is unconditioned by the structures of ordinary reality. What better figure could express the utter discontinuity of this state with everyday consciousness than madness? But, as we have seen, this is not simply a pleasant metaphor. For Śiva's devotees appear to be literally mad. They weep and laugh hysterically. They indulge in highly unusual behavior.

To sum up the meaning of Māṇikkavācakar's madness in philosophical terms, it is the mode of being which is appropriate to the *jīvan-mukta*. It is how one appears who exists in the sphere of saṃsāra but is no longer bound by its constraints. Madness is to normality what *mokṣa* is to saṃsāra. Madness is salvation. Māṇikkavācakar is implicitly claiming that to live authentically in relation to what is ultimately real, i.e., to Śiva, is to exist in a state of ecstasy which those still caught in saṃsāra call madness. Or to turn the symbol of madness around, in a mad world sane men will appear to be crazy. When seen from the perspective of the complex of philosophical-theological ideas in the *Tiruvācakam*, Māṇikkavācakar's madness can only be understood in the context of salvation's relation to the saṃsāric order. In short, saṃsāra, conditionedness, karma, attachment, the *devas*, and normality, on the one side, stand opposed to and are transcended by *mokṣa*, unconditionedness, freedom from karma, love, Śiva, and madness, on the other.

There is a sense in which madness is similar to play, to *līlā*. In fact, in the *Tiruvācakam* they can be viewed as two aspects of the same phenomenon. Madness has no rules,

Actions labelled 'mad' at least in everyday parlance, are those considered to be irrational, not motivated by practical concern with the 'real' world of 'fact' and social conventions. Madness appears to have no goal. Like play, mad behavior seems to be an end in itself. From the standpoint of sane practical activity, both madness and play are often perceived to be self-indulgent, economically and socially unproductive, not really meaningful modes of existence. In certain respects both seem to be reversions to the pre-adult, unsocialized world of the child. The playful madman does not participate in the ordinary shared structures of reality established by social consensus. His actions do not anticipate the future but rather are spontaneous, natural, *sahaja* (to use a Sanskrit term, but one not found in our text). Like the child he is struck by the immediacy of experience, seeing the world as if for the first time.

This mad and playful world of immediate experience is, of course, echoed in the pages of many mystical texts, and not a few mystics have borne the charge of lunacy. Recently there has also been a certain vogue for ecstasy among western psychologists and social critics, not to mention the general populace (one can even find a 'serious' sociologist proposing play as the new methodology, or rather anti-methodology, for doing social science).[25] Thus, a psychologist like R.D. Laing writes:

> We live in a secular world. To adapt to this world the child abdicates its ecstasy. ("*L'enfant abdique son extase*": Mallarmé.). . .
>
> From the alienated starting point of our pseudosanity, everything is equivocal. Our sanity is not "true" sanity. . . . True sanity entails in one way or another the dissolution of the normal ego, that false self competently adjusted to our alienated social reality; the emergence of the "inner" archetypal mediators of divine power, and through this death a rebirth, and the eventual re-establishment of a new kind of ego-functioning, the ego now being the servant of the divine, no longer its betrayer.[26]

While Laing quite likely never heard of Māṇikkavācakar, his remarks just quoted seem an appropriate commentary on our poet's experience. Even though Māṇikkavācakar did not live in a world as secularized as ours, the pressures to abdicate ecstasy were doubtless strong, otherwise his behavior would not have been so readily called mad. Assuming that, in his mad ebullience, Māṇikkavācakar recovered something of his pre-socialized self, one does not want to leave the impression that he simply regressed to an infantile mode of existence. Rather, that return gains significance only after the discriminating intellect has been developed and the self has learned to adapt to its social environment. Return is thus an upward spiraling. To close this section on this note, the following quotation:

> Ecstasy, *ex stasis*, is the transport out of a biologically and culturally ordered mode of thought and perception into the mystic mode. In that mode man returns to the primal state of affairs. But the return is on a higher level. It is both a circle (revolution) and a linear progression (evolution): an upward spiraling. Man regains his primitive condition, but rather than being unconscious or unaware of it, as animals are, he is super-conscious of it. It is paradoxical: *By recovering his animal nature, man becomes God.*[27]

Possession

If Māṇikkavācakar sometimes appears to be mad, his is far from an isolated case in the Hindu tradition. The presence of devotional madness similar to Māṇikkavācakar's is widely attested in other well-known bhaktas, both Śaiva and Vaiṣṇava, both preceding and succeeding our poet.[28] Among Tamil Śaivas, madness is mentioned in the works of most of the major devotional poets. For example, Kāraikkālammaiyār's behavior prompted the charge that she was possessed by a demon (*pēy*). Appar says that Śiva reveals release (*mutti*) to his devotees who have become like madmen (*pittar*).[29] Campantar refers to Śiva's devotees as "madmen who madly parade about" (*pittu ulāviya pittarkaḷ*).[30] Tāyumāṉavar tells of bhaktas fainting in ecstasy and how he himself cried and raved and was filled with madness (*Tāyumāṉavar Pāṭal* 77, 83).[31]

Moving to the Vaiṣṇavas, there is Kulacēkarāḻvār, who calls "everyone mad but the madmen who with tearful eyes and thrilled body, pine for Him, and sing and dance and worship Vishnu" (*Perumāḷ Tirumoḻi* II, 9). And of the later North Indian ecstatic bhaktas, Caitanya is probably the most conspicuous example. In the *Caitanya Caritāmṛta*, the best known of the biographies of Caitanya, he is made to say, "I repeated Kṛṣṇa's name incessantly, and my mind became unhinged. I could not be calm—I became mad, and so I laugh and weep and dance and sing. . . . Once, my mind was calm, but in the name of Kṛṣṇa rationality has disappeared" (*Caitanya Caritāmṛta Ādi* 7:74f).[33] Even one of the 'modern' saints of the "Hindu Renaissance", Ramakrishna, was thought to be crazy by some of his contemporaries.[34]

Historically, what are the origins of this ecstatic devotional madness? Since ecstatic bhakti seems to have arisen in South India and gradually spread northward throughout the subcontinent, the roots of this phenomenon could well lie in South Indian soil.[35] Undoubtedly, religious ecstasy was known in India long before the rise of the Tamil bhakti movements in the seventh through ninth centuries. One need only remember the *munis* of *Ṛg Veda* 10:136 and the various *śramaṇas* of later centuries in order to see how long-standing the search for ecstasy has been in Indian religions. But ecstatic madness achieved not by means of some psycho-physical, ascetical technique but rather through interaction with a personal deity, theistically conceived, does seem to be a distinctively Tamil contribution to the development of the Hindu tradition. It should be stressed that the restrained, almost austere devotion of the *Bhagavad Gītā* is not in question here. The decidedly emotional pulsating bhakti of the *Tiruvācakam*, shared by other early Tamil devotional hymns, is our focus.

When reading the poets of the Tamil bhakti movements one is often struck by the similarity between ecstatic devotion and possession by a god, and this is particularly true of the *Tiruvācakam*. The sense of being overpowered, enslaved, and even entered by Śiva is much like that of possession. And here may well lie a clue to the roots of at least certain aspects of Tamil bhakti; for of the relatively few formal religious practices mentioned in the Caṅkam corpus, a number of them refer to ecstatic behavior occurring when an individual has been possessed by a deity, particularly the god Murukan̲, who is the most indigenously Tamil of the gods appearing in the Caṅkam texts. Lest the following argument be misconstrued, it is emphasized that a monocausal explanation of all ecstatic Hindu bhakti is not intended. Rather, as has been true several times before, the aim is to understand the *Tiruvācakam* in light of its historical context. That the factor under consideration is evidenced in other Hindu devotional literature and practice does not mean that other, or at least supplementary, influences may not help account for devotional madness in these cases.

The evidence in the *Tiruvācakam* for stating that Māṇikkavācakar experienced periods of possession by Śiva is overwhelming. A verb which has appeared again and again in passages translated is *āṭkoḷ* (sometimes *āṇṭukoḷ*), including two of those just quoted with regard to madness.[36] *Āṭkoḷ* is a reflexive form of the verb *āḷ* (to rule, reign over, govern), another verb frequently found in the text. *Āṭkoḷ* thus literally means "to rule for oneself", or even more literally "to take to oneself in order to rule over (a person)". In passages from the *Tiruvācakam* quoted here, *āṭkoḷ* has been consistently translated by "enslave", although "accept as one's slave", "take possession of", or "possess" are renderings sometimes encountered in other translations. All these translations are acceptable, for in the *Tiruvācakam* this is clearly how Śiva acts toward Māṇikkavācakar. In a sense, the bystanders' derisive observation that Śiva's bhakta appears as if possessed by a demon (4:68) is not far off the mark, because this is exactly what Śiva does—he possesses Māṇikkavācakar, overwhelms him, enters him, and takes control of his life.

This is not a gentle process. Thus, Śiva is said to "vigorously rule" the poet (*tiṇṇamē āḷ*–28:5). He must pull and drag (*īrttu īr*) Māṇikkavācakar and melt (*urukku*) his bones, so that his sacred feet resembling the savor of sugarcane may be revealed to the poet, whose mind is like iron (38:1). And on numerous occasions Māṇikkavācakar says that Śiva enters (*puku*) him.[37] Indeed, the god enters him to such an extent that Śiva fills his body and soul without remainder (34:6 translated on p. 81).

These reterences to bengi enslaved and entered by Śiva

would not be quite so impressive were they not accompanied by mention of various forms of ecstatic behavior commonly associated with possession, features for the most part already discussed in the previous sections of this chapter. A particularly noteworthy aspect of Māṇikkavācakar's behavior which connects with South Indian traditions of possession is dancing. Eight of the passages cited as evidence for "melting" and "madness" also mention dancing.[38] In fact, a common modern Tamil word for someone who is possessed by a deity is *cāmiyāṭi*, literally a "god-dancer", and ethnographic accounts report that the god is said to descend (*iṟaṅku*) on the individual.[39] The association of possession with dancing, indeed frenzied dancing, is hardly a recent development in Tamil culture.

Possession and ecstatic dancing were prominent features of early Tamil cultic practice, so far as we are able to glimpse the shape of religious ritual in early Tamilnad from occasional references in Caṅkam poetry.[40] Such examples of dancing and possession are especially associated with the god Murukaṉ, and these forms are noticeably brought together in the god-possessed dance of the Vēlaṉ, the priest of Murukaṉ. Vēlaṉ means "spearman", because like Murukaṉ himself, this religious functionary carries a spear. Murukaṉ too is called Vēlaṉ (e.g., see 9:3 translated above on p. 175), thus confirming the temporary identity of deity and god-possessed priest. The Vēlaṉ's dance is sometimes called the *veṟiyāṭṭu* or *veṟi ayartal*.[41] The word *veṟi* indicates the ecstatic nature of the dance; for it connotes drunkenness, intoxication, giddiness.[42] *Veṟi* can also signify fermented palm toddy, the source of intoxication, although there seems to be no evidence suggesting that the *veṟiyāṭṭu* was accompanied by the ingestion of the physical intoxicant.[43] The Vēlaṉ's *veṟi*, his madness, apparently did not depend on any external stimulant but was due entirely to his poss ssion by Murukaṉ.

A number of Caṅkam passages indicate that the Vēlaṉ uttered oracles and could effect cures when possessed. In *akam* poetry the ecstatic dancing of the Vēlaṉ priest frequently occurs in the context of attempts to diagnose the unmarried heroine's love-sickness, which itself is often mistakenly attributed to her being possessed by Murukaṉ.[44] In one instance, where the Vēlaṉ has been summoned to determine the cause of the girl's malady, it is said that he "makes the large floor resplendent with his frenzied dancing [*veṟiyayar*], moving like a puppet [*pāvai*] manipulated by a skillful puppeteer [*vallōṉ*]."[45] The ecstatic behavior associated with possession by Murukaṉ is further confirmed by a reference in *Puṟanāṉūṟu* 259 to a bull who "jumps and frolics like a pulaitti [a low-caste woman] whose body has been taken over by Murukaṉ."[46] In *Paṭṭiṉap-pālai* 155 female worshippers of Murukaṉ are pictured as dancing the *veṟiyāṭṭu*.

Another form of religious dancing associated with Murukaṉ's cult, although not directly involving possession as does the dancing of the Vēlaṉ priest, is the *kuravai*, usually a dance for women. *Maturaikkāñci* 612-617 gives a description of this occasion.

> The girls wearing *kuṟiñci* flowers that blossom in the rainy season worship with zeal and concentration this god who is extremely handsome by wearing the blooms of *kaṭampa*. They join their hands and embracing one another, dance the *kuravai*—which is performed in the village common ground—and indulge in other noisy dances and songs.[47]

Although in certain sections the *Tirumurukāṟṟuppaṭai* depicts an already rather Brahmanized form of worship, it speaks of the performance of the *kuravai* dance at Murukaṉ's shrines too. In this case, Murukaṉ himself is felt to participate in the dancing, directing his attention to the "tender-shouldered women with whom he frisks about holding them in his great, drum-like arms."[48] Mention of ecstatic dancing also occurs elsewhere in the Caṅkam corpus.[49]

In the *Cilappatikāram*, there are several examples of possession by a deity. Here it appears primarily as a local phenomenon and occurs outside the purview of the Jain and Buddhist practices mentioned in this epic. For example, the whole twelfth canto depicts how a forest woman of the Maṟavar tribe performs a frenzied dance, becomes possessed by a goddess, and then communicates the wishes of the deity to the assembled group, and subsequently how a young Maṟavar girl impersonates the goddess. In the seventeenth canto a group of cowherd women perform a dance, which while not actually involving possession, dramatizes an event in the legends about Kṛṣṇa. The dance is designed to quiet the cattle who had suddenly become strangely agitated. And, at the end of the epic, the possession of a Brahmin woman named Tēvantikai by the god Pācaṇṭaṉ (30:69), her patron deity, is graphically described.[50] It is not insignificant that possession by a god often occurs among women. Likewise, Māṇikkavācakar frequently thinks of himself as a female who is to be ruled by, subservient to, and completely self-negating before Śiva.

The claim that Māṇikkavācakar's madness and his possession by Śiva reflect pre-bhakti Tamil traditions of ecstatic god-possession is strengthened by the presence among other Tamil bhaktas of similar behavior. Two of the earliest figures in the Tamil bhakti movements suffered the same accusation as Māṇikkavācakar, namely, that they were demon-possessed. Kāraikkālammaiyār's case has already been mentioned; and the very name of Pēyāḻvār, a Vaiṣṇava, is indicative of his apparently frenzied, "demon-like" behavior. Or moving to the centuries following the bhakti movements, one finds the motif of possession continuing to occupy a not unimportant place in the Śaiva Siddhānta. In expounding the Siddhānta concept of *jñāna-samādhi*, the pinnacle of religious experience, Aruḷnanti in his *Civañāṉacittiyār* writes that those who attain this goal "become like children and mad men and possessed persons, and they may delight in singing and dancing also" (3:8:32).[51] In the *Tiruvaruṭpayaṉ* ("The Fruit of Holy Grace") Umāpati also utilizes the motif of demon possession and elaborates it so as to find in it a key image for describing the nature of salvation.

> Till you are in a state like that of one possessed
> [*pēyoṉṟuntaṉmai*],
> remain destitute of all action.
> *Com*. One possessed by a spirit is under that spirit's absolute control, and is incapable of any independent action; so remain thou inactive, till all thine acts are under the control of the King.
> *Sum*. Here we are told what mature *Samādhi* is.[52]

Philosophically, it is significant that Śaiva Siddhānta retains the reference to possession; for Siddhānta's understanding of the *advaita* relationship between Śiva and the human soul is that of maximum personal involvement rather than ontological identity. Also, the idea of possession serves well both the Tamil Śaiva poets and philosophers with regard to their emphasis on the primacy of Śiva's grace at every moment of the soteriological process.

Possession remains an important aspect of South Indian folk religion, as the ethnographic literature makes plain.[53] Dancing and trembling are the most typical signs of ecstasy. Māṇikkavācakar too sometimes mentions how Śiva's devotees tremble in ecstatic devotion (*kampi*–4:61; 6:27; *patai*–5:21, 31; 23:2).[54] But while there are many similarities between the characteristics of Māṇikkavācakar's devotion and those of the South Indian tradition of god-possession, there is one significant difference. In no case does Māṇikkavācakar —or any other devotee — use his possession as a means for divination, curing, or mediumship. Māṇikkavācakar's possession, his god-intoxication, has no reference to third parties. It is solely the manifestation of his communion with Śiva, which is an end in itself.

Although bhakti, with its emphasis on achieving the ultimate goal of release rather than mere mundane, pragmatic ends, is in this important respect different from the possession of the Vēlaṉ priest or the modern *cāmiyāṭi*, it is apparent how the long-standing Tamil propensity to see the gods as powers periodically taking possession of individual humans, who at these times act very differently from 'normal' people, prepared the ground for ecstatic bhakti such as that found in the *Tiruvācakam*. In this regard the indebtedness of Tamil bhakti to its South Indian cultural milieu has not gone unrecognized by other scholars. Hart has written that, "the custom of ecstasy in worship survived in Tamilnad to produce the Nāyaṉmārs and Āḻvars, who went about Tamilnad singing ecstatic songs about Śiva and Vishnu, and were largely responsible in later times for the position of pre-eminence those gods attained as well as for the Bhakti movement, which produced the *Bhāgavata Purāṇa* and spread all over India."[55] And Louis Dumont, arguing from a structural rather than historical perspective, says of Tamil bhakti as "classically" expressed in the *Bhāgavata Purāṇa:*

> This mystic ecstasy puts us in mind of what we have called possession, which so far we have not encountered at a learned level. Even some of the recommended means for achieving this condition recall the situations where possession is habitually produced in village festivals. . . . It is true that. . . . the bhakta does not prophesy as does the possessed. Yet it remains that both possession, a functional feature of folk religion, and bhakti, a characteristic of many sects, rest upon a common psychological condition, and that bhakti takes up in more or less sublimated form an aspect of common religion ignored by Brahmanic orthodoxy.[56]

In this section, the intent has been to trace the connections between bhakti and possession more closely than has been done before. Certainly, it seems that Māṇikkavācakar's intensely personal theism and supercharged emotions are more comprehensible when viewed against the background of Tamil emphasis on possession by a god than they are if construed solely as developments internal to the Brahmanical tradition.

Guru and Other Devotees

Another factor which quite likely contributed to the prominent mention in the *Tiruvācakam* of Śiva's possessing his devotees is the concept of the guru-śiṣya relationship. As previously mentioned, Māṇikkavācakar had a very decisive experience at the port of Peruntuṟai where he met a guru whom he took to be Śiva in the form of a human teacher and to whom Māṇikkavācakar committed himself as a disciple.[57] A śiṣya is supposed to surrender himself completely to his guru. The guru 'indwells' his disciple. In effect, the śiṣya negates himself. He lives only for his guru. As can readily be inferred, there is some overlap between this attitude and that of possession by a god.

Whereas Śaivism lacks the Vaiṣṇava concept of God's *avatāras*, allowance is made for Śiva's intervention in human affairs, most typically in the form of a particularly holy teacher. Śaiva Siddhānta formalizes this idea and provides rationalizations for why **Śiva** should act in this manner.[58] Aruḷnanti, the author of several important Siddhānta treatises, considered his guru Meykaṇṭa, who wrote the *Civañāṉapōtam*, the basic Śaiva Siddhānta text, to be a manifestation of Śiva.[59] Guru-bhakti is, of course, an important aspect of many Vaiṣṇava sects too.[60] The centrality of the guru in Māṇikkavācakar's experience and in the later bhakti tradition is significant for what it says about religious communication in India (and this is true of non-bhakti traditions—indeed, of many 'non-religious' traditions too). One does not learn so much from a book, even though a text may be available. Rather, one receives instruction from a person whose level of spiritual achievement enables him to interpret the tradition according to the capacity of the individual disciple. Indeed the guru's very presence communicates. Gurus give *darśana* to their followers just as devotees have *darśana* of the god in a temple. Bhakti is not mediated through books but through persons.

In chapter 4 we noted how Māṇikkavācakar is released by Śiva from traditional social roles. The hierarchical network of kinship and caste is replaced by a dyadic relationship with Śiva or with Śiva as guru. This relationship is certainly not one between equals, but it is fully personal, intimate, and unstructured in its unpredictability — at least this appears to have been Māṇikkavācakar's experience. But, this is not the only relationship Māṇikkavācakar deems important. He is not a *saṃnyāsin*, either in his attitude to his natural surroundings or in his desire for fellowship with other bhaktas. Although there is one instance where the poet says that he considers his kin (*uṟavu*) to be a potsherd begging bowl (*ōṭu*) and a quilt cloth made of rags (*kavanti*) (40:1), taken out of context this verse misses the new relations he values with other devotees. Māṇikkavācakar does reject traditional society, but he is not cut from the mould of the stereotypical cross-grained *saṃnyāsin*. He does not retire from the company of others, neither does he perform *tapas*, nor does he fast, and clearly he takes no vow of silence.

There is a community of Śiva's bhaktas. One does not become a devotee in isolation. Thus, every verse of the twenty-sixth hymn, except for the last, ends with the phrase, "we saw the wonder of how You ruled (*āḷ*) me and joined me to Your devotees" (26:1–9). When Śiva enslaves Māṇikkavācakar, he also completely transforms the poet's social ambience. The devotees (usually *aṭiyār*),[61] the 'slaves' of Śiva, are very much a community but one whose 'rules' seem to be quite different from those of the rest of Hindu society. Indeed, it would appear that for Māṇikkavācakar, only another devotee of Śiva can make a social claim on the poet which he would recognize as being legitimate. This sentiment is articulated quite forcefully in the following three verses:

> The King of all came and enslaved [*aṇṭukoḷ*] me.
> We're not subject to anyone.
> We don't fear anything.
> We've joined His devotees.
> We'll dive (into the sea of bliss) again and again
> and cavort there with His devotees.
>
> (5:30)[62]

> Each to himself is his own kin [*cuṟṟam*].
> Each to himself is his own law.
> "Who are we?", "What is ours?", "What is bondage [*pācam*"?]
> To make these delusions [*māyam*] go away
> join with ancient devotees of the King,
> accept His will as your intention.
> If you enter the way which leads to Lord Puyaṅkaṉ's golden feet,
> He will remove what is false.
>
> (45:3)

> I won't accept the position of Indra, Viṣṇu, or Brahmā.
> Even if my family [*kuṭi*] goes to ruin,
> I won't befriend anyone except Your devotees.
> Even if I enter hell,
> I won't ridicule You if I'm there by Your holy grace [*aruḷ*].
> O God [*iṟaivaṉ*]!
> I don't think about any other god [*teyvam*] but You.
> O our pre-eminent One [*uttamaṉ*]!
>
> (2:5)

In the realm of bhakti, social distinctions are abandoned. But as these verses indicate, Śiva does not simply sever old ties, he replaces them with new relationships of an entirely different sort. A bhakta may give up family, kin, and caste, but he joins Śiva's devotees, indeed he will befriend no one but those who are devoted to Śiva. The relationships of family and caste are exchanged for membership in the band of Śiva's bhaktas. Māṇikkavācakar expresses this change of society by saying:

> The Lord allowed forlorn me to obtain bliss
> and caused me to enter His gracious band of devotees,
> thus bringing me into good relationships [*uṟavu*].
>
> (42:7)[63]

How does one characterize the "good relationships" which Māṇikkavācakar enjoys with the other bhaktas? One aspect is Māṇikkavācakar's willingness to serve other devotees of Śiva. Hence, the poet says that Śiva "made me a slave (*aṭiyaṉ*) of his most loving devotees (*aṭiyār*)" (5:29, translated above on pp. 168), and that he "joined me to the feet of his devotees" (41:8), another indication that Māṇikkavācakar shows reverence to other bhaktas. In certain respects, one should conduct oneself toward Śiva's devotees as one would treat Śiva himself. The best example of this attitude is found at 7:9, where the female devotees are depicted seeking good husbands:

> O most ancient Being
> older than the most ancient being!
> And again O One
> whose nature is all that is recent and new!
> We excellent devotees
> who acquired You as our lord
> shall bow down [*paṇi*] before Your devotees' feet.
> Only them shall we accommodate,
> and they will be our husbands.
> In whatever way they are pleased to tell us,
> we shall serve them as slaves [*toḻumpāyp paṇicey*].
> If You, our King, will grant us this,
> we'll be free of any want.
>
> (7:9)[64]

The service rendered to other devotees mirrors the service performed to Śiva. The bhaktas, insofar as they are possessed by the god, themselves embody Śiva and thus provide access to him. The mutual service of the devotees to each other is consequently both preparation for and extension of the love due to God himself. Māṇikkavācakar's mention of service toward Śiva's devotees is far from unique in Tamil Śaivism. According to several of the biographies related in the *Periya-purāṇam*, a number of the Nāyaṉmārs' most distinctive feature was the unusual service they rendered to other devotees.[65]

Although Māṇikkavācakar serves the other devotees and they presumably serve him, such relationships are quite different from those of rank-determined reciprocity. These "good relationships" are characterized by lack of structure and habituated action. They are face-to-face, dyadic relationships based on love (*aṉpu*) rather than interaction founded upon a social network ordered by birth. When he speaks of his association with Śiva's devotees, Māṇikkavācakar sometimes uses the noun *kūṭṭam* (e.g., 13:7; 21:8; 25:9) and its cognate verbs *kūṭu* (e.g., 5:55; 34:5; 50:2) and *kūṭṭu* (e.g., 6:44; 26:1–9; 41:8). The connotation here is that Māṇikkavācakar is joining a confederation, a fellowship, of devotees. The fellowship of the bhaktas, as opposed to the society of kin and caste, represents social freedom, spontaneity, and community; for as Māṇikka-vācakar reminds his hearers, the devotees are not subject to anyone, have no fear, and engage in blissful play (5:30, translated above on pp. 196). They are like children who play rather than work and who are free to interact without concern for social status.

In his book *The Ritual Process*, Victor Turner sets forth a theory about the opposition between social structure and *communitas*, which is suggestive for interpreting the social aspect of Māṇikkavācakar's bhakti. *Communitas*, as opposed to everyday social structure, represents personal interaction between individuals not wearing their usual social masks. This is the sphere of Martin Buber's "I" and "thou". Turner argues that societies exhibit a dialectic between these two types of human relatedness and that *communitas* is especially evident in ritual situations and among certain types of religious groups. In this regard, the early followers of Francis of Assisi are cited as a classic example of *communitas*.[66] Likewise, Māṇikkavācakar, in leaving behind the social hierarchy of kinship and caste, enters the egalitarian, unstructured companionship of Śiva's devotees where each serves the other and all are the slaves of God. The opposition between structure and *communitas* at a social level is directly related to the opposition between saṃsāra and *mokṣa*, betweed sanity and madness at an ontological-epistemological-psychological level. Indeed, several of the category oppositions which Turner sees as parallel to that between *communitas* and structure are equally descriptive of the dynamics of Māṇikkavācakar's experience and expression — for example, the following, where correlates of the *communitas* category are listed first: homogeneity/heterogeneity, absence of status/status, sexual continence/sexuality, humility/just pride of position, no distinctions of wealth/distinctions of wealth, total obedience (to Śiva)/obedience only to superior rank, unselfishness/selfishness, sacredness/secularity, suspension of kinship rights and obligations/kinship rights and obligations, continuous reference to mystical powers (and experience)/intermittent reference to mystical powers (and experience), foolishness/sagacity, and simplicity/complexity.[67]

Turner's argument is, of course, based mainly on recent ethnographic data, whereas in the case of Māṇikkavācakar, one is limited almost entirely to the level of ideology; for we really do not know if the bhaktas exemplified the kind of *communitas* which the *Tiruvācakam* and other Tamil Śaiva devotional hymns would lead us to expect. Be that as it may, the polarities which emerge from Māṇikkavācakar's thinking are so similar to the oppositions postulated by Turner that it seems we are almost certainly dealing with structurally analogous sets of phenomena. In fact, Turner discusses Caitanya and his followers as a religious group demonstrating his theory.[68]

The critique of social stratification discussed in chapter 4 and the egalitarian, socially unstructured nature of bhakti are not unexpectedly related to Māṇikkavācakar's understanding of the deity. For Śiva is addressed not merely as father, mother and kinsman, as previously noted, but also as "the One who has no kin" (*kiḷai ilāṉ*–5:28) and "the God to the people of every country" (*ennāṭṭavarkkum iṟaivaṉ*–4:165). Even though he sometimes appears as a Brahmin, Śiva does not symbolize hierarchy, is not himself bound to a particular caste, clan, or tribe. From Śiva's point of view — and from the point of view of those enslaved by him — a hierarchical, structured ordering of society reflects a kind of false consciousness, a social awareness which does not correlate with the vision of a god who knows no boundaries, social or otherwise.

Māṇikkavācakar's release from relationships based on caste and kinship is simply one aspect of the total freedom effected by the working of Śiva's grace; for such structured relationships are but one facet of the bondage which includes karma, sensuality, egoism, and "sanity". As A. K. Ramanujan has pointed out with respect to the Vīraśaivas, bhakti stands opposed to all that would render the universe safe and manipulable — from the closely defined relationships of caste to established forms of temple ritual to the concept of inexorable karmic causality.[69] It is this world-view of reasonableness, normality, and habit which bhakti blows wide open. Bhakti itself is release.

Notes

1. There are many references to melting in the *Tiruvācakam*. Several verbs are used, all of which connote melting or becoming soft and ripe. These verbs with examples of each are: *uruku* (to melt, to glow with love)–1:57; 3:150, 175; 4:61, 80; 5:14, 56, 95, 100; 22:2; 23:2; 25:4; 26:1; 27:8; 35:10; *urukku* (causative of *uruku*)–5:58; 36:1; 37:10; 38:1; 40:3; *neku* (to become soft, to melt)–4:80; 5:29, 36, 60, 100; 23:1; 27:8; 32:6; 35:7, 10; 38:7; *kaci* (to melt, to grow tender-hearted)–1:57; 5:56; 15:4; 22:2; *kuḻai* (to become soft, pulpy, tender)–4:67; 15:14. This last verb is also used in a negative sense in its transitive form, where it means 'bruise' or 'mash'; see 33:1, 10. Without using any of the above verbs, 8:5 says Śiva kneaded Māṇikkavācakar's stone-like nature causing him to become like ripe fruit (*kaṉi*). The poet commonly likens his unregenerate self to stone (e.g., 5:37, 56; 15:14) or iron (e.g., 5:22, 80; 38:1).

2. In addition to terms signifying the mind or heart (e.g., *akam, uḷḷam, uḷ, neñcu, maṉam*), the following words also appear as objects of verbs designating melting: *ākkai* (body)–22:2; *ūṉ* (flesh)–5:58; *eṉpu* (bones)–3:150; 4:80; 5:31; 37:10; 38:1; 40:3.

3. See Knox, R.A. *Enthusiasm: A Chapter in the History of Religion* (Oxford: Oxford University Press, 1950), pp. 588–589.

4. James, *Varieties of Religious Experience*, pp. 212–213.

5. On the background of this word, see Dhavamony, *Love of God*

according to Śaiva Siddhānta, pp. 24–28, 31.

6. Cf. "unwavering *kaṟpu*" (30:6) discussed on p. 123 and p. 134-135 (n. 39).

7. Tirumūlar, *Tirumantiram* (Madras: South India Saiva Siddhanta Works Publishing Society, 1962), vol. 1, p. 112.

8. *Kātal* usually connotes love between the sexes, although these instances are not the only place in the *Tiruvācakam* or in other Tamil devotional literature where this term is used to express religious emotion. Other references to *kātal* include 5:29, 56; 9:14; 30:6; 36:5. See Dhavamony's comments on *kātal* in *Love of God according to Śaiva Siddhānta*, p. 27.

9. The seventeenth hymn, the "Aṉṉaippattu" (The Mother Decad), pictures the devotee as a young female confessing her love for Śiva to her mother. The erotic aspect is more pronounced than in most other hymns. At 36:5 the devotees are advised to "make love" (*kātal cey*) with Śiva if they are to be released.

10. For example, see Dimock, "Doctrine and Practice among the Vaiṣṇavas of Bengal", pp. 41–63; and Klaus Klostermaier, "The Bhaktirasāmṛtasindhubindu of Viśvanātha Cakravartin", *Journal of the American Oriental Society* 94, no. 1 (January–March 1974): 96–107.

11. Examples of these terms include: *patti*–2:119; 3:42; 11:12; 31:7; 42:6; 44:1; 51:1; *nēcam*–1:65; 5:24; 7:2; 9:4; *nēyam*-1:13; *pācam*–7:2.

12. Cf. *toṇṭar* (slaves), e.g., 5:42; 6:32; 7:10; 9:7; 36:3; 46:2.

13. In addition to the verse translated, see the following instances where *toḻu* or one of its cognates appears along with the mention of Śiva's feet: 5:88; 6:47; 10:7; 20:1, 9; 42:8; 45:6.

14. Of the numerous references to Śiva's feet by far the most frequently used term is *aṭi*, either unmodified (e.g., 1:5; 14:3; 34:2) or in conjunction with any of several common attributes, e.g., *malar aṭi* (flower feet) e.g., 4:9; 16:2; 23:2; *sēvaṭi* (red feet) e.g., 3:61; 25:8; 47:3; *poṉṉaṭi* (golden feet) e.g., 1:32; 41:1; 45:7; *tiruvaṭi* (sacred feet) e.g., 5:5; 12:10; 20:1; *iṇai aṭi* (pair of feet) e.g., 7:20; 23:1; 47:10. Other terms for Śiva's feet with a few examples of each are: *kaḻal*, which connotes the feet with anklets–1:91; 9:14; 45:1; *pātam*–2:137; 5:60; 35:1; *tāḷ*–1:1; 8:11; 50:5; *kāl*–5:8; 9:18; 29:7; *caraṇam*–4:105; 10:9; 30:6. This last term permits an apt *double entendre*, since it transliterates both the Sanskrit *caraṇa* (foot) and *śaraṇa* (refuge).

15. Three of the passages previously translated mention Māṇikka-vācakar's having Śiva's feet on his head: 5:31 on p. 170, 13:1 on p. Ch. 81 and 40:7 on p. 141; see also 25:8; 27:3; 35:6; 38:4. The hymn 42 bears the title "Ceṉṉippattu" (The Head Decad). Each of the verses ends with a refrain "At His red feet our heads rest".

16. It has been claimed that the Sanskrit *pūjā* is of Dravidian origin, stemming from the words *pū* (flower) and *cey* (to do, make); thus, "to do with flowers".

17. A modern edition to Cēkkiḻār's work has been published under

the title *Tiruttoṇṭar Mākkatai* (The Great Story of the Holy Devotees) ed. Pa. Irāmanāta Piḷḷai and Cu. A. Irāmacāmip Pulavar (Madras: South India Saiva Siddhanta Works Publishing Society, 1970). The story of Caṇṭēcuvarar is found on pp. 234–243. Pope recounts the same story in a long footnote on pp. 185–187 of his translation of the *Tiruvācakam*. There is also a German translation of the complete *Periyapurāṇam* in Schomerus, *Śivaitische Heiligenlegenden*, which includes the story of Caṇṭēcuvarar on pp. 104–107.

18. Cēkkilār, *Tiruttoṇṭar Mākkatai*, p. 242.

19. The story of Kaṇṇappan forms Chapter 10 of the *Periyapurāṇam*. See ibid., pp. 122–156. Pope again relates the account in an extended footnote: *Tiruvāçagam*, pp 141–145. Also, see Schomerus, *Śivaitische Heiligenlegenden*, pp. 88–94.

20. Cf. 5:26, translated above on p. 103 which states that Māṇikkavācakar's thoughts, sight, worship, speech, indeed all his five senses, are directed toward Śiva (also, see 28:5). For a fascinating parallel in western mystical literature to such all-consuming love to God, see a poem by the fourteenth-century English mystic, Richard Rolle in *The Fire of Love*, trans., Clifton Wolters (Baltimore: Penguin Books, 1972), pp. 52-53.

21. For example, *piccu*–3:107; 8:2, 5; 24:3; *piccaṉ*–5:96; *pittu*–7:15; 9:10; 44:4; 47:6; *pittaṉ*–26:4; 31:7; *uṉmattam* 17:10; *uṉmattaṉ*–32:2; 34:3; and *mattam* 5:3; 34:3; 47:6. All these words are Sanskrit derived. *Pittu*, *piccu*, and their cognates stem from the Sanskrit *pitta*, meaning "bile". *Uṉmattam* derives from *unmatta*—"insane", "frantic", "intoxicated" (from *ud*+$\sqrt{mad}$—"to be or become distracted, mad"), and *mattam* from *matta*—"excited", "drunk".

22. Pope, *Tiruvāçagam*, pp. 111-113. As described in the *Periyapurāṇam*, Kāraikkālammaiyār's behavior is quite extraordinary, to be sure. Most commentators, however, do not share Pope's view that Māṇikkavācakar had the mother of Kāraikkāl in mind when he composed this verse, and the passage is so interpreted here (see p. 164, n. 30).

23. For example see 27:7-8, translated above on p. 170 and 3:150-156 on p. 181. Such physical manifestations of devotional ecstasy are significant, because Indian aesthetic theory considers them to be involuntary signs of inner emotion which cannot be simulated (Barbara Stoler Miller, *Phantasies of a Love Thief: The Caurapañcāśikā Attributed to Bilhaṇa* [New York: Columbia University Press, 1971], p. 11). Also see Klostermaier, "The Bhaktirasāmṛtasindhubindu", p. 103-107; and Adalbert Gail, *Bhakti im Bhagavatapurāṇa: Religionsgeschichtliche Studie zur Idee der Gottesliebe in Kult and Mystik der Viṣṇuismus* (Wiesbaden: Otto Harrassowitz, 1969), pp. 95-96.

24. This is quite different, however, from groups such as the Pāśupatas, who for religious reasons systematically sought to offend their fellows through studied outrageous behavior. See Daniel H.H. Ingalls, "Cynics and Pāśupatas: The Seeking of Dishonor", *Harvard*

Theological Review 55 (1962), 281-298; and Lorenzen, *Kāpālikas and Kālāmukhas*, pp. 185-191. Cf. also the "contrariness" of the Bengali Bāuls: Charles H. Capwell, "The Esoteric Belief of the Bauls of Bengal", *Journal of Asian Studies* 33, no. 2 (February 1974): 255-264.

25. Derek L. Phillips, *Abandoning Method: Sociological Studies in Methodology* (San Francisco: Jossey-Bass, 1973), pp. 158-165.

26. R.D. Laing, *The Politics of Experience* (New York: Pantheon Books, 1967), p. 101.

27. John White, *The Highest State of Consciousness*, ed. John White (Garden City, N.Y.: Doubleday & Company, 1972), p. xii.

28. For a good survey of madness among Hindu saints, particularly those of the bhakti traditions, see Kinsley, "Through the Looking Glass", pp. 286–305.

29. Tamil text quoted in Dhavamony, *Love of God According to Śaiva Siddhānta*, p. 157.

30. Campantar *Tēvāram* 2:105:6; *patikam* 241 in Tiruñāṉacampantar, *Tēvārappatikaṅkaḷ* ed. Catāciva Ceṭṭiyār (Madras: South India Saiva Siddhanta Works Publishing Society, 1927), p. 543.

31. T. Issac Tambyah, trans., *Psalms of a Saiva Saint* (London: Luzac & Co., 1925), pp. 42, 45.

32. Quoted in Jesudasan, *History of Tamil Literature*, p. 99.

33. Quoted in Edward C. Dimock, Jr., *The Place of the Hidden Moon: Erotic Mysticism in the Vaiṣṇava-sahajiyā Cult of Bengal* (Chicago: Univertity of Chicago Press, 1966), p. 115.

34. For example, see Christopher Isherwood, *Ramakrishna and His Disciples* (New York: Simon and Schuster, 1965), pp. 64–68; Swami Nikhilananda, trans., *The Gospel of Sri Ramakrishna*, abridged ed. (New York: Ramakrishna-Vivekananda Center, 1958), pp. 324-369; Swami Vivekananda, *Ramakrishna and His Message* (Calcutta: Advaita Ashrama, 1972), p. 28.

35. The southern origins of bhakti are attested in the *Bhāgavata Purāṇa* and particularly in its appendix, the *Bhāgavatamāhātmya*, on which see the passage quoted on p. Ch. 42.

36. The two verses translated in the last section are 7:15 on pp. 181 and 47:6 on p. 182. The occurrence of *āṭkoḷ/āṇṭukoḷ* and *āḷ* is so common throughout the text that in lieu of citing further examples here, the notation of these verbs whenever they appear in translated passages serves to indicate the frequency with which Māṇikkavācakar uses them. Also relevant are nouns derived from these verbs: thus, *āṇṭamai* (5:35), meaning "lordship, ruling"; *āḷāṉavar* (4:198) and *āḷāṉār* (38:2) for Śiva's devotee "servants"; and a series of nouns used to designate Śiva as ruler, sovereign, king: *āṇṭāṉ* (2:40; 5:24; 40:1-10), *āḷvāṉ* (45:3, 5, 7), *āḷuṭaiyaṉ* (19:2), and *āḷi* (18:6).

37. For example, 5:29; 8:2; 18:4; 22:3; 23:1; 31:3; 34:6; 38:7; 41:5.

38. 4:61-62; 5:14, 95, 100; 7:15; 9:10; 15:4; 27:8.

39. Diehl, *Instrument and Purpose*, pp. 177 and 234. Strictly speaking, this phenomenon is different from shamanism, although there

are a number of common elements. Lacking are the aspects of "ascent" and "magical flight" stressed by Eliade in his classic study of Central and North Asian shamanism: Mircea Eliade, *Shamanism: Archaic Techniques of Ecstasy*, trans., Willard R. Trask, Bollingen Series, no. 76 Princeton: Princeton University Press, 1972). Also, in a narrowly literal sense of the word, "ecstasy" does not apply to the phenomena of madness or possession; for strictly defined, it means to stand outside of oneself. 'Ecstasy' has been used here, however, in its everyday meaning, signifying intense emotional exaltation approaching a trance-like state.

40. We are referring now to specifically cultic behavior as reported in the Caṅkam texts rather than to notions of sacred power and the kinds of precautions that were deemed necessary to control such power in everyday life. The relative lack of reference in Caṅkam poetry to the gods, to ritual, and to acseticism has given rise to the idea that this literature is "secular", a claim that George Hart's writings attempt to refute.

41. See *Akanāṉūṟu* 98:19; 114:2; 182:17; 242:11; *Puṟanāṉūṟu* 362:22; *Kuṟuntokai* 53:8; 318:3; and *Tirumurukāṟṟuppaṭai* 223, as cited in Kailasapathy, *Tamil Heroic Poetry*, p. 64. For additional references, see Subrahmaniam, *Pre-Pallavan Tamil Index*, pp. 785-786.

42. *Veṟi* is used no less than five times in the *Tiruvācakam*, in each instance to describe another noun. Twice *veṟi* modifies the "flower feet" of Śiva (5:52; 6:44) and once his flowing hair (35:8). Another time *veṟi* simply describes a flower (3:90) and, finally, the mouths of bees (6:5). In these cases the meaning of *veṟi* is probably "fragrance" or "honey", but it is not inconceivable that at least in the three instances relating to Śiva, Māṇikkavācakar is playing on this word; thus, "intoxicatingly fragrant flowery feet". This, after all is how Śiva affects his devotees: he intoxicates them.

43. The *kuravai* dance mentioned below, also performed in connection with Murukaṉ's cult, is, however, in one instance said to be accompanied by the drinking of a honey liquor (*tēkkaḷ tēṟal—Tiṟumurukāṟṟappaṭai* 195). But the Vēlaṉ is not pictured as indulging in this drinking.

44. This is a means of making her feelings public so that a marriage will be arranged. See *Naṟṟiṇai* 268; *Akanāṉūṟu* 22; 98; *Aiṅkuṟunūṟu* 241-250; and also *Kuṟuntokai* 23, where the diviner is female. See Manickam, *Tamil Concept of Love*, pp. 45-46; Hart, *Poems of Ancient Tamil*, pp. 28-29; and Subrahmaniam, *Saṅgam Polity*, p. 365.

45. *Akanāṉūṟu* 98:18-20 in Hart, *Poems of Ancient Tamil*, pp. 28-29. The word Hart translates as "skillful puppeteer" (*vallōṉ*) also can mean "God", at least in the later literature. For the text of this poem, see Po. Vē. Cōmacuntaraṉ, ed. and commentator, *Akanāṉūṟu: Kaḷiṟṟiyāṉai Nirai* (Madras: South India Saiva Siddhanta Works Publishing Society, 1970), pp. 350-351.

46. Hart, *Poems of Ancient Tamil*, p. 122.

47. Tanslated in Kailasapathy, *Tamil Heroic Poetry*, pp. 63-64 Also see *Kuriñcippāṭṭu* 175 which mentions the dancing of Murukaṉ's female worshippers, without, however, designating it as *veṟiyāttu* or *kuravai*.

48. My translation of *Tirumurukāṟṟuppaṭai* 215-216. For the text, see Chelliah, *Pattupattu*, p. 354.

49. See Hart, *Poems of Ancient Tamil*, p. 29 for references to *Puṟanāṉūṟu* 22; 129 and *Kuṟuntokai* 105; 366.

50. This deity is identified with Pācaṇṭaccāttaṉ, one of the names of Aiyaṉār. See Po. Vē. Cōmacuntaraṉ, ed. and commentator, *Cilāppatikāram: Vañcikkāṇṭam* (Madras: South India Saiva Siddhanta Works Publishing Society, 1972), p. 190.

51. Nallaswami Pillai, *Sivajnana Siddhiyar*, p. 237. Tāyumāṉavar, a Tamil Śaiva poet who lived in the seventeenth or eighteenth century, ascribes the same three characteristics to *jñanins*, viz., that they are like little children (*pālar*), demon-possessed persons (*pēyar*), and madmen (*pittar*). See verse 778 in *Tāyumāṉavar Pāṭal*, ed. K. Nagalinga Mudaliyar (Madras, 1906).

52. *Tiruvaruṭpayaṉ* 8:7 as translated in the prefatory "appendix" of Pope, *Tiruvāçagam*, p. lvii. Quotations from the Tamil text of this passage are found in Dhavamony, *Love of God According to Śaiva Siddhānta*, p. 285.

53. For example, see Louis Dumont, *Une sous-caste de l'Inde du sud: Organisation sociale et religion des Pramalai Kallar* (Paris: Mouton, 1957), pp. 350-352; Clarence Maloney, "Religious Beliefs and Social Hierarchy in Tamil Nāḍu, India", *American Ethnologiṣt* 2, no. 1 (February 1975): 188; and moving outside the Tamil-speaking areas of South India, see Edward B. Harper, "Shamanism in South India", *Southwestern Journal of Anthropology*: 13 (1957) 167-187; and E. Kathleen Gough, "Cults of the Dead among the Nāyars", *Traditional India: Structure and Change*, ed. Milton Singer (Philadelphia: American Folklore Society, 1959), p. 243.

54. Frits Staal claims that since the Vedic seers (and at a later time, Brahmins in general) are called *vipra*, which connotes trembling while inspired by the gods, therefore possession is as much a part of the 'Sanskritic' tradition as it is a so-called 'non-Sanskritic' phenomenon. But, for purposes of the argument here, this is not a very helpful point, since what was true of the Vedic *ṛṣis* is of little assistance in explaining the behavior of a poet almost 2,000 years later, especially when during the intervening centuries most *vipras* had long ceased to quiver. See J.F. Staal, "Sanskrit and Sanskritization", *Journal of Asian Studies* 22, no. 3 (May 1963): 267.

55. Hart, *Poems of Ancient Tamil*, p. 29.

56. Louis Dumont, "World Renunciation in Indian Religions", *Religion/Politics and History in India: Collected Papers in Indian Sociology* (Paris: Mouton, 1970), p. 57.

57. There are many references to Śiva's appearance to Māṇikkavācakar as a guru, e.g., 1:3, 59; 2:42, 54; 3:149; 4:76, 91, 180: 5:91; 8:1, 3: 10:14; 11:1; 13:13; 18:10; 20:8, 9; 23:10; 25:3; 29:1-10; 42:4: 44:3; 50:4. Virtually any mention of Peruntuṟai can be construed as an allusion to Māṇikkavācakar's encounter with Śiva in his guru form. Each verse of hymn 29 contains a phrase about Śiva's "abiding beneath the flowering *kuruntam* tree in holy Peruntuṟai", a reference to Māṇikkavācakar's meeting with the guru.

58. See *Civañāṉapōtam* 8 and commentary and *Tiruvarutpayaṉ* Chap. 5, the latter summarized in Piet, *Śaiva Siddhānta Philosophy*, pp. 134-135.

59. *Irupāvirupatu* 1:1. On this verse see the translation by J.M. Nallaswami Pillai, "Irupa-iru-pahtu of St. Arul Nandi Sivachariar", *Siddhānta Deepika* 13 (1912-1913): 199; and on the entire text, see Dhavamon, *Love of God according to Śaiva Siddhānta*. pp. 245-251.

60. The most conspicuous modern example is that of the Bengali strand of Vaiṣṇavism initiated by Caitanya. On guru-bhakti in the *Bhāgavata Purāṇa*, see Gail, *Bhakti im Bhāgavatapurāṇa*, pp. 86-88.

61. References to the devotees are quite frequent in the text. *Atiyār* and variants are by far the most typical terms (e.g., 2:144; 5:17, 29, 35, 89; 6:22, 25; 8:9; 13:7; 16:6; 18:5; 20:6, 8.9; 21:5; 26:1-9; 36:5; 37:4; 41:8; 43:5; 45:4; 49:5), Other words for the devotees include *toḻumpar* (see p. 173), *toṇṭar* (see n. 12 on p. 201), *aṉpar* (see p. 171), *pattar* (see p. 173), *kātalar* (see p. 172). and *āḷāṉār/āḷāṉvar* (see n. 36 above on p. 203).

62. This is the verse which appears to rely on one of Appar's stanzas (*Tēvāram* 6:98:1), on which see p. 48. There is a German translation of this entire *patikam* by Appar in Lehmann, *Die śivaitische Frömmigkeit der tamulischen Erbauungsliteratur*, pp. 17-19.

63. Cf. *Civañāṉapōtam* 12, which recommends the company of Śiva's devotees because others cause *aññāṉām* (Skt. *ajñāna*) to arise. See Gordon Matthews, trans., *Śiva-ñāna-bōdham: A Manual of Śaiva Religious Doctrine* (Oxford: Oxford University Press, 1918), pp. 27-28 and p. 76.

64. This verse is still often sung in Tamilnad by young unmarried women at the beginning of the marriage season in the month of Mārkaḻi (December-January) as a prayer for a good husband. I am indebted to Professor M. Shanmugam Pillai for this information.

65. See particularly the stories of Iyapṟakaināyaṉār (Chap. 3) Mūrkkanāyaṉār (Chap. 32), Ciṟuttoṇṭanāyaṉār (Chap. 36), Kalikkam panāyaṉār (Chap. 44), and Muṉaiyaṭuvāṉāyaṉār (Chap. 52). The chapters are those as given in Cēkkiḻār, *Tiruttoṇṭar Mākkatai*.

66. Victor Turner, *The Ritual Process: Structure and Anti-Structure* (Chicago: Aldine Publishing Company, 1969), pp. 140-154.

67. Ibid., pp. 106-107.

61. Ibid., pp. 155-164.

69. A.K. Ramanujan, "Structure and Anti-Structure: The Vīraśaiva Example" (Paper delivered at the meeting of the Society for South India Studies, Chambersberg, Penna., March 17, 1973). Ramanujan makes much the same point in the introduction to his translation of Vīraśaiva *vacanas*, *Speaking of Śiva*, pp. 29-31.

Epilogue

This essay began with a quotation from T. S. Eliot's *Four Quartets*. That passage continues:

> For most of us, there is only the unattended
> Moment, the moment in and out of time,
> The distraction fit, lost in a shaft of sunlight,
> The wild thyme unseen, or the winter lightning
> Or the waterfall, or music heard so deeply
> That it is not heard at all, but you are the music
> While the music lasts. These are only hints and guesses,
> Hints followed by guesses . . . . [1]

The timeless moment must indeed for most of us remain a series of hints. "Saints", however, experience eternity more fully, consciously; and when a "saint" through a dint of personality or power of expression is able to communicate something of his experience to others, we gain further hints that allow us to guess what such experience is like. But, just as interesting as the moment out of time itself is its context. Eternity does not break into a vacuum. Mystics are also temporal beings, beings in history.

It has been the aim of this essay to understand the particularity of a "saint". Thus, attention has been focused on the dynamics of his experience and the cultural and historical dimensions of his expression. It is in these aspects, despite the great difference from much that is western and "modern", that Māṇikkavācakar's humanity is most readily grasped. Thus, we meet a person plagued by a sense of the unsatisfactoriness of things, a sense of conditionedness and fragmentation. Although, the words used to describe this basic human problem (e.g., *viṉai, piṟappu, malam, pācam*) are different from western terminology and are similar to other Hindu texts, one comes to see Māṇikkavācakar as someone wrestling with much the same concern as many of his modern Western counterparts. Also, Māṇikkavācakar is a poet who infuses his language with a sense of individuality which makes it impossible simply to label him a 'typical' Hindu. Māṇikkavācakar's solutions to these fundamental human problems also ring rather strange to western ears. But it is hoped that the inner logic of his world view, the logic of a mad, dancing god who possesses his devotees and thereby releases them from a 'sane' but alienting ordinary 'reality', has become compelling when viewed on its own terms. In short, it is hoped that the 'foreign' has become imaginatively possible, vital, and perhaps even real. Recalling Eliade's dictum that "the historian of religions himself will feel the consequences of his own hermeneutical work",[2] it has been the goal here to vivify the religious meanings of Māṇikkavācakar's *Tiruvācakam*, which if realized does not leave the writer or his readers unchanged. In so far as our investment of imaginative capital has been returned with interest, that is, to the degree that Māṇikkavācakar's world has ceased to be a mere curiosity of another time and place, this study will have been successful.

Historically, Māṇikkavācakar's uniqueness is best seen in his ability to integrate Tamil religio-cultural values into a Brahmanical framework which is oriented toward the attainment of an ultimate goal. Thus, his multivalent attitudes toward nature and woman reflect a synthesis of divergent influences representing varying origins and emphases. And it must be stressed that this is a synthesis, not an amalgamation. Tamil traditions are brought into a harmonious balance with Brahmanical values. Nowhere is this more evident than in the combination of elements stemming from the popular South Indian tradition of possession by a god, on the one hand, with Brahmanical theism and its emphases on devotion and release, on the other. From this synthesis sprang a new and important branch on the many-limbed tree of Indian religion, namely, the cult of ecstatic devotion to a god. For ecstatic bhakti, mad', bhakti, popular bhakti, gradually spread northward from

Tamilnad throughout the entire Indian subcontinent until it became one of the dominant currents of the Hindu tradition, a particularly good example of how Sanskritic and local elements combine to form something new yet continuous with the received tradition.

While the Tamil bhakti movements are often considered to have had a Sanskritizing effect on Tamil religion and culture, one must not lose sight of the concomitant indigenization of Brahmanical traditions, a process well exemplified by the *Tiruvācakam*. Both the Brahmanical and indigenous Tamil traditions contributed to and were themselves modified in the evolution of this new form of Hindu religiosity. Indeed, it is this very refraction of Brahmanical, Sanskritic concepts through the various prisms of vernacular language and local tradition which results in the many-faceted phenomenon which the West has labelled "Hinduism", a cultural and religious synthesis which must be considered one of the great accomplishments of Indian civilization. The endless malleability of the Hindu tradition, its capacity for assimilating new ideas and practices while still conserving key insights (e.g., Śiva in the Vedas and the *Tiruvācakam*), is clearly evident in Māṇikkavācakar's poetry.

The course of Māṇikkavācakar's thought in history is, as noted at the outset, a topic for future research. A close study alone of the further Brahmanization of his thought in the Śaiva Siddhānta system would necessitate a lengthy monograph in itself. But, even in this instance, it must be noted that this is not a simple uni-directional process; for Śaiva Siddhānta is Hindu philosophy in Tamil rather than in Sanskrit. Perhaps even more intriguing to the historian of religions, is the fascination this poet has had for the popular mind. The evolution of Māṇikkavācakar's own cult and the continued high esteem in which his hymns are held indicate to what extent the *Tiruvācakam* has come to represent a self-understanding, a statement of identity, which has served as a point of orientation for generations of Tamils. While the world of the Caṅkam classics had disappeared by the ninth century, not a few of its most salient cultural impulses found new expression in Tamil bhakti. Unlike the Caṅkam texts, which had been all but forgotten until less than 100 years ago and now have come to enjoy again the status of classics, venerated but effectively dead,[3] the literature of bhakti has never gone into eclipse. And of the bhakti hymns, the *Tiruvācakam* especially has found widespread acceptance in Tamilnad as genuinely living literature. Perhaps this is not least of all due to the confluence in these hymns of the two major currents which together combine to form the distinctively Tamil expression of the Hindu tradition. These, of course, are the pre-Sanskritic values of ancient Tamilnad and the Brahmanical tradition which entered South India from the North during the course of the early and middle centuries of the first millennium A.D. That Māṇikkavācakar's was a successful synthesis is attested by the continued hold the *Tiruvācakam* exercises on the imagination of many Tamils.

Although full exploration of Māṇikkavācakar's esteemed position in Tamilnad lies beyond the scope of this essay and awaits further research, some of the reasons for his popularity have been adumbrated here. For it is in the *Tiruvācakam* itself that the root causes of Māṇikkavācakar's long-standing popularity are to be found. Thus, although this study has focused on a particular individual, we have in the process learned something about what for want of a better term may be called the 'Tamil mind'. The experience expressed in the *Tiruvācakam* has been paradigmatic for many Tamil-speaking devotees of Śiva over the past 1000 years. Nowhere is the conviction about the *Tiruvācakam's* exemplary nature better stated than in a verse by Tuṟaimaṅkalam Civappirakācar, a seventeenth-century Śaiva poet. It is with this passage that I should like to conclude this essay; for according to it, hearers, and by extension one supposes, modern readers of the *Tiruvācakam*, are all ineluctably drawn into its divine madness.

> If the Vedic utterances said to be words
> Of the three-eyed First-Cause
> With body shared by the resplendent bejewelled One,
> Or the vocal honey which emanated from the blossomy mouth
> Of the eminent one of Vātavūr [i.e., Māṇikkavācakar]
> Praised from days of yore —
> If you ask which of these is the eminent one,
> We have not seen anyone stand do
> With eyes streaming with tears

And mind thawing and thawing and melting
While the Vedas are chanted:
But if the *Tiruvācakam* is but once recited,
The hearers become love-filled ones,
With even granite-like mind melting and swelling up,
With the eyes, surpassing the well in sandy soil
Which, the moment it is dug overflows with water,
Welling up and gushing with tears,
With body, its hair standing on end,
Quivering in every fibre.
No one is exception to this
In this world of men.[4]

Notes

1. Eliot, *The Complete Poems and Plays*: 1909–1950, p. 136.
2. Eliade, *The Quest*, p. 62.
3. On the "rediscovery" of Caṅkam literature in the late nineteenth Century, see the first chapter in Zvelebil, *Tamil Literature*, pp. 5-18.
4. Cited and translated by Vanmikanathan, *Pathway to God through Tamil Literature: I — Through the Thiruvaachakam*, p. 102.

Synopsis of the *Tiruvācakam's* Contents

The form of this synopsis will be to list the hymn number and title followed by an English translation of the title, the place of composition ascribed by tradition, and very brief comments on the nature of the poem. The places of composition show that the hymns as presently arranged do not purport to follow a chronological order and consequently should not be read as though they represented an evolutionary pattern of mystical progress.

Hymn 1 — Civapurāṇam (The Story of Śiva), Peruntuṟai. 95 lines in *veṇkalippā* meter which summarize major ideas of Śaiva theology.

Hymn 2 — Kīrttit Tiruvakaval (The Sacred Akaval of Praise), Tillai. 146 lines extolling Śiva's activities, particularly at various places in Tamilnad.

Hymn 3 — Tiruvaṇṭap Pakuti (The Sacred Poem on the Universe), Tillai. 182 lines interspersing sections of epigrammatic praise with passages describing Śiva's operation of grace and the ecstasy of his devotees.

Hymn 4 — Pōṟṟit Tiruvakaval (The Sacred Akaval of Praise), Tillai. There are 225 lines mainly of ejaculatory praise of Śiva but also including passages on Viṣṇu's and Brahmā's inability to reach Śiva's feet and a stylized history of the devotee's life.

Hymn 5 — Tiruccatakam (The Sacred 100 Stanzas), Perunturai. 100 four-line *antāti* stanzas arranged in ten decads in various meters giving an account of the poet's spiritual progress.

Hymn 6 — Nīttal Viṇṇappam (The Petition on Being Abandoned), Uttarakōcamaṅkai. Fifty quatrains in *antāti* form in which Māṇikkavācakar implores Śiva not to abandon him; contains some of the most affecting poetry in the text.

Hymn 7 — Tiruvempāvai (The Sacred Hymn of "Our Lady"), Tiruvaṇṇāmalai. Twenty four-line verses sung by maidens going to take their morning bath; each stanza ends with the untranslatable rhythmic refrain *ēl ōr empāvai*.

Hymn 8 — Tiruvammāṉai (The Sacred Ammāṉai), Tiruvaṇṇāmalai. Twenty six-line stanzas sung by women while sitting in a circle playing a ball game called *ammāṉai*; each verse ends with the refrain *pāṭutum kaṇ ammāṉay* ("Look, Ammāṉai, let us sing").

Hymn 9 — Tirupporcuṇṇam (The Sacred Golden Powder), Tillai. Twenty quatrains for singing while preparing a bath powder for Śiva with a pestle; each stanza ends with the refrain *cuṇṇam iṭittum nāmē* ("Let us pound the powder").

Hymn 10 — Tirukkōttumpi (The Sacred Kingly Bee), Tillai. Twenty quatrains addressed to a humming bee as a messenger to Śiva; each verse ends with the refrain *ūtāy kōttumpī* ("Hum, O Kingly Bee").

Hymn 11 — Tirutteḷḷēṇam (The Sacred Teḷḷēṇam), Tillai. Twenty quatrains for singing while playing *teḷḷēṇam*, a game for girls involving singing and hand-clapping; each stanza ends with the refrain *teḷḷēṇam koṭṭāmō* ("Let us clap Teḷḷēṇam").

Hymn 12 — Tiruccāḻal (The Sacred Cāḻal), Tillai. Twenty quatrains each consisting of a two-line challenge and two-line response as the question and answer *cāḻal* game for girls; each verse ends with the exclamation *cāḻalō*.

Hymn 13 — Tiruppūvalli (The Sacred Creeper Flowers), Tillai. Twenty quatrains to be sung while picking flowers for Śiva; each stanza ends with the refrain *pūvalli koyyāmō* ("Let us pluck the creeper flowers").

Hymn 14 — Tiruvuntiyār (The Sacred Unti), Tillai. Twenty three-line verses celebrating Śiva's triumphs to accompany playing a women's game similar to badminton; the second and third lines of each stanza end with the words *untī paṟa* ("O Unti, fly").

Hymn 15 — Tiruttōṇōkkam (The Sacred Tōṇōkkam), Tillai. Fourteen quatrains to accompany the playing of *tōṇōkkam*, a game for girls which has the participants placing their hands on each others' shoulders.

Hymn 16 — Tiruppoṉṉūcal (The Sacred Golden Swing), Tillai. Nine six-line stanzas to be sung while swinging; each verse ends with the refrain *poṉ ūcal āṭāmō* ("Let us move the golden swing").

Hymn 17 — Aṉṉaippattu (The Mother Decad), Tillai. Ten quatrains addressed by a girl to her mother confessing her love for Śiva; the second and fourth lines of each stanza end with the words *aṉṉē eṉṉum*. ("'O mother,' she says").

Hymn 18 — Kuyiṟpattu (The Cuckoo Decad), Tillai. Ten quatrains addressed to a cuckoo as a messenger to Śiva; each verse ends with the word *kūvāy* ("Call [Śiva]").

Hymn 19—Tiruttacāṅkam (The Sacred Ten Features), Tillai. Ten quatrains in dialogue form between a devotee and a parrot with each verse mentioning one of Śiva's ten features—name, country, city, river, mountain, steed, weapon, drum, garland, and flag.

Hymn 20—Tiruppaḷḷiyeḻucci (The Sacred [Song] of Rising from Bed), Peruntuṟai. Ten quatrains sung to the god to awaken him in the morning; each verse ends with the refrain *paḷḷi eḻuntu aruḷāyē* ("Graciously arise from Your bed").

Hymn 21—Kōyil Mūtta Tiruppatikam (The Ancient Sacred Temple Song), Tillai. Ten quatrains in *antāti* form on the Naṭarāja temple at Cidambaram.

Hymn 22—Kōyil Tiruppatikam (The Sacred Temple Song), Tillai. Ten quatrains in *antāti* form on Śiva, the god of the Cidambaram temple.

Hymn 23—Cettilāppattu (The Decad on Not Growing Weak), Peruntuṟai. Ten quatrains, each containing a refrain praising Śiva as dwelling in Peruntuṟai.

Hymn 24—Aṭaikkalappattu (The Refuge Decad), Peruntuṟai. Ten quatrains, each concluding with the refrain *uṭaiyāy aṭiyēṉ uṉ aṭaikkalamē* ("O Master, O the Refuge of me Your devotee").

Hymn 25—Ācaippattu (The Decad of Longing), Peruntuṟai. Ten quatrains, each ending with the refrain *ācaippaṭṭēṉ kaṇṭāy ammāṉē* ("O Father, look, I yearn").

Hymn 26—Aticayappatu (The Wonder Decad), Peruntuṟai. Ten quatrains, each except for the last stanza ending with the refrain *āṇṭu taṉ aṭiyaril kūṭṭiya aticayam kaṇṭāmē* ("We saw the wonder of how You ruled me and joined me to Your devotees"), the last verse has only the final two words of the refrain.

Hymn 27—Puṇarccippattu (The Decad on Union), Peruntuṟai. Ten quatrains, each ending *eṉṟa kollō eṉ pollā maṇiyaip puṇarntē* ("Ah, when shall I be united with my uncut Gem?").

Hymn 28—Vaḻāppattu (The Decad on Weariness with Life), Peruntuṟai. Ten quatrains, all except the second ending with the refrain *vāḻkilēṉ kaṇṭāy varuka eṉṟu aruḷ puriyāyē* ("Look, I cannot live; exercise Your grace and say 'come'").

Hymn 29—Aruṭpattu (The Grace Decad), Peruntuṟai. Ten quatrains, each except for the last ending with the refrain *aṭiyēṉ ātarittu aḻaittāl atu eṉtuvē eṉṟu aruḷāyē* ("If I Your devotee ardently call upon You, graciously say 'What is it?'"); the final verse has only the last two words of the refrain.

Hymn 30—Tirukkaḻukkuṉṟap Patikam (The Song on Tirukkaḻukkuṉṟam), Tirukkaḻukkuṉṟam. Seven quatrains, each ending *kāṭṭiṉāy kaḻukkuṉṟilē* ("You revealed Yourself in Kaḻukkuṉṟam.")

Hymn 31—Kaṇṭappattu (The Vision Decad), Tillai. Ten quatrains relating what Māṇikkavācakar saw in Cidambaram; each stanza ends with the verb *kaṇṭēṉē* ("I saw").

Hymn 32—Pirārttaṉaippattu (The Decad of Supplication), Peruntuṟai. Eleven quatrains in *antāti* form calling upon Śiva.

Hymn 33—Kuḻaittappattu (The Decad of Being Bruised), Peruntuṟai. Ten quatrains in *antāti* form, the title being taken from the first and last word of the poem.

Hymn 34—Uyiruṇṇippattu (The Decad on Him Who Eats the Soul), Peruntuṟai. Ten quatrains with rhyme at the beginning of each line.

Hymn 35—Accappattu (The Fear Decad), Tillai. Ten quatrains, each ending with the refrain *amma nām añcum āṟē*. ("Ah, how we are frightened then").

Hymn 36—TiruppāṇṭipPatikam (The Song about the Sacred Pāṇṭiyaṉ), Peruntuṟai. Ten quatrains praising Śiva as the lord of Pāṇṭiyan region.

Hymn 37—Piṭittapattu (The Decad of Holding Fast [to Śiva]), Tiruttōṇippuram (i.e., Cīkāḻi). Ten quatrains, each ending with the refrain *cikkeṉap piṭittēṉ eṅku eḻuntu aruḷuvatu iṉiyē* ("I seized You tightly; henceforth where will You graciously arise?").

Hymn 38—Tiruvēcaṟavu (The Sacred Adoration), Peruntuṟai. Ten quatrains praising Śiva for revealing himself to Māṇikkavācakar.

Hymn 39—Tiruppulampal (The Sacred Wailing), Tiruvārūr. Three four-line verses with second syllable rhyme praising Śiva in a rather ejaculatory manner.

Hymn 40—Kulāppattu (The Decad on Resplendent [Tillai]), Tillai. Ten quatrains, each ending with the refrain *kulāt tillai aṇṭāṉaik koṇṭu aṉṟē* ("Is it not so that I acquired resplendent Tillai's Lord?").

Hymn 41—Aṟputappattu (The Miracle Decad), Peruntuṟai. Ten quatrains praising Śiva for releasing Māṇikkavācakar from various problematic aspects of his existence, each stanza ending with the refrain *aṟputam aṟiyēṉē* ("I do not comprehend the miracle").

Hymn 42—Ceṉṉippattu (The Head Decad), Peruntuṟai. Ten quatrains, each ending with a refrain declaring that the devotees' heads will rest upon Śiva's feet which includes the repeated words *cēvaṭikkaṇ nam ceṉṉi maṉṉi* ("At His red feet our heads rest").

Hymn 43—Tiruvārttai (The Sacred Word), Peruntuṟai. Ten quatrains, each ending with the refrain *aṟivār empirāṉ āvārē* ("Only those who know become [one with] our Lord").

Hymn 44—Eṇṇap Patikam (The Song of Expectation), Tillai. Six quatrains with typical second-syllable rhyme in which Māṇikkavācakar pleads with Śiva to allow him to reach the final goal.

Hymn 45—Yāttiraippattu (The Pilgrimage Decad), Tillai. Ten quatrains in *antāti* form picturing the devotee's journey to Śiva's feet; each verse mentions Śiva as Puyaṅkaṉ.

Hymn 46—Tiruppaṭaiyeḻucci (The Setting-Out of the Sacred Army), Tillai. Two four-line verses featuring martial imagery.

Hymn 47—Tiruveṇpā (The Sacred Veṇpā), Peruntuṟai. Eleven quatrains in *veṇpā* meter with a caesura before the last word of the second line.

Hymn 48—Paṇṭāyanāṉmaṟai (The Ancient Four Vedas), Peruntuṟai. Seven *veṇpā* quatrains whose title is based on the opening words of the first stanza.

Hymn 49—Tiruppaṭaiyāṭci (The Reign of the Sacred Army), Tillai. Eight eight-line verses on the experience of final bliss; this difficult hymn effects a high pitch of emotional intensity, largely because in each stanza the first seven of the eight lines end with *ākātē* ("It shall not be").

Hymn 50—Āṉantamālai (The Garland of Bliss), Tillai. Seven quatrains imploring Śiva to let Māṇikkavācakar join the god.

Hymn 51—Accōp Patikam (The "Accō" Song), Tillai. Nine quatrains, each of which addresses Śiva with a different title; each stanza ends with the refrain *aruḷiya āṟu ār peṟuvār accōvē* ("O wonder! Who but I knows such grace?").

Bibliography

I. Texts and Translations of the Tiruvācakam

Citpavāṉantar, Cuvāmi, ed. and commentator. *Tiruvācakam.* Tirupparāyturai: Srīrāmakiruṣṇa Tapōvaṉam, 1970.

Irāmanāta Piḷḷai, Pa., ed. and commentator. *Tiruvācakam.* Madras: South India Saiva Siddhanta Works Publishing Society, 1968.

Navanīta Kiruṣṇa Pāratiyār, Ka. Cu., ed. and commentator. *Tiruvācakam,* Māviṭṭapuram, Sri Lanka: Patmā Patippakam, 1954.

Pope, G. U., trans. and commentator. *The Tiruvāçagam or 'Sacred Utterances' of the Tamil Poet, Saint, and Sage Māṇikka-vāçagar.* Oxford: Clarendon Press, 1900.

Schomerus, H. W., trans. and commentator. *Die Hymnen des Māṇikka-vāśaga (Tiruvāśaga).* Jena: Eugen Diederichs, 1925.

Vanmikanathan, G., trans. and commentator. *Pathway to God through Tamil Literature: I — Through the Thiruvaachakam.* New Delhi: Delhi Tamil Sangam, 1971.

II. Texts and Translations of Other Tamil Literary and Philosophical Works

Cēkkiḻār, *Tiruttoṇṭar Mākkatai* [Periyapurāṇam]. Edited by Pa. Irāmanāta Piḷḷai and Cu. A. Irāmacāmip Pulavar. Madras: South India Saiva Siddhanta Works Publishing Society 1970.

Chelliah, J. V., ed. and trans. *Pattapattu: Ten Tamil Idylls*. Madras: South India Siddhanta Works Publishing Society, 1962.

Cōmacuntaraṉ, Po. Vē., ed. and commentator. *Akanāṉūṟu: Kaḷṟṟiyāṉai Nirai*. Madras: South India Saiva Siddhanta Works Publishing Society, 1970; *Cilappatikāram*. Madras: South India Saiva Siddhanta Works Publishing Society, 1972.

Filliozat, J., trans. *Un texte de la religion Kaumāra, le Tirumurukāṟṟuppaṭai*. Pondichéry: Institut français d'indologie, 1973; *Un texte tamoul de dévotion Vishnouite, le Tiruppāvai d'Āṇṭaḷ*. Pondichéry: Institut français d'indologie, 1972.

Gros, François, trans. *Le Paripāṭal: Texte tamoul*. Pondichéry: Institut français d'indologie. 1968.

Kaṭavuḷmāmuṉivar, *Tiruvātavūraṭikaḷ Purāṇam*. Edited by Pu. Ci. Puṉṉaivaṉanāta Mutaliyār. Madras: South India Saiva Siddhanta Works Publishing Society, 1967.

Kingsbury, F., and Phillips, G. E., trans. *Hymns of the Tamil Śaivite Saints*. Calcutta: Association Press, 1921.

Māṇikkavācakar, *Tirukkōvaiyār*. Edited by Po. Vē. Cōmacuntaraṉ. Madras: South India Saiva Siddhanta Works Publishing Society, 1970.

Matthews, Gordon, trans. *Śiva-ñāna-bōdham: A Manual of Śaiva Religious Doctrine*. Oxford: Oxford University Press, 1948.

Nallaswami Pillai, J. M., trans. "Irupa-iru-pahtu of St. Arul Nandi Sivachariar". *Siddhanta Deepika* 13 (1912–1913): 199–202, 370–373, 397–399, 439–550; *Sivajnana Siddhiyar of Arunandi Sivacharya*. Madras: Meykandan Press, 1913.

Ramanujan, A. K., trans. *The Interior Landscape: Love Poems from a Classical Tamil Anthology*. Bloomington, Indiana: Indiana University Press, 1967.

Ramaswamy Iyengar, D., trans. *Thiruppavai*. 2d ed. Madras: Sri Vishishtadvaita Pracharini Sabha, 1967.

Schomerus, H. W., trans. *Śivaitische Heilegenlegenden* (*Periya-*, purāṇa und Tiruvātavūrar-purana). Jena: Eugen Diederichs, 1925.

Tambyah, T. Issac, trans. *Pslams of a Saiva Saint* [Tāyumāṉavar]. London: Luzac & Co., 1925.

Tāyumāṉavar, *Tāyumāṉavar Pāṭal*. Edited by K. Nagalinga Mudaliyar. Madras, 1906.

Tirumūlar, *Tirumantiram*. 2 vols. Madras: South India Saiva Siddhanta Works Publishing Society, 1962.

Tiruñāṉacampantar, *Tēvārappatikaṅkaḷ*. Edited by Catāciva Ceṭṭiyār. Madras: South India Saiva Siddhanta Works Publishing Society, 1927.

Tirunāvukkaracu, *Tēvārappatikaṅkaḷ*. Madras: Āṟumukavilāca Accukkūṭam, 1898.

Tiruvaḷḷuvar, *Tirukkural*. Translated by G. U. Pope, W. H. Drew, John Lazarus, and F. W. Ellis. Madras: South India Saiva Siddhanta Works Publishing Society, 1970.

III. Other Works

Allchin, Bridget and Raymond, *The Birth of Indian Civilization*. Baltimore: Penguin Books, 1968.

Arbman, Ernst. *Rudra, Untersuchungen zum altindisoehn Galuben und Kultus*. Uppsala Universitets Ärsskrift. Uppsala: A. B. Akademiska Bokhandeln, 1922.

Babb, Lawrence A. *The Divine Hierarchy: Popular Hinduism in Central India*. New York: Columbia University Press, 1975; "Marriage and Malevolence: The Uses of Sexual Opposition in a Hindu Pantheon". *Ethnology* 9 (1970): 137–148.

Balasubramaniam, K. M. "Saint Manickavachakar's Tiruvembavai". In *Madurai Sri Meenakshi Sundareswarar Mahakumbabishekam Souvenir*, edited by P.T. Rajan, pp. x–xii. Madurai: Thiruppani Committee Sri Meenakshi Devasthanam, 1963.

Basham, A. L. *The Wonder That Was India*. Rev. ed. New York: Hawthorn Books, 1963.

Bhandarkar, R. G. *Vaiṣṇavism, Śaivism and Minor Religious Systems*. Strassburg: Karl J. Trübner, 1913.

Blake, William. *The Poetry and Prose of William Blake*. Edited by David V. Erdman. Garden City, N.Y.: Doubleday & Company, 1965,

Bloomfield, Maurice. trans., *Hymns of the Atharva-Veda*. The Sacred Books of the East, vol 42. 1897. Reprint. Delhi: Motilal Banarsidass, 1964.

Bolle, Kees W. "Speaking of a Place". In *Myths and Symbols: Studies in Honor of Mircea Eliade*, edited by Joseph M. Kitagawa and Charles H. Long, pp. 127–139. Chicago: University of Chicago Press, 1969.

Brown, Cheever Mackenzie. *God as Mother: A Feminine Theology in India, An Historical and Theological Study of the Brahmavaivarta Purāṇa*. Hartford, Vermont: Claude Stark & Co., 1974.

Capwell, Charles H. "The Esoteric Belief of the Bauls of Bengal". *Journal of Asian Studies* 33 (1974): 255–264.

Carman, John Braisted. *The Theology of Rāmānuja: An Essay in Interreligious Understanding*. New Haven: Yale University Press, 1974.

Ceṅkalvāraya Piḷḷai, Va. Gu. *Tiruvācaka Oḷiner̤i*. Madras: South India Saiva Siddhanta Works Publishing Society, 1967.

Clothey, Fred W. "Pilgrimage Centers in the Tamil Cultus of Murukan". *Journal of the American Academy of Religion* 40 (1972): 79–95.

Coomaraswamy, Ananda K. *The Dance of Shiva*. New York: Noonday Press, 1957.

Cragg, Kenneth. *The House of Islam*. 2d ed. Encino, Calif.: Dickenson Publishing Company, 1975.

Das, R. K. *Temples of Tamilnad*. Bombay: Bharatiya Vidya Bhavan, 1964.

Deleury, G. A. *The Cult of Viṭhobā*. Poona: Deccan College, 1960.

Dessigane, R., Pattabiramin, P. Z., and Filliozat, J. *La Legende des Jeux de çiva a Madurai: D'aprés les textes et les peintures* 2 vols. Pondichéry: Institut français d'indologie, 1960.

Dhavamony, Mariasusai. *Love of God according to Śaiva Siddhānta: A Study in the Mysticism and Theology of Śaivism*. Oxford: Clarendon Press, 1971.

Dickinson, Emily. *The Poems of Emily Dickinson*. Edited by Thomas H. Johnson. 3 vols. Cambridge, Mass.: Harvard University Press, Belknap Press, 1958.

Diehl, Carl Gustav. *Instrument and Purpose: Studies on Rites and Rituals in South India*. Lund: CWK Gleerup, 1956.

Dilthey, Wilhelm. *Pattern and Meaning in History: Thoughts on History and Society*. Edited and introduced by H. P. Rickman. New York: Harper & Row, 1962.

Dimock, Edward C., Jr. "Doctrine and Practice among the Vaiṣṇavas of Bengal". In *Krishna: Myths, Rites, and Attitudes*, edited by Milton Singer, pp. 41–63. Chicago: University of Chicago Press, 1968; *The Place of the Hidden Moon: Erotic Mysticism in the Vaiṣṇava-sahajiyā Cult of Bengal*. Chicago: University of Chicago Press, 1966.

Dorai Rangaswamy, M. A., *The Religion and Philosophy of Tēvāram: With Special Reference to Nampi Ārūrar (Sundarar)*, Book 1. Madras: University of Madras, 1958.

Dumont, Louis. *Une sous-caste de l'Inde du sud: Organisation sociale et religion des Pramalai Kallar*. Paris: Mouton, 1957.

Dumont, Louis. "World Renunciation in Indian Religions". *Religion/Politics and History in India; Collected Papers in Indian Sociology*, pp. 33-60. Paris: Mouton, 1970.

Edgerton, Franklin, trans. and commentator. *The Bhagavad Gītā*. 2 vols. Cambridge, Mass.: Harvard University Press, 1944.

Eggeling, Julius, trans. *The Śatapatha-brāhmaṇa*. Part I. The Sacred Books of the East, vol. 12. 1882, Reprint. Delhi: Motilal Banarsidass, 1963; *The Śatapatha-brāhmaṇa*. Part III. The Sacred Books of the East, vol. 41. 1894. Reprint. Delhi: Motilal Banarsidass, 1963.

Eliade, Mircea. *The Quest: History and Meaning in Religion*. Chicago: University of Chicago Press, 1969; *Shamanism: Archaic Techniques of Ecstasy*. Translated by Willard R. Trask. Bollingen Series, no. 76. Princeton: Princeton University Press, 1972.

Eliot, T. S. *The Complete Poems and Plays:* 1909–1950. New York: Harcourt, Brace & World, 1971.

Gail, Adalbert. *Bhakti im Bhāgavatapurāṇā: Religionsgeschichtliche Studie zur Idee der Gottesliebe in Kult und Mystik der Viṣṇuismus*. Wiesbaden: Otto Harrassowitz, 1969.

Godakumbura, C. E. *Sinhalese Literature*. Colombo: Colombo Apothecaries' Co., 1955.

Gonda, Jan. *Die Religionen Indiens I: Veda und älterer Hinduismus*. Stuttgart: W. Kohlhammer Verlag, 1960; *Die Religionen Indiens II: Der jüngere Hinduismus*. Stuttgart: W. Kohlhammer Verlag, 1963.

Gough, E. Kathleen. "Cults of the Dead among the Nāyars". In *Traditional India: Structure and Change*, edited by Milton Singer, pp. 240–272. Philadelphia: American Folklore Society, 1959.

Graefe, P. "Legends as Mile-Stones in the History of Tamil Literature". In *Professor P. K. Gode Commemoration Volume*, edited by H. L. Hariyappa and M. M. Patakar, pp. 129–146. Poona Oriental Series, no. 93. Poona: Oriental Book Agency, 1960.

Grierson, George. "Bhakti-Marga". In *Encyclopedia of Religion and Ethics*, edited by James Hastings, vol. 2, pp. 539–551. Edinburgh: T. & T. Clark, 1909.

Harle, James C. *Temple Gateways in South India; The Architecture and Iconography of the Cidambaram Gopuras*. Oxford: Bruno Cassirer, 1963.

Harper, Edward B. "Shamanism in South India". *Southwestern Journal of Anthropology* 13 (1957): 267–287.

Hart, George L., III. "Ancient Tamil Literature: Its Scholarly Past and Future". In *Essays on South India*, edited by Burton Stein, pp. 41–63. Asian Studies at Hawaii, no. 15.

Honolulu: The University Press of Hawaii, 1975; "Cosmic Imagery in Kamban". Paper delivered at the Twenty-Seventh Annual Meeting of the Association for Asian Studies, 25 March 1975, in San Francisco; *The Poems of Ancient Tamil: Their Milieu and Their Sanskrit Counterparts*. Berkeley: University of California Press, 1975; "Some Aspects of Kinship in Ancient Tamil Literature". In *Kinship and History in South Asia*, edited by Thomas T. Trautmann, pp. 29–60. Michigan Papers on Southeast Asia, no. 7. Ann Arbor: Center for South and Southeast Asian Studies, The University of Michigan, 1974; "Some Related Literary Conventions in Tamil and Indo-Aryan and their Significance". *Journal of the American Oriental Society* 94 (1974); 156–167; "Women and the Sacred in Ancient Tamilnad". *Journal of Asian Studies* 32 (1973): 233–250.

Hopkins, Thomas J. "The Social Teaching of the *Bhāgavata Purāṇa*". In *Krishna: Myths, Rites, and Attitudes*, edited by Milton Singer, pp. 3–22. Chicago: University of Chicago Press, 1968.

Hume, Robert Ernest, trans. *The Thirteen Principal Upanishads*. 2d ed., rev. New York: Oxford University Press, 1931.

Ingalls, Daniel H. H. "Cynics and Pāśupatas: The Seeking of Dishonor". *Harvard Theological Review* 55 (1962): 281–298; "Kālidāsa and the Attitudes of the Golden Age". *Journal of the American Oriental Society* 96 (1976): 15–26.

Isherwood, Christopher. *Ramakrishna and His Disciples*. New York: Simon and Schuster, 1965.

James, William. *The Varieties of Religious Experience*. New York: New American Library, 1958.

Jesudasan, C. and Hephzibah. *A History of Tamil Literature*. Calcutta: Y.M.C.A. Publishing House, 1961.

Kailasapathy, K. *Tamil Heroic Poetry*. Oxford: Clarendon Press, 1968.

Karve, I. "On the Road: A Maharashtrian Pilgrimage". *Journal of Asian Studies* 22 (1962): 13–29.

Keith, Arthur Berriedale. *The Religion and Philosophy of the*

Veda and Upanishads. 2 vols. 1925. Reprint. Delhi: Motilal Banarsidass, 1970; trans. *Rigveda Brahmanas: The Aitareya and Kauṣītaki Brāhmaṇas of the Rigveda*. Harvard Oriental Series, vol. 25. Cambridge, Mass.: Harvard University Press, 1920.

Keller, C. A. "A Literary Study of the Tirumurukarruppadai". In *Proceedings of the First International Conference Seminar of Tamil Studies*, vol. 2, pp. 55–62. Kuala Lumpur: International Association of Tamil Research, 1969; "Some Aspects of Manikkavasagar's Theology". In *Proceeeings of the Second International Conference Seminar of Tamil Studies*. vol. 2, edited by R. E. Asher, pp. 55–63. Madras: International Association of Tamil Research, 1971.

Kinsley, David R. *The Sword and the Flute: Kālī and Kṛṣṇa, Dark Visions of the Terrible and the Sublime in Hindu Mythology*. Berkeley: University of California Press, 1975; "'Through the Looking Glass': Divine Madness in the Hindu Religious Tradition". *History of Religions* 13 (1974): 270–305; "'Without Kṛṣṇa There Is No Song'". *History of Religions* 12 (1272): 149–180.

Klostermaier, Klaus. "The Bhaktirasāmṛtasindhubindu of Viśvanāth Cakravartin". *Journal of the American Oriental Society* 94 (1974): 96–107.

Knox, R. A. *Enthusiasm: A Chapter in the History of Religion*. Oxford: Oxford University Press, 1950.

Krishnaswami Aiyangar, S. *Manimekhalai in its Historical Setting*. London: Luzac & Co., 1928.

Kulke, Hermann. *Cidambaramāhātmya: Eine Untersuchung der religionsgeschichtlichen und historischen Hintergründe für die Entstehung der Tradition einer südindischen Tempelstadt*. Wiesbaden: Otto Harrassowitz, 1970.

Laing, R. D. *The Politics of Experience*. New York: Pantheon Books, 1967.

Larson, Gerald James. "The *Bhagavad Gītā* as Cross-Cultural Process: Toward an Analysis of the Social Locations of a Religious Text". *Journal of the American Academy of Religion* 43 (1975): 651–669.

Lehmann, Arno. *Die sivaitische Frömmigkeit der tamulischen Erbauungsliteratur*. Berlin-Hermsdorf: Heimatdienstverlag, 1947.

Long, J. Bruce. "Siva and Dionysos — Visions of Terror and Bliss", *Numen* 18 (1971): 180–209; "Visions of Terror and Bliss: A Study of Rudra-Śiva in Pre-Purāṇic Hinduism". Ph.D. dissertation, University of Chicago, 1970.

Lorenzen, David N. *The Kāpālikas and Kālāmukhas: Two Lost Śaivite Sects*. Berkeley: University of California Press, 1972.

Mahadevan, T. M. P. *Ten Saints of India*. Bombay: Bharatiya Vidya Bhavan, 1965.

Maloney, Clarence. "Religious Beliefs and Social Hierarchy in Tamil Nāḍu, India". *American Ethnologist* 2 (1975): 169-191.

Manickam, V. Sp. *The Tamil Concept of Love*. Madras: South India Saiva Siddhanta Works Publishing Society, 1962.

Martin, James L. "The Cycle of Festivals at Pārthrsārathīswami Temple". In *Asian Religions: 1971*, edited by Bardwell L. Smith, pp. 223–240. Chambersburg, Penna.: American Academy of Religion, 1971.

Meenakshisundaran, T. P. *A History of Tamil Literature*. Annamalainagar: Annamalai University, 1965.

Miller, Barbara Stoler. *Phantasies of a Love Thief: The Caurapañcāśikā Attributed to Bilhaṇa*. New York: Columbia University Press, 1971.

Miller, Jeanine. "Forerunners of Yoga: The *Keśin* Hymn". In *Yoga and Beyond; Essays in Indian Philosophy* by George Feuerstein and Jeanine Miller. New York: Schocken Books, 1972.

Monier-Williams, Monier. *A Sanskrit-English Dictionary*. Rev. ed. Oxford: Clarendon Press, 1899.

Mowry, M. Lucetta. "The Structure of Love in Māṇikkavācakar's *Tiruvācakam*". In *Structural Appoaches to South India Studies*, edited by Harry M. Buck and Glenn E. Yocum, pp. 207–224. Chambersburg, Penna.: Wilson Books, 1974.

Müller, F. Max, trans. *The Upaniṣads*. Part II. 1884. Reprint.

New York: Dover Publications, 1972; *Vedic Hymns*. Part I. The Sacred Books of the East, vol. 32. 1891. Reprint. Delhi: Motilal Banarsidass, 1964.

Narayana Ayyar, C. V. *Origin and Early History oj Śaivism in South India*. Madras University Historical Series, no. 6. Madras: University of Madras, 1936.

Natarajan, B. *The City of the Cosmic Dance*. New Delhi: Orient Longman, 1974.

Navaratnam, Ratna. *A New Approach to Tiruvacagam*. 2d ed. Annamalainagar: Annamalai University, 1971.

Nikhilananda, Swami, trans. *The Gospel of Sri Ramakrishna*. Abridged ed. New York: Ramakrishna-Vivekananda Center, 1958.

Nilakanta Sastri, K. A. *The Cōḷas*. 2d ed. Madras University Historical Series, no. 9. Madras: University of Madras, 1955; *The Culture and History of the Tamils*. Calcutta: K. L. Mukhopadhyay, 1963; *Development of Religion in South India*. Bombay: Orient Longman, 1963; *A History of South India from Prehistoric Times to the Fall of Vijayanagar*. 3rd ed. Madras: Oxford University Press. 1966; *The Pāṇḍyan Kingdom: From the Earliest Times to the Sixteenth Century*. 1929. Reprint. Madras: Swathi Publications, 1972.

O'Flaherty, Wendy Doniger. *Asceticism and Eroticism in the Mythology of Śiva*. London: Oxford University Press, 1973.

Oldenberg, Hermann, trans. *Vedic Hymns*. Part II. The Sacred Books of the East, vol. 46. 1897. Reprint. Delhi: Motilal Banarsidass, 1964.

Otto, Rudolf. *The Idea of the Holy*. Translated by John W. Harvey. New York: Oxford University Press, 1958; *Mysticism East and West: A Comparative Analysis of the Nature of Mysticism*. Translated by Bertha L. Bracey and Richenda C. Payne. New York: Meridian Books, 1957.

Phillips, Derek L. *Abandoning Method: Sociological Studies in Methodology*. San Francisco: Jossey-Bass, 1973.

Piet, John H. *A Logical Presentation of the Śaiva Siddhānta Philosophy*. Madras: Christian Literature Society for India, 1952.

Pillay, K. K. *South India and Ceylon*. Madras: University of Madras, 1963.

Rajamanickam, M. *The Development of Saivism in South India (A. D. 300–1300)*. Dharmapuram: Gnanasambandam Press, 1964.

Ramachandra Dikshitar, V. R. *Studies in Tamil Literature and History*. Madras: University of Madras, 1936.

Ramana Maharshi. *The Collected Works of Ramana Maharshi*. Edited by Arthur Osborne. New York: Samuel Weiser, 1972.

Ramanujan, A. K. trans. *Speaking of Śiva*. Baltimore: Penguin Books, 1973; "Structure and Anti-Structure: The Vīraśaiva Example". Paper delivered at the meeting of the Society for South India Studies, 17 March 1973, in Chambersburg, Penna.

Rice, Edward P. *A History of Kanarese Literature*. 2d ed. Calcutta: Association Press, 1921.

Rolle, Richard. *The Fire of Love*. Translated by Clifton Wolters. Baltimore: Penguin Books, 1972.

Schomerus, Hilko Wiardo. *Indien und das Christentum, I Teilt Indische Frömmigkeit*. Halle-Saale: Buchhandlung des Waisenhauses, 1931; *Meister Eckehart und Māṇikka-Vāśagar: Mystik auf deutschem und indischem Boden*. Gütersloh: Verlag C. Bertelsmann, 1936; *Der Śaiva-Siddhānta: Eine Mystik Indiens*. Leipzig: J. C. Hinrichs, 1912.

Schweitzer, Albert. *Indian Thought and Its Development*. Translated by Mrs. Charles E.B. Russell. Boston: Beacon Press, 1936.

Singaravelu, S. *Social Life of Tamils: The Classical Period*. Kuala Lumpur: Department of Indian Studies, University of Malaya, 1966.

Singer, Milton. "The Rādhā-Krishna *Bhajanas* of Madras City". In *Krishna: Myths, Rites, and Attitudes*, edited by

Milton Singer, pp. 90–138. Chicago: University of Chicago Press, 1968.

Smith, Wilfred Cantwell. "Methodology and the Study of Religion: Some Misgivings". In *Methodoligical Issues in Religious Studies*, edited by Robert D. Baird, pp. 1–30. Chico, Calif.: New Horizons Press, 1975; "The Study of Religion and the Study of the Bible". *Journal of the American Academy of Religion* 39 (1971): 131–140.

Solomon, Ted J. "Early Vaiṣṇava Bhakti and its Autochthonous Heritage". *History of Religions* 10 (1970): 32–48.

Somasundaram Pillai, J.M. *Siva-Nataraja—the Cosmic Dance in Chid-Ambaram*. Annamalainagar: J.M. Somasundaram Pillai, 1970; *The University's Environs: Cultural and Historical*. 4th ed. Annamalainagar: Annamalai University, 1963.

Spencer, George W. "The Politics of Plunder: The Cholas in Eleventh-Century Ceylon". *Journal of Asian Studies* 35 (1976): 405–419; "The Sacred Geography of the Tamil Shaivite Hymns". *Numen* 17 (1970): 232–244.

Srinivasa Aiyangar, M. *Tamil Studies*. Madras: Guardian Press, 1914.

Srinivasa Raghavan, A. "Mystical Symbolism in the Work of the Alwars". In *Proceedings of the First International Conference Seminar of Tamil Studies*. Vol. 2. Kuala Lumpur: International Association of Tamil Research, 1969.

Staal, [J.] Frits. *Exploring Mysticism: A Methodoligical Essay*. Berkeley: University of California Press, 1975; "Sanskrit and Sanskritization". *Journal of Asian Studies* 22 (1963); 261–275.

Stace, Walter T., ed and commentator. *The Teachings of the Mystics*. New York: New American Library, 1960.

Stein, Burton. "Social Mobility and Medieval South Indian Hindu Sects". In *Social Mobility in the Caste System in India*, edited by James Silverberg, pp. 78–94. The Hague: Mouton, 1968.

Streng, Frederick J. *Understanding Religious Life*. 2nd ed. Belmont, Calif.: Dickenson Publishing Company, 1976.

Streng, Frederick J., Lloyd, Charles L., Jr., and Allen, Jay T. *Ways of Being Religious*. Englewood Cliffs, N.J.: Prentice-Hall, 1973.

Subrahmaniam, N. *Pre-Pallavan Tamil Index*. Madras: University of Madras, 1966; *Śaṅgam Polity: The Administration and Social Life of the Śaṅgam Tamils*. Bombay: Asia Publishing House, 1966.

Sullivan, Herbert P. "A Re-Examination of the Religion of the Indus Civilization". *History of Religions* 4 (1964): 115–125.

Tamil Lexicon, 6 vols. Madras: University of Madras, 1924-1936.

Taylor, Edward. *The Poems of Edward Taylor*. Edited by Donald E. Stanford. New Haven: Yale University Press, 1960.

Thani Nayagam, Xavier S. *Landscape and Poetry: A Study of Nature in Classical Tamil Poetry*. 2d ed. London: Asia Publishing House, 1966.

Turner, Victor. *The Ritual Process: Structure and Anti-Structure*. Chicago: Aldine Publishing Company, 1969.

Vaiyapuri Pillai, S. *History of Tamil Language and Literature (Beginning to 1000 A.D.)*. Madras: New Century Book House, 1956.

Van der Leeuw, G. *Religion in Essence and Manifestation*. Translated by J.E. Turner. 2 vols. New York: Harper & Row, 1963.

Varadarajan, M. *The Treatment of Nature in Sangam Literature*. Madras: South India Saiva Siddhanta Works Publishing Society, 1969.

Vaudeville, Charlotte. "Evolution of Love-Symbolism in Bhagavatism". *Journal of the American Oriental Society* 82 (1962): 31–40.

Vivekananda, Swami. *Ramakrishna and His Message*. Calcutta: Advaita Ashrama, 1972.

Walker, Benjamin. *The Hindu World*. 2 vols. New York: Frederick A. Praeger, 1968.

Warren, Henry Clarke, trans. *Buddhism in Translations*. 1896. Reprint. New York: Atheneum, 1973.

White, John, ed. *The Highest State of Consciousness*. Garden City, N.Y.: Doubleday & Company, 1972.

Whitney, William Dwight, trans. *Atharva-Veda Saṃhitā*. Edited by Charles Rockwell Lanman. 2 vols. Harvard Oriental Series, vols. 7–8. Cambridge, Mass.: Harvard University, 1905.

Zaehner, R. C., trans. and commentator. *The Bhagavad-Gītā*. Oxford: Clarendon Press, 1969; *Hindu Scriptures*. London: J. M. Dent & Sons, 1966.

Zimmer, Heinrich. *Myths and Symbols in Indian Art and Civilization*. Edited by Joseph Campbell. New York: Harper Torchbooks, 1962.

Zvelebil, Kamil V. *The Poets of the Powers*. London: Rider and Company, 1973; *The Smile of Murugan: On Tamil Literature of South India*. Leiden: E. J. Brill, 1973; *Tamil Literature*. Leiden: E. J. Brill, 1975.

Index